The Book of Oriental Literature
The Diary of a Slave
The Golden East
The Golden Treasury of Indian Literature
The Lion of the Frontier
The Prince Aga Khan
The Spirit of the East
The Tragedy of Amanullah
The Wanderings of Asaf
The White Terror of the Khyber
Through the Garden of Allah
Vietnam
Westward to Mecca

The Dermis Probe
The Elephant in the Dark
The Englishman's Handbook
The Exploits of the Incomparable Mulla Nasrudin
The Farmer's Wife
The Horrible Dib Dib
The Hundred Tales of Wisdom
The Idries Shah Compendia Series
The Idries Shah Anthology
The Idries Shah Study Guides
The Lion Who Saw Himself in the Water
The Magic Horse
The Magic Monastery
The Man and the Fox
The Man With Bad Manners
The Natives Are Restless
The Old Woman and the Eagle
The Onion
The Pleasantries of the Incredible Mulla Nasrudin
The Secret Lore of Magic
The Silly Chicken
The Subtleties of the Inimitable Mulla Nasrudin
The Sufis
The Tale of the Sands
The Treasury Collection
The Way of the Sufi
The World of Nasrudin
Thinkers of the East
Wisdom of the Idiots
Witches and Sorcerers
World Tales

By Tahir Shah

Beyond the Devil's Teeth
Casablanca Blues
Casablanca Blues: The Screenplay
Congress With a Crocodile
Cultural Research
Eye Spy
Godman
Hannibal Fogg and the Supreme Secret of Man
House of the Tiger King
In Arabian Nights
In Search of King Solomon's Mines
Jinn Hunter: Book One – The Prism
Jinn Hunter: Book Two – The Jinnslayer
Jinn Hunter: Book Three – The Perplexity
Journey Through Namibia
Paris Syndrome
Scorpion Soup
Sorcerer's Apprentice
Spectrum Guide to Jordan
Tales Told to a Melon
The Anthologies: Africa
The Anthologies: Ceremony
The Anthologies: Childhood
The Anthologies: City
The Anthologies: Danger
The Anthologies: East
The Anthologies: Expedition
The Anthologies: Frontier
The Anthologies: Hinterland

The Anthologies: India
The Anthologies: Jungle
The Anthologies: Morocco
The Anthologies: People
The Anthologies: Quest
The Anthologies: South
The Anthologies: Taboo
The Arabian Nights Adventures
The Caliph's House
The Clockmaker's Box
The Man Who Found Himself
The Middle East Bedside Book
The Misadventures of the Mystifying Nasrudin
The Peregrinations of the Perplexing Nasrudin
The Reason to Write
The Tahir Shah Fiction Reader
The Tahir Shah Travel Reader
The Voyages and Vicissitudes of Nasrudin
Three Essays
Timbuctoo
Timbuctoo: The Screenplay
Trail of Feathers
Travels With Myself
Travels With Nasrudin

A Son of a Son
Volume I

A Son of a Son

Volume I

A Century of Collected Work

THE SIRDAR IKBAL ALI SHAH

IDRIES SHAH

TAHIR SHAH

MMXXI

Secretum Mundi Publishing Ltd.
Kemp House
City Road
London
EC1V 2NX
United Kingdom

www.secretum-mundi.com
info@secretum-mundi.com

First published by Secretum Mundi Publishing Ltd, 2021

A SON OF A SON: A Century of Collected Work
VOLUME I

Version 08042021

© THE SIRDAR IKBAL ALI SHAH

© IDRIES SHAH

© TAHIR SHAH

The Sirdar Ikbal Ali Shah, Idries Shah & Tahir Shah
assert the right to be identified as the Author of the Work
in accordance with the Copyright, Designs and Patents Act 1988.
A CIP catalogue record for this title is available from the British Library.

ISBN 978-1-912383-81-8

معَ كاملِ الاحترام، أُهدي هذا العمل المتواضع

إلى صاحبِ السُموِّ الملكيّ

الأمير محمد بن سلمان آل سعود

If the father cannot, the son will finish the task.

Persian saying

CONTENTS

Introduction   1

Author Biographies   15

An Editorial Note   21

The Magic Horse   23

Witchcraft and Necromancy in Afghanistan   38

The Arabian Nights Adventures   59

The Teaching-Story   72

Redtape-istan   113

The Princess of Zilzilam   131

The Fakirs and Their Doctrines   148

Desert Ways   168

Children of the Devil   187

Maruf the Cobbler   210

In Arabia   219

Insider Information   229

Mulla Nasrudin   258

The Slaver is Ambushed   275

House of the Tiger King   284

Reflections   299

The Sheikh, the Sun, and the Sack   310

Flight of the Birdmen   321

Hypocrisy   331

Fairies and Fairy-tales of Persia 347
A Conversation Paid for in Postage Stamps 371
Understanding the Path 378
Opium Den Drama 408
Godman 425
The Legend of the Cattleman 440
The Bolshevik School of Spies 465
The Clockmaker's Box 480
Tales of a Parrot 483
The Haunted Carpet 501
Bibliography 513

INTRODUCTION

THIRTY-THREE YEARS AGO, an elderly friend of my parents invited me to tea at The Traveller's Club on Pall Mall. I knew nothing about him except that he had been an inseparable friend of my grandfather, the Sirdar Ikbal Ali Shah.

As plates of prim sandwiches with their crusts cut off were served along with pots of orange pekoe tea, we made polite conversation. Doing as my father had trained me to do, I listened three times as much as I spoke. And, whenever given the opportunity to talk about myself, I turned the conversation around, so my host might have an opportunity to tell me about his life.

I learned that during a long and distinguished career the gentleman had worked for the British Foreign Office in various capacities. Now in his eighties, he was at last able to reflect on travels through Asia, Africa, and the Americas.

When I asked for the high point of his professional life, his eyes seemed to glaze over.

'Pursuing your grandfather,' he said dreamily.

'Pursuing him?'

'Oh yes. Pursuing him to the ends of the earth.'

'Don't quite follow you,' I responded.

1

The elderly gentleman reached for a scone, lathering it in cream and jam.

'I was spying on him,' he said.

'Spying on him for…?'

'For the British Crown.'

'But why?'

'Because the top bods in Whitehall assumed he was up to no good.'

'What would have given them that opinion?'

'The fact that he travelled everywhere – from the wilds of Central Asia, down to the southern reaches of Tierra del Fuego… all under the cover of being a writer.'

'That's what he was.'

'*I* know that, and *you* know that, but the paper-pushers of the Foreign Office didn't believe it for a moment. You see the Sirdar knew people at the very highest levels. He was a close confidante of Mustafa Kemal Ataturk of Turkey, and King Ibn Saud, the Prince Aga Khan, Amanullah of Afghanistan, and was even best friends with King Zog of Albania.'

'Was that really so unusual?'

My host took a bite of his scone, washing it down with a gulp of orange pekoe.

'At the time it was.'

'What was your exact brief?' I asked.

'To follow the Sirdar from a discreet distance, and report back on everything.'

'*Everything?*'

'On where he went and who he met, on what books he was reading, and even on what he was writing in his journals.'

'How long did you follow him?'

'Let me think… First there was a prolonged journey through Afghanistan, Persia, Iraq and the Holy Land. Then a long stay in Saudi Arabia and the Sudan, and after that a North African journey, east to west. A year or so later he and your father made the voyage down to Buenos Aires. All in all, I'd say I shadowed him for about eight years, off and on.'

'Surely he knew you were there.'

The elderly gentleman smiled retiringly.

'From the first moment of the first day,' he replied.

'*So?*'

'So he allowed me to do my job. And, rather than making it arduous, he made it very easy. In circumstances when he knew I was listening in, he would speak especially clearly. Or, when he was sitting in a café making notes as was his habit, he would slip inside to wash his hands, leaving his notebook on the table just long enough for me to take a peek.'

My gaze followed a waiter as he crossed the salon, a silver tray laden with tea balanced on an upturned hand.

'There's something I don't quite understand,' I said. 'You see, my father told me that you were his father's closest friend.'

'Oh but I was,' the gentleman shot back fast.

'How could you have been though, if you were spying on him?'

'I am pleased you asked me that. Very pleased indeed. If you would permit me, I will answer with a description of something that happened one night a little south of Samarkand.

'For weeks the Sirdar had blazed a trail through Afghanistan, with me hot on his heels, dressed in local attire. We had crossed the border north of Mazar-i-Sharif – first him, then I at a distance. I was doing my best to monitor him while sending reports back to London whenever possible. As I described, I was sure he was on to me, because he was so accommodating. He had put up in a caravanserai at the small Uzbek town of Kitab.'

'*Kitab*... the Arabic for "book"?'

'Yes, that's right... As I was to learn, he was drawn there by its reputation as being a centre of the sky-searchers, what's now known as astronomers. It was mid-winter and I was frozen to the bone. To make matters worse, my funds had run out, and there was no hope of getting any more until we reached Samarkand. So I was forced to camp in the stables, with nothing to eat, while your grandfather sat in the teahouse beside a roaring fire, with a feast laid out before him.

'I remember watching him through the window, marvelling at the way he engaged with everyone there – regaling them with tales of his journeys. My face was pressed up to the glass, my body shaking with cold, as the snow began falling more heavily.

'I was about to prise myself away and limp back into the stable block, when I heard a voice speak a name, *my* name. The next thing I knew, the Sirdar had invited me inside to the fire, fed me a meal of mutton and rice, and given me his own blanket.'

'Did he know who you were?'

'Oh yes, of course he did. And he was most courteous. He commended me for following the "breadcrumbs" he had left so diligently, and apologized for travelling at such a furious pace. When I was warm and well fed, he made a proposal.'

'What was it?'

'He suggested that we travel together as equals rather than as adversaries.'

'But was that allowed?'

'Strictly speaking it was not, but if Whitehall didn't know, they didn't know. And from that moment we became inseparable friends. We soon found we shared common interests in all sorts of things, from philosophy and folklore, to architecture, literature and phonetics.'

'Didn't the mandarins in Whitehall ever get suspicious?'

My host smiled from the corner of his mouth.

'Apparently not. We continued to travel together for years.'

I enquired about the journey to Latin America just after the War. As I'd hoped, the elderly gentleman's eyes glinted with delight.

'Your father was about your age,' he said. 'As thin as a rake, and intensely studious. Your grandfather took him as his private secretary, leaving his younger brother at home in Oxford to finish his studies. The Sirdar was on a mission to find a source of halal meat for troops from the Indian Army. As with so many of his projects, it was misunderstood from the start by the Foreign Office. They were certain he was up to no good, which of course he was not.'

'My father loves to go on about Buenos Aires in the late forties,' I chipped in.

'Quite rightly so. It was the most magnificent of cities. The Sirdar, your father, and I strolled down the tree-lined streets with our mouths wide open in wonder. We had of course come from the winter of a land torn to shreds by war. Each afternoon we would sit at Café Richmond on Calle Florida and discuss the state of the world.'

'I hardly knew my grandfather,' I said. 'All I remember is the blurred outline of a man sitting in the garden of his home in Tangier, with the scent of orange blossom.'

The elderly gentleman smiled very slowly, as though he were feasting on a memory.

'There was no one else like him,' he said. 'He was sophisticated, but could get on with anyone. At heart he was an Oriental, but was one with an interest in the ways of the Occident. He was devout, but not in an obvious or superficial way. His faith was between him and God, with no one else in between.'

'How was he with my father?'

'Reserved. One might even say he was cruel. But that was the only way he knew to be.'

The gentleman brushed a crumb of cake from his lapel as his mind focused.

'One afternoon at Café Richmond,' he said, 'the Sirdar took something from his pocket and placed it on the table. It was a *tusbi*, a rosary, the kind carried by Sufis. The ninety-nine beads were beautifully fashioned from red amber. Over the years I'd seen glimpses of it from time to time, whether it be in Bokhara, Khartoum, or Marrakech.

'He was in an especially reflective mood that day. He said: "Each one of us is a bead on a string, a bead touching the one before and the one after." He touched a bead and said, "That's me." Then pointed to the one beside it, and said "That is you, Idries." Then, in a voice that was so soft as to be almost mute, he said, "And that bead to the left of you, Idries, will be your son."'

'*Me*?'

The elderly gentleman smiled again, pleased he'd made an impact.

'You are yourself,' he told me, 'but at the same time, you are part of a chain of transmission. The chain stretches back to antiquity, and forward as well, far into the future. It's for you to build on the foundations left by others, and to allow others to build upon you.'

Thanking my host for his stories and his wisdom, I made my excuses. After all, I didn't want to overstay the hospitality.

As I stood up to leave, he touched a hand to my wrist.

'I've got something for you,' he said.

Before I could reply, he tugged an object from his jacket pocket and pressed it into my hand.

An exquisite *tusbi* made from red amber beads.

'I visited the Sirdar on Halloween in 1969,' he said. 'Less than a week before he died. You had been taken to him a few days before that. He was thrilled.'

'Thrilled with what?'

'Thrilled to have a grandson… thrilled to have the next bead on the *tusbi*. Looking back, it was as though he had sensed his death was near – although he could surely not have known quite how near it was. Before I left Tangier, he gave me this rosary, and he made me promise I'd give it to you on a quiet afternoon such as this, when you were ready.'

'Ready for what?'

'Ready to start your life as a writer.'

Three days after meeting the elderly gentleman who'd pursued my grandfather and become his greatest friend, I found a listing in the British Library catalogue for a book 'of poetry in prose' called *Eastern Moonbeams*. Launched in Edinburgh in 1918, it was the very first book my grandfather ever published. The British Library had misplaced their copy, so I searched for one.

…for thirty-two years.

Over the years I began to imagine that the edition didn't exist at all. But then, a few months ago, my long quest paid off. Something stirred me in the middle of the night, caused me to flip open my laptop, and to search eBay for the hundred thousandth time. To my amazement, there it was… *Eastern Moonbeams*, priced at £6.99.

Far more than a book, it's a symbol.

A symbol of the point at which a family of oral storytellers changed medium – from spoken words to written script.

The volume is small and rectangular, about the size of a bar of chocolate. Printed on exquisite laid paper, it contains an introduction by the legendary folklorist, Donald

Mackenzie. There's none of the rip-roaring bravado found in my grandfather's later books. *Eastern Moonbeams* is a work that tiptoed into the medium rather than taking it by storm.

The publisher was John Orr of Edinburgh, which appears to be so small a house that they released almost no other work at the time. Although romantic and saccharine, the poetry in prose form was elegant. Holding it in my hand, as I have done so often since it first reached me, I have tried to imagine how my grandfather felt on first reading his name on the front.

My inkling is that publishing the little book had been the idea of my Scottish grandmother, Elizabeth MacKenzie. The two had met the year before, at a sale of flags and teacake for the war effort. My grandmother, who later recounted the episode in her lightly fictionalized autobiography *My Khyber Marriage*, was instantly smitten by the dashing young medical student from the wilds of the Hindu Kush.

In the forty-two years of their marriage, my grandmother wrote journalistic pieces and published books. Although a fiercely independent woman, she was resigned to playing the supportive wife she was expected to be. So, hanging back in the shadows, she typed out my grandfather's work, edited it, and allowed him to shine.

Over four decades he churned out more than seventy books, and many hundreds of pieces of journalism published in every conceivable language. An expert on Central Asia and the Middle East, he was a representative at the League of Nations, an emeritus professor, and a confidante to heads of state.

But above all, he was a writer.

Looking at his life and career as I so often do, I see my own life mirrored in his. No surprise of course, because I've been inspired by his love of travel and adventure, and by the desperate need for freedom. He lived by a pair of mantras, passed down to my father, and then on to me.

The first: 'Time spent on reconnaissance is seldom wasted.'

The second: 'Write, write, write, and the doors will open themselves.'

There was never any question my father would follow in his footsteps as a writer. But, looking at it as I am doing now, I realize it was my aunt, Amina, who was expected to be the budding author. She once told me how, when aged eighteen in the summer of 1937, my grandfather had brought her two packets wrapped in brown paper and string.

The first contained an Underwood typewriter.

In the second was a ream of paper.

'He instructed me to write a book,' she once explained, 'and that if I did, he would get it published. And that's just what happened. I typed away all summer in the garden. As the leaves began to turn, I handed him a manuscript of my first collection of tales – *Tiger of the Frontier*.'

The book was launched the next year by Sampson Low, one of my grandfather's publishers. While I'm certain there were enormous expectations on her, Aunt Amina wrote relatively little else in her long and amazing life. The handful of books she published showed off her bedazzling sense of imagination – the very same we knew from the stories she told us.

My father was far too sensible to have the same gift of imagination. Practical, level-headed, and thoroughly reserved, he weighed situations up with great care before he acted. What he lacked in imagination, he made up in industriousness. I've written elsewhere how the soundtrack to my childhood at Langton House was that of a manual typewriter clattering away like machine-gun fire.

He wrote like a man who'd been told his family would be executed at dawn were he not to complete the job at hand. I used to watch him. It was one of the most extraordinary things I've ever seen. When he typed, his hands weren't those of an ordinary mortal. Rather, they were the hands of a sorcerer. In the rare moments when they weren't bashing the keys, they were flexing and gnashing, as though filled with an unruly lifeblood of their own.

Considering it now, I get the feeling Aunt Amina was expected to be the writer. Five years older than my father, she was a gifted storyteller. But, in the same way cooking a meal requires various flavours, being a writer takes the collision of various elements.

In *The Reason to Write* I set down a great many thoughts about writing. One of the central points was that – while almost anyone can knock out a book if they put their mind to it – very few people are what I call 'real' writers.

Looking at my father and grandfather, I can safely say that they were real writers. They both had the fixation and the

11

obsession. But, most of all, they had the intense dedication needed to make it as a wordsmith. From my life writing books I've come to regard it as the single most important factor which guarantees success.

Doing the grind.

It's that simple.

Grind away, even when you're half-blind from editing the manuscript, and when your head pounds, and bother to put in that last damn comma even when you know that no one will notice whether it's there... and you deserve to be where you yearn to be.

Again, I've written about my own path on the writing journey in *The Reason to Write*, so no need to expand on it here. What I want to note is that there's something so incredibly satisfying about building on foundations laid down over centuries by members of my family.

I see it as passing on a baton – a baton handed from one generation to the next – first orally, and then in print.

Over a span of more than a century, my grandfather, father, and I have published hundreds of books. We are merely the newest branches of a tree, the roots of which stretch downward deep into the soil.

Our recent contribution has spanned three generations, and a hundred years. Beginning with *Eastern Moonbeams* – it has encompassed literature, travel, philosophy, psychology, *belle-lettres*, and folklore.

As I sit here, writing books and thinking about the world, every word I type is connected to every word uttered by my father, grandfather, and by the generations who came before us.

In the following pages I have assembled fragments of the combined corpus of a century. My hope is that it's as much of a joy to read as it has been to assemble.

Tahir Shah

AUTHOR BIOGRAPHIES

The Sirdar Ikbal Ali Shah (1894-1969)

Eldest son of the Nawab Amjad Ali Shah, the Sirdar Ikbal was born at the ancestral seat of Sardhana, into the Afghan nobility, the Sadaat of Paghman. He was educated at the Aligarh University, before travelling to Scotland during the Great War to begin studies for a medical career.

While in Edinburgh he published *Eastern Moonbeams*, a small book of 'poetry in prose' that began not only his own literary career, but a century-long journey of literary production. The Sirdar fell in love with the daughter of a Scottish aristocrat, Elizabeth Luiza MacKenzie. They were married, and began a life together of travel and adventure, and one that bridged West with East.

In a world ravaged by rebellion and war, the Sirdar Ikbal Ali Shah was deeply conscious of the fact that a particular kind of cultural information was needed if Occident and Orient were to coexist in the new order. Welcomed in the ruling courts of Europe, the Near East, and Central Asia, he became a close friend and confidant to many of the leaders of the day – among them Mustafa Kemal Ataturk of Turkey,

15

King Abdullah of Jordan, King Fuad of Egypt, the Aga Khan, and the founder of Saudi Arabia, King Ibn Saud.

During the inter-war years, the Sirdar Ikbal played a role at the League of Nations in Geneva, his efforts seeking to foster unity between all Muslim peoples. His writtenwork from this time includes hundreds of articles which appeared in the international media, as well as a great many radio pieces for the BBC.

The Sirdar is widely regarded as one of the leading exponents from the first half of the twentieth century to present Sufi thought and culture within the West, and to stress the notion of tolerance that lies at the heart of the Islamic faith.

Idries Shah (1924-1996)

Born at the Himalayan hill station of Shimla, Idries Shah was the eldest son of the Sirdar Ikbal Ali Shah. Brought up in Central Asia, the Near East, and in Europe, he acted as his father's secretary from a young age, and was groomed to build on the foundations of bridging Orient with Occident that his father and his mother had laid.

Idries Shah frequently observed that one of the key reasons he was so well positioned to fulfil this role was that his childhood and adolescence had been so unusual. Embracing an astonishing variety of people, places, traditions, and disparate cultures, Shah gained a unique understanding of human society – from both East and West.

Immersing himself in the first part of his career in informal belief systems, Idries Shah devoted the central part of his life to explaining the thinking within the Sufi tradition to others. Stripping away what he regarded as misleading distractions – such as music and dance – that frequently accompany Sufi groups, Shah presented the elemental thought of the tradition in a new way.

Publishing scores of books on these and related themes over a forty-year career, Shah found himself at the heart of what was to become an era of fresh thinking. Having sold in their millions, his books are studied at postgraduate level at universities the world over.

Although basing himself in the United Kingdom for much of his adult life, Shah travelled and lectured widely. During the years of the Soviet invasion in Afghanistan, he took a leading role in assisting the Mujahedeen militia in the war-stricken country of his ancestors, and raising international awareness to the conflict.

As far as Idries Shah was concerned, there was nothing quite so important as demonstrating to others that the Sufi Path, which has assisted countless generations in the East, could help the Occident in the very same way.

A SON OF A SON I

Tahir Shah (1966–)

Tahir Shah was born in London, and raised primarily at the family's home, Langton House, in the English countryside – where founder of the Boy Scouts, Lord Baden Powell, was also brought up.

Along with his twin and elder sisters, Tahir was continually coaxed to regard the world around him through Oriental eyes. This included being exposed from early childhood to Eastern stories, and to the back-to-front humour of the wise fool, Nasrudin.

Having studied at a leading public school, Bryanston, Tahir took a degree in International Relations, his particular interest being in African dictatorships of the mid-1980s. His research in this area led him to travel alone through a wide number of failing African states, including Uganda, Sierra Leone, and Zaire.

After university, Tahir embarked on a plethora of widespread travels through the Indian subcontinent, Latin America, and Africa, drawing them together in his first travelogue, *Beyond the Devil's Teeth*. In the years that followed, he published more than a dozen works of travel. These quests – for lost cities, treasure, Indian magic, and for the secrets of the so-called Birdmen of Peru – led to what is surely one of the most extraordinary bodies of travel work ever published.

In the early 2000s, with two small children, Tahir moved his young family from an apartment in London's East End to a supposedly haunted mansion in the middle of a Casablanca

19

shantytown. The tale of the adventure was published in his bestselling book, *The Caliph's House*.

In recent years, Tahir Shah has released a cornucopia of work, embracing travel, fiction, and literary criticism. He has also made documentaries for National Geographic TV and the History Channel, and published hundreds of articles in leading magazines, newspapers, and journals. His oeuvre is regarded as exceptionally original and, as an author, he is considered a champion of the new face of publishing.

AN EDITORIAL NOTE

IN EDITING THIS selection of combined work written over the span of a hundred years, I have sought out some pieces with care, and chosen others at random. The extracts are presented here in a largely arbitrary order, but in a rotating sequence of father, grandfather, and son.

As the reader will see, the particular way the material has been handled depends on who has written it, and when. This collection is not intended to be comprehensive or inclusive in any way, but rather to provide a sense of three generations writing over the days, months, and years of an entire century.

My grandfather, the Sirdar Ikbal Ali Shah, published his first book at the end of the Great War, and continued writing until the late fifties.

My father, Idries Shah, began publishing almost exactly the same time his own father ceased. And I began my book-writing journey in earnest in the early nineties, just when my father's prodigious output had recently been completed.

A Son of a Son is inspired by the Persian saying, told to me so often by my father during my childhood – 'If the father cannot, the son will finish the task.' In the spirit of the aphorism, I have not broadened the selection to include work by my grandmother, my aunt, or by the other writers in our family.

The Magic Horse

THIS TALE IS of great importance because it belongs to an instructional corpus of mystical materials with inner content but – beyond entertainment value – without immediate external significance.

The teaching-story was brought to perfection as a communication instrument many thousands of years ago. The fact that it has not developed greatly since then has caused people obsessed by some theories of our current civilizations to regard it as the product of a less enlightened time. They feel that it must surely be little more than a literary curiosity, something fit for children, the projection, perhaps, of infantile desires, a means of enacting a wish-fulfilment.

Hardly anything could be further from the truth than such pseudo-philosophical, certainly unscientific, imaginings. Many teaching-stories are entertaining to children and to naive peasants. Many of them in the forms in which they are viewed by conditioned theorists have been so processed by unregenerate amateurs that their effective content is distorted. Some apply only to certain communities, depending upon special circumstances for their correct unfolding: circumstances whose absence effectively prevents the action of which they are capable.

So little is known to the academics, the scholars and the intellectuals of this world about these materials, that there is no word in modern languages which has been set aside to describe them.

But the teaching-story exists, nevertheless. It is a part of the most priceless heritage of mankind.

Real teaching-stories are not to be confused with parables; which are adequate enough in their intention, but still on a lower level of material, generally confined to the inculcation of moralistic principles, not the assistance of interior movement of the human mind. What we often take on the lower level of parable, however, can sometimes be seen by real specialists as teaching-stories, especially when experienced under the correct conditions.

Unlike the parable, the meaning of the teaching-story cannot be unravelled by ordinary intellectual methods alone. Its action is direct and certain, upon the innermost part of the human being, an action incapable of manifestation by means of the emotional or intellectual apparatus.

The closest that we can come to describing its effect is to say that it connects with a part of the individual which cannot be reached by any other convention, and that it establishes in him or in her a means of communication with a non-verbalized truth beyond the customary limitations of our familiar dimensions.

Some teaching-stories cannot now be reclaimed because of the literary and traditionalistic, even ideological, processing to which they have been subjected. The worst of such processes is the historicizing one, where a community comes to believe that one of their former teaching-stories represents literal historical truth.

This tale is given here in a form which is innocent of this and other kinds of maltreatment.

*

ONCE UPON A time, not so very long ago, there was a realm in which the people were exceedingly prosperous. All kinds of discoveries had been made by them, in the growing of plants, in harvesting and preserving fruits, and in making objects for sale to other countries, and in many other practical arts.

Their ruler was unusually enlightened, and he encouraged new discoveries and activities, because he knew of their advantages for his people.

He had a son named Hoshyar, who was expert in using strange contrivances, and another – called Tambal – a dreamer, who seemed interested only in things which were of little value in the eyes of the citizens.

From time to time the king, who was named King Mumkin, circulated announcements to this effect:

'Let all those who have notable devices and useful artefacts present them to the palace for examination, so that they may be appropriately rewarded.'

Now there were two men of that country – an ironsmith and a woodworker – who were great rivals in most things, and each delighted in making strange contraptions. When they heard this announcement one day, they agreed to compete for an award, so that their relative merits could be

SHAH

decided once and for all, by their sovereign, and publicly recognized.

Accordingly, the smith worked day and night on a mighty engine, employing a multitude of talented specialists, and surrounding his workshop with high walls so that his devices and methods should not become known.

At the same time the woodworker took his simple tools and went into a forest where, after long and solitary reflection, he prepared his own masterpiece.

News of the rivalry spread, and people thought that the smith must easily win, for his cunning works had been seen before, and while the woodworker's products were generally admired, they were only of occasional and undramatic use.

When both were ready, the king received them in open court.

The smith produced an immense metallic fish which could, he said, swim in and under the water. It could carry large quantities of freight over the land. It could burrow into the earth; and it could even fly slowly through the air. At first the court found it hard to believe that there could be such a wonder made by man: but when the smith and his assistants demonstrated it, the king was overjoyed and declared the smith among the most honoured in the land, with a special rank and the title of 'Benefactor of the Community'.

Prince Hoshyar was placed in charge of the making of the wondrous fishes, and the services of this new device became available to all mankind.

Everyone blessed the smith and Hoshyar, as well as the benign and sagacious monarch whom they loved so much.

In the excitement, the self-effacing carpenter had been all but forgotten. Then, one day, someone said: 'But what about the contest? Where is the entry of the woodworker? We all know him to be an ingenious man. Perhaps he has produced something useful.'

'How could anything possibly be as useful as the Wondrous Fishes?' asked Hoshyar. And many of the courtiers and the people agreed with him.

But one day the king was bored. He had become accustomed to the novelty of the fishes and the reports of the wonders which they so regularly performed. He said: 'Call the woodcarver, for I would now like to see what he has made.'

The simple woodcarver came into the throne-room, carrying a parcel wrapped in coarse cloth. As the whole court craned forward to see what he had, he took off the covering to reveal – a wooden horse. It was well enough carved, and it had some intricate patterning chiselled into it, as well as being decorated with coloured paints, but it was only... 'A mere plaything!' snapped the king.

'But, Father,' said Prince Tambal, 'let us ask the man what it is for...'

'Very well,' said the king, 'what is it for?'

'Your Majesty,' stammered the woodcarver, 'it is a magic horse. It does not look impressive, but it has, as it were, its own inner senses. Unlike the fish, which has to be directed, this horse can interpret the desires of the rider, and carry him wherever he needs to go.'

'Such a stupidity is fit only for Tambal,' murmured the chief minister at the king's elbow. 'It cannot have any real advantage when measured against the wondrous fish.'

The woodcarver was preparing sadly to depart when Tambal said: 'Father, let me have the wooden horse.'

'All right,' said the king, 'give it to him. Take the woodcarver away and tie him on a tree somewhere, so that he will realize that our time is valuable. Let him contemplate the prosperity which the wondrous fish has brought us, and perhaps after some time we shall let him go free, to practise whatever he may have learned of real industriousness, through true reflection.'

The woodcarver was taken away, and Prince Tambal left the court carrying the magic horse.

Tambal took the horse to his quarters, where he discovered that it had several knobs, cunningly concealed in the carved designs. When these were turned in a certain manner, the horse – together with anyone mounted on it – rose into the air and sped to whatever place was in the mind of the person who moved the knobs.

In this way, day after day, Tambal flew to places which he had never visited before. By this process he came to know a great many things. He took the horse everywhere with him. One day he met Hoshyar, who said to him: 'Carrying a wooden horse is a fit occupation for such as you. As for me, I am working for the good of all, towards my heart's desire!'

Tambal thought: 'I wish I knew what was the good of all. And I wish I could know what my heart's desire is.'

When he was next in his room, he sat upon the horse and thought: 'I would like to find my heart's desire.' At the same time he moved some of the knobs on the horse's neck. Swifter than light the horse rose into the air and carried the prince a thousand days' ordinary journey away, to a far kingdom, ruled by a magician-king.

The king, whose name was Kahana, had a beautiful daughter called Precious Pearl, Durri-Karima. In order to protect her, he had imprisoned her in a circling palace, which wheeled in the sky, higher than any mortal could reach. As he was approaching the magic land, Tambal saw the glittering palace in the heavens, and alighted there.

The princess and the young horseman met and fell in love.

'My father will never allow us to marry,' she said, 'for he had ordained that I become the wife of the son of another magician-king who lives across the cold desert to the east of our homeland. He has vowed that when I am old enough I shall cement the unity of the two kingdoms by this marriage. His will has never been successfully opposed.'

'I will go and try to reason with him,' answered Tambal, as he mounted the magic horse again.

But when he descended into the magic land there were so many new and exciting things to see that he did not hurry to the palace. When at length he approached it, the drum at the gate, indicating the absence of the king, was already beating.

'He has gone to visit his daughter in the Whirling Palace,' said a passer-by when Tambal asked him when the king might be back, 'and he usually spends several hours at a time with her.'

Tambal went to a quiet place where he willed the horse to carry him to the king's own apartment. 'I will approach him at his own home,' he thought to himself, 'for if I go to the Whirling Palace without his permission he may be angry.'

He hid behind some curtains in the palace when he got there, and lay down to sleep.

Meanwhile, unable to keep her secret, the princess Precious Pearl had confessed to her father that she had been visited by a man on a flying horse, and that he wanted to marry her. Kahana was furious.

He placed sentries around the Whirling Palace and returned to his own apartment to think things over. As soon as he entered his bedchamber, one of the tongueless magic servants guarding it pointed to the wooden horse lying in a corner. 'Aha!' exclaimed the magician-king. 'Now I have him. Let us look at this horse and see what manner of thing it may be.'

As he and his servants were examining the horse, the prince managed to slip away and conceal himself in another part of the palace.

After twisting the knobs, tapping the horse and generally trying to understand how it worked, the king was baffled. 'Take that thing away. It has no virtue now, even if it ever had any,' he said. 'It is just a trifle, fit for children.'

The horse was put into a store-cupboard.

Now King Kahana thought that he should make arrangements for his daughter's wedding without delay, in case the fugitive might have other powers or devices with which to try to win her. So he called her to his own palace and sent a message to the other magician-king, asking that the prince who was to marry her be sent to claim his bride.

Meanwhile Prince Tambal, escaping from the palace by night when some guards were asleep, decided that he must try to return to his own country. His quest for his heart's desire now seemed almost hopeless. 'If it takes me the rest of my life,' he said to himself, 'I shall come back here, bringing troops to take this kingdom by force. I can only do that by convincing my father that I must have his help to attain my heart's desire.'

So saying, he set off. Never was a man worse equipped for such a journey. An alien, travelling on foot, without any kind of provisions, facing pitiless heat and freezing nights interspersed with sandstorms, he soon became hopelessly lost in the desert.

Now, in his delirium, Tambal started to blame himself, his father, the magician-king, the woodcarver, even the princess and the magic horse itself. Sometimes he thought he saw water ahead of him, sometimes fair cities, sometimes he felt elated, sometimes incomparably sad. Sometimes he even thought that he had companions in his difficulties, but when he shook himself he saw that he was quite alone.

He seemed to have been travelling for an eternity. Suddenly, when he had given up and started again several times, he saw something directly in front of him. It looked like a mirage: a garden, full of delicious fruits, sparkling and almost, as it were, beckoning him towards them.

Tambal did not at first take much notice of this, but soon, as he walked, he saw that he was indeed passing through such a garden. He gathered some of the fruits and tasted them cautiously. They were delicious. They took away his fear as well as his hunger and thirst. When he was full, he lay down in the shade of a huge and welcoming tree and fell asleep.

When he woke up he felt well enough, but something seemed to be wrong. Running to a nearby pool, he looked at his reflection in the water. Staring up at him was a horrible apparition. It had a long beard, curved horns, ears a foot long. He looked down at his hands. They were covered with fur.

Was it a nightmare? He tried to wake himself, but all the pinching and pummelling had no effect. Now, almost bereft of his senses, beside himself with fear and horror, thrown into transports of screaming, racked with sobs, he threw himself on the ground. 'Whether I live or die,' he thought, 'these accursed fruits have finally ruined me. Even with the greatest army of all time, conquest will not help me. Nobody would marry me now, much less the Princess Precious Pearl. And I cannot imagine the beast who would not be terrified at the sight of me – let alone my heart's desire!' And he lost consciousness.

When he woke again, it was dark, and a light was approaching through the groves of silent trees. Fear and hope struggled in him. As it came closer he saw that the light was from a lamp enclosed in a brilliant starlike shape, and it was carried by a bearded man, who walked in the pool of brightness which it cast around.

The man saw him. 'My son,' he said, 'you have been affected by the influences of this place. If I had not come past, you would have remained just another beast of this enchanted grove, for there are many more like you. But I can help you.'

Tambal wondered whether this man was a fiend in disguise, perhaps the very owner of the evil trees. But as his sense came back, he realized that he had nothing to lose.

'Help me, father,' he said to the sage.

'If you really want your heart's desire,' said the other man, 'you have only to fix this desire firmly in your mind, not thinking of the fruit. You then have to take up some of the dried fruits, not the fresh, delicious ones, lying at the foot of all these trees, and eat them. Then follow your destiny.'

So saying, he walked away.

While the sage's light disappeared into the darkness, Tambal saw that the moon was rising, and in its rays he could see that there were indeed piles of dried fruits under every tree.

He gathered some and ate them as quickly as he could.

Slowly, as he watched, the fur disappeared from his hands and arms. The horns first shrank, then vanished. The beard fell away. He was himself again. By now it was first light, and in the dawn he heard the tinkling of camel bells. A procession was coming through the enchanted forest.

It was undoubtedly the cavalcade of some important personage, on a long journey. As Tambal stood there, two outriders detached themselves from the glittering escort and galloped up to him.

'In the name of the prince, our lord, we demand some of your fruit. His celestial Highness is thirsty and has indicated a desire for some of these strange apricots,' said an officer.

Still Tambal did not move, such was his numbed condition after his recent experiences. Now the prince himself came down from his palanquin and said:

'I am Jadugarzada, son of the magician-king of the east. Here is a bag of gold, oaf. I am having some of your fruit, because I am desirous of it. I am in a hurry, hastening to claim my bride, Princess Precious Pearl, daughter of Kahana, magician-king of the west.'

At these words Tambal's heart turned over. But, realizing that this must be his destiny which the sage had told him to follow, he offered the prince as much of the fruit as he could eat.

When he had eaten, the prince began to fall asleep. As he did so, horns, fur and huge ears started to grow out of him. The soldiers shook him, and the prince began to behave in a strange way. He claimed that he was normal, and that they were deformed.

The councillors who accompanied the party restrained the prince and held a hurried debate. Tambal claimed that all would have been well if the prince had not fallen asleep. Eventually it was decided to put Tambal in the palanquin to play the part of the prince. The horned Jadugarzada was tied to a horse with a veil thrown over his face, disguised as a serving-woman.

'He may recover his wits eventually,' said the councillors, 'and in any case he is still our prince. Tambal shall marry the girl. Then, as soon as possible, we shall carry them all back to our own country for our king to unravel the problem.'

Tambal, biding his time and following his destiny, agreed to his own part in the masquerade.

When the party arrived at the capital of the west, the king himself came out to meet them. Tambal was taken to the princess as her bridegroom, and she was so astonished that she nearly fainted. But Tambal managed to whisper to her rapidly what had happened, and they were duly married, amid great jubilations.

In the meantime the horned prince had half recovered his wits, but not his human form, and his escort still kept him under cover. As soon as the feasting was over, the chief of the horned prince's party (who had been keeping Tambal and the princess under a very close watch) presented himself to the court. He said: 'O just and glorious monarch, fountain of wisdom; the time has now come, according to the pronouncements of our astrologers and soothsayers, to conduct the bridal pair back to our own land, so that they may be established in their new home under the most felicitous circumstances and influences.'

The princess turned to Tambal in alarm, for she knew that Jadugarzada would claim her as soon as they were on the open road – and make an end of Tambal into the bargain.

Tambal whispered to her, 'Fear nothing. We must act as best we can, following our destiny. Agree to go, making only the condition that you will not travel without the wooden horse.'

At first the magician-king was annoyed at this foible of his daughter's. He realized that she wanted the horse because it was connected with her first suitor. But the chief minister of the horned prince said: 'Majesty, I cannot see that this is anything worse than a whim for a toy, such as any young girl might have. I hope that you will allow her to have her plaything, so that we may make haste homeward.'

So the magician-king agreed, and soon the cavalcade was resplendently on its way. After the king's escort had withdrawn, and before the time of the first night-halt, the hideous Jadugarzada threw off his veil and cried out to Tambal:

'Miserable author of my misfortunes! I now intend to bind you hand and foot, to take you captive back to my own land. If, when we arrive there, you do not tell me how to remove this enchantment, I will have you flayed alive, inch by inch. Now, give me the Princess Precious Pearl.'

Tambal ran to the princess and, in front of the astonished party, rose into the sky on the wooden horse with Precious Pearl mounted behind him.

Within a matter of minutes the couple alighted at the palace of King Mumkin. They related everything that had happened to them, and the king was almost overcome with delight at their safe return. He at once gave orders for the hapless woodcarver to be released, recompensed and applauded by the entire populace.

When the king was gathered to his fathers, Princess Precious Pearl and Prince Tambal succeeded him. Prince Hoshyar was quite pleased, too, because he was still entranced by the wondrous fish.

'I am glad for your own sakes, if you are happy,' he used to say to them, 'but, for my own part, nothing is more rewarding than concerning myself with the wondrous fish.'

And this history is the origin of a strange saying current among the people of that land, yet whose beginnings have now been forgotten. The saying is: 'Those who want fish can achieve much through fish, and those who do not know their heart's desire may first have to hear the story of the wooden horse.'

From: *Caravan of Dreams*
Idries Shah

Witchcraft and Necromancy
in Afghanistan

IN AFGHANISTAN, WITCHES are held to be in league with
Satan, from whom they derive their powers, and a *saher* or
necromancer is no true Muslim, for, although there appears
to be a belief in the existence of necromancy, he who
practises it is a *kaffir* (infidel), and no true follower of the
laws taught by Mohammed.

The Yogi from India and its borderland are known to be
cognizant of the art of necromancy, and those who come in
contact with them learn the nefarious practice. Yogi are, of
course, Hindus, and, according to the belief of the Afghans,
cannot call any superior beings such as angels and jinns
to their assistance, hence they rely on 'Paleed', an unclean
spirit.

Although it is averred that necromancy is rare in
Afghanistan, the women in the backwoods of the country
seem to possess knowledge of certain practices by which
influence can be exercised over other minds. How they
became possessed of it is hard to say; it is certain, however,
that a class of 'wise women' exists in the country, who
impart their knowledge to the rest. It is extremely perilous
to a woman practising necromancy for any man to discover

that she is so engaged, or even for men to hear rumours of her being thus occupied, for the result is that she is soon dispatched 'to the care of Satan's family in the Eternal Fires'.

Witchcraft in Afghanistan assumes many forms and is often resorted to in cases where revenge is desired. To obtain this result, women mould crude dolls of wax, into which a pin is stuck each day. The effect believed to be produced by this action is to bring misfortune and disease on the individual whom it is desired to injure. Together with the pinsticking, the person seeking revenge burns some pungent substance, and holds the doll in the smoke whilst reading certain imprecations. Whosoever becomes an adherent of Satan and desires to practise witchcraft must renounce all religious observances and beliefs, and assume filthy habits, otherwise the charms will not take effect, and the Devil will take fright on hearing the name of Allah pronounced.

To subdue a husband or mother-in-law it is considered most efficacious to cause them to eat the flesh of an owl. Whilst the classical conception of the owl is that of the bird of wisdom, the popular conception, shared also by the Afghans, is the reverse. To be hailed as an owl in Afghanistan, as here, is equivalent to being called an ass. This has led to the superstition amongst the Afghans that the constant administering to any person of the flesh of a roasted owl will result in the conquest even of the most intractable temperaments. But great caution must be exercised in the preparing of the fateful dish so as to escape detection, for otherwise the days of the woman responsible for it would undoubtedly be numbered.

In the case of a theft occurring in the house, it is usual for the women to seek to find the thief either through the services of a *saher* or by taking the matter into their own hands and subjecting the household to a severe scrutiny in a manner to be presently explained.

If the *saher* is employed, on the case being related to him he chants an incantation over some water, which must be used as a gargle by everybody in the house. It has no effect on the innocent, but causes the gums of the thief to bleed profusely.

If the affair is to be dealt with at home, the lady of the house takes an old slipper and drives a big nail through the centre; the shoe is then held by means of the head of the nail, and two women balance it on their index fingers. A circle is then drawn on the ground and the assistance of the Devil is invoked. The lady of the house strikes the circle with the fellow slipper of the one poised on the women's fingers, and whilst the servants and others stand before her in a row, she exclaims 'Oh, Nona – I take the name of your husband and ask you who is the thief. Is it So-and-So or...?' (naming names).

If the shoe does not move on the mentioning of a name, the owner is deemed innocent, and the process is repeated until, on the utterance of some name, the shoe moves, describing a right angle. This is considered to be a proof of guilt, and the detected thief is made to restore the stolen property. 'Nona' is the name of a great necromancer, quite unknown to authentic history.

Some women have been known to send burning missiles, containing a curious medley of rubbish, to the homes of those with whom they have had a quarrel. The writer has seen one of these which failed on its mission and lay in a field. These missiles are formed of round earthen pots with narrow mouths and a capacity for containing about half a gallon of water. The pots are filled with rotten eggs, honey or syrup, lentils and small pieces of glass, sharp nails and powder of either lead oxide or carmine. The exterior of the pot is sometimes encircled with white chalk. This missile is doubtless intended to act as an explosive, and, if falling in close proximity to anyone, the glass and nails might inflict serious injuries. The mode of procedure in the dispatch of these messengers of evil is peculiar. Either a necromancer or a witch is entrusted with the work. The pot, having been prepared, is placed, on some dark night, in the centre of four cross roads. Certain charms are read over it, and the name and address of the person on whom it is intended to fall is also repeated. Upon this, the pot is said to rise in the air and travel towards the enemy's house, looking like a ball of fire in its flight.

Needless to say, it is much to be questioned whether such pots do actually fly and fall upon the houses. Necromancers work on the minds of superstitious women under their influence, and cause them to believe in the flight of such pots by sending up a *borj* into the air. A *borj* means a dome or heavenly body. Probably what really happens is that a witch – or, at any rate, a woman with the pretensions of exercising that ignoble calling – tells her clients that the

41

pot will pass over their house at such and such a time, on such and such a night, and that if they look out they will see it flying. In the meantime she prepares a dome-shaped structure supported by very fine bamboo fibre, and covers it with fine red tissue paper. In the centre of this she fixes a bundle of rags which have been soaked in oil. The circumference of such a *borj* is often as much as two feet.

When a woman has made a balloon of this description, she carries it to some spot near her house, and lights a smoky fire, holding the balloon over it till it is inflated with smoke, then she ignites the rags and lets off the balloon. As it rises, the light of the burning rags gives it the appearance of a ball of fire, and the women, watching it passing over the houses, say that it is the pot on its journey to strike their enemy's abode.

Some men are known to undertake to harm a client's enemy on payment of a given sum. They go into the woods and take up their abode in some lonely spot where no human face is seen.

Here they employ themselves rigorously in chanting incantations to invoke the powers of evil. They say that one effect producible is to create *kulla pundee* (*kulla* – cheeks or face; *pundee* – from *pumdeedun*, meaning swelling). The face of a man against whom such a charm is exercised begins to swell. This increases day by day till, it is said, pus fills the cheeks and the man dies. Women may be heard imputing the illnesses of their husbands or brothers to the insidious charms of necromancers. Also, in the case of a death during or after childbirth, they say that a *kuftara* (a witch) caused the haemorrhage which killed the patient.

Frogs are also used, especially by ladies of position, to bring harm or at least disfavour on other people. It often happens that a husband decides a quarrel between his wife and his sister, or mother, in his wife's favour; the opposing party naturally becomes jealous, and enchantment is frequently resorted to for the purpose of creating trouble between husband and wife. Two frogs, one male and one female, are procured. The figure of a black ox is painted on the back of the male specimen and a cow's face on the back of the female. Then both are tied back to back and placed in an earthenware pot which is buried amongst a heap of burning faggots. Soon the frogs are burned and reduced to fine powder. This powder effects the desired result, for, whenever this is thrown on any person without that person being aware of it, its effect is to turn away his or her affection from whomsoever of the opposite sex has hitherto been most deeply loved. The heart of a sheep and the horns of a bull are also employed to attain the same object, but they are believed to be less efficacious.

So far I have dealt with the spells cast by *saher*, pointing out that they necessitated the employment of *kalamatal kuffr* - words of infidelity contrary to the laws of Mohammed. The second form of enchantment known in Afghanistan is spoken of as *ufsoon*. This is in so far permissible that it may or may not be *kaffr* (unclean), for it derives its origin from Son 'Samaree' who lived and practised the art in the days of Moses, and being associated with that prophet, it is considered less worthy of censure.

All that is ascertainable of 'Samaree' is that he moulded a cow in silver and gold, and declared that he could make it speak. One day, thanks to the powers that he had gained by *ufsoon*, he saw the angel Gabriel alight from his horse and visit Moses in the mosque, and deliver God's message. 'Samaree' collected the sand from under the hoofs of Gabriel's horse, and on the following morning, having gathered the people together, he threw the sand into the cow's mouth, and the cow at once began to speak. 'Samaree' hereupon led away the followers of Moses, making them believe that he had the power to put life into matter. Moses prayed to God, who commanded 'Samaree' to be turned into a stone figure, which he would always remain. This led to the warning to the descendants of 'Tiflay Chihil Roza' ('Son' or 'Child of Forty Days') that they should always recollect the fate of 'Samaree' if they ventured to entertain the idea of learning necromancy. Adam is termed the 'Child of Forty Days' because it is believed that it took forty days to create him.

In Afghanistan, witches (or *kuftaras*) are said to be able to assume any form or shape. They dwell in lonely roads or underground, where acacias grow. They haunt men, women, and children, and pursue them with the intention of devouring their livers and hearts. There are said to be several ways of recognizing them. One is that they always seek to hide their faces; if seen, the face has the appearance of that of an old woman of about eighty. They have very large, fiery eyes, many wrinkles, and hollow cheeks. Their teeth are very large and prominent. They entice little children from the villages to their dens and woodland haunts, and then pounce on them.

*

A STUDY OF the charms, spells, and divinations of Afghanistan seems to show that they are to a great extent the outcome of the religious traditions and old beliefs of the country, though, as is only to be expected, a large number are exotic and can be traced to Indian and Persian ideas. In the provinces of Herat, for instance, it is noticeable that the charms have a distinctly Shiatic character; in the north they bear marks of a Kirghiz origin, while in the east and south they have a strong Hindu and Baluch colouring. Kabul itself seems to be the meeting-place of the ideas and traditions of all these races. As in the case of superstitions, the women have borne by far the greater share in the perpetuation of the charms and spells.

The charms have, in most cases, been written by mullas or *faqeers*, and the people place an unquestioning belief and unflinching trust in them. The majority of them, which are called *taweez*, are passages from the Qur'an, though a few are invocations in the names of saints or pious leaders of sects whose lives are regarded as offering noble examples to their fellow beings.

In certain parts of the country the writing of charms and spells is taken up by some mullas as their profession, and, indeed, in the regions of Badakhshan and the country adjoining to Swat and Bonair in the north-east, this is their only vocation in life. In other districts, however, they add to their other qualifications a knowledge of medicine and take the place of the village doctor.

Only those disciples of the mullas who win their favour by their obedience and by the proof they give in their lives that they are worthy to be entrusted with the secret art are initiated into its mysteries. In order to acquire the necessary knowledge, they must subject themselves to a course of self-discipline and abnegation, during which they must go through special forms of prayer known as *chillas*, meaning forty days' prayer, and observe certain rules of fasting. These rules vary considerably; in some cases the aspirants are forbidden to eat meat or eggs, in others they may eat lamb, but no fish or eggs. During this period, which is called the *wazeefa*, the aspirants must retire from contact with their fellow beings to a cell, where, in addition to the prayers already mentioned, they must recite a certain number of times such passages from the Qur'an or other holy writings as may be given them for the purpose by their *peer* (or the spiritual leader).

As the days pass, the result of this self-discipline is manifested in the appearance of forms and apparitions, some in the shape of animals, others like ethereal beings that vanish in an instant. These forms are said to mock at the student and try to frighten him, but he sits with closed eyes on his prayer carpet, and draws around him a circle called *diara*. So long as he remains within his *diara* no harm can touch him, but the minute he puts his foot outside the circle he will be destroyed. Such, at least, is the belief.

The efforts of these evil beings reach their climax on the day preceding that on which the *wazeefa* is to end. Assuming, therefore, that the *wazeefa* is to last for a period of eleven days, on the tenth day the student will be in a state of the greatest terror, for all the spirits of jinns which he is to subjugate will be seated close to him, though outside the safety circle, in the most hideous forms of giants, lions, serpents, and other wild creatures, which it is possible to conceive. On the last night of the *wazeefa* their craft and cunning will know no bounds, and they will leave no form of horror untried in order to frighten the man into abandoning the safety of his circle. If, however, he succeeds in resisting, and provided that he has faithfully fulfilled all the other conditions, these same fearsome forms will, at the end of the eleven days, or the stipulated time, kneel down before him with folded hands and receive his commands.

Each charm has a certain number of beings subservient to it. The severity and duration of *wazeefa* vary according to the power of the jinns, for the more powerful the being, the harder is the task of overcoming him and the greater the command of the art required. In some cases, the mullas can send these jinns or spirits as their servants to perform tasks for their clients; in others they write a charm which is possessed of a curative value with regard to certain diseases; while in yet others the same power may be employed to bring harm to an enemy by causing his house to be burned, or bringing some severe or fatal disease or even insanity upon him. Many a good lady has invoked the aid of the charms to subdue her husband.

The *wazeefas* are divisible into two principal branches: the *jamalee* and *jalallee*. The *jamalee* pertains to ethereal or celestial light, and is consequently a mild form; its control is not difficult, and no real danger threatens the learner. *Jalallee*, on the other hand, is connected with wrath, anger, and severity, and is a much more violent phase of the *wazeefas*. Those, therefore, who wish to take it up must have great strength of mind, for the beings will make so many attacks, that, unless the student can offer an exceptionally powerful resistance, he will either be killed or driven insane. All the more important jinns and spirits are under the control of *jalallee*.

How far these people do actually perform what they profess to do is a matter which perplexes the mind of one who has been born and bred in this bed of charms and divination. One fact, at any rate, is undeniable. That is, that they are always on the look-out to take advantage of circumstances which may enhance their reputation; whether they have ever killed a man by the mere force of a charm, or turned a husband into the romantic lover of the wife whom he hated, is very questionable.

Nevertheless, an unquestioning belief in the charms written by pious masters of art is pretty general in both sexes. Wrestlers fasten them in a capsule of silver on the left wrist in the belief that their power will carry them victoriously through all their contests. Women frequently sew them into their husband's garments when they go forth to fight; this is, in fact, their most popular use, for the possession of such a charm is a sure protection against wounds. An oft-related story from the memoirs of the late Ameer Abdur Rahman Khan may be recalled. The Ameer writes that once when he was reviewing his troops, a soldier deliberately fired at him. The bullet passed through the back of his chair and killed a page-boy who was standing behind him. 'I used not to believe in charms,' said the Ameer, 'but I owe my life to a charm which a mulla had given me and which I was wearing at the time. I tested the efficacy of it by tying it round the neck of a goat and firing several shots at him, none of which hit him.' I refrain from commenting on what the wise Ameer said, and leave it at that.

A bullet which has passed through a human body or has lodged itself and been extracted from muscle substance is very highly prized. It is, they say, saturated in warm blood, and if worn in a pendant will act as a protection against all unforeseen troubles and mishaps.

While it is quite easy for anyone to read or even write a charm, it will have no effect unless written by one who has undergone the prescribed course of discipline, and who, in addition, has received permission from a mulla or person of equal standing to write such charms. The paper on which they are written must be kept folded, otherwise the beneficial properties will escape.

Ladies often hire the services of a man versed in the art to devote himself to the exercise of spells and charms, in order, by thus propitiating God, to obtain the blessing of a child. The man engaged for the work will either sit in a *chilla* in the cell of a mosque, or go down to the banks of a river to read his charms, or in some cases he may be allotted a room in his client's house, where he can shut himself up without fear of being disturbed. During this time the whole of his board and lodging, as well as clothing expenses, are paid by the lady employing him. Nor does the financial side of the transaction end there, for each week a number of goats must be provided to be thrown into the running stream as a sacrifice, while almost every day *neyaz*, or offerings of sweetmeats or fruits, must be made to the saints. After a prayer has been said, these offerings are distributed amongst the members of the family and the priest, who often retains more than half.

There is no doubt that these parasites influence the womenfolk very profoundly, and play upon their superstitious minds. If a *wazeefa* fails to obtain the desired object it must be repeated, so that it is no exaggeration to say that these mullas are more or less permanent dependants of any household which employs them.

On some occasions, charms must be written with musk and rose-water and placed inside a new earthenware pot. It is then put into a room where no one but the priest is allowed to go; the mouth of the pot is closed, and for eleven days the priest must seat himself in the room after the last prayer of the day has been said and recite the charm one hundred and one times, or, better still, eleven hundred times. After each of these recitals he retires to bed without speaking to anyone; when the eleven days are over, the lid of the pot is raised and seven coins are discovered inside; two of these are given to the poor, the rest the priest retains for his own use. This procedure may be repeated one hundred and one times.

Should the *amal*, as this prayer is called, not achieve the desired effect, it is attributed to failure in adhering in some respect to the strict regulations regarding fasting and general behaviour while the *amal* is performed, or to the fact that permission to use the *amal* has not been obtained from the mulla to whom it belongs; this last condition is essential to success.

Charms are frequently given as a means of relieving pain; in certain districts, in fact, they are the only treatment applied. When used for this purpose, a charm is burned and the vapour inhaled by the patient, while another is rubbed in water which the patient is made to drink. To protect children from the evil eye a charm or two is placed in a pendant worn round the neck. On occasions of domestic discord, a wife will often place a charm beneath a stone, when it is thought that the pressure of the stone on the paper will influence the husband's mind and render him obedient to his wife. When a man is setting forth on a journey, charms are fastened to his arms as a sure means of protection. If the journey is through water, and it is likely to be a long time before the traveller returns home, a large number of relations and friends come to bid him farewell; they tie charms or gold coins, wrapped in gorgeous silk, on his arms while one of them holds the Qur'an in his hand, and as the traveller steps out of his house he passes under the Holy Book and kisses it.

When, as often happens, a grave charge is brought against a man in the civil or military courts, a member of his family takes a vow to pray, on the bank of a river, for the acquittal of his relation. Each morning he goes down to the river, taking with him some dough made of a mixture of milk and fine flour. After washing himself in the stream, he settles down to his prayers. At the end of each prayer he picks out a small piece of the dough and, rolling it in his fingers like a pill, throws it into the stream. This procedure is followed every day until the heart of the judge, or of those upon whom the fate of his relation may depend, is so 'softened' under the influence of a higher power that he releases the prisoner. In cases of fatal or lingering illness, too, this is a common form of procedure, for it is believed that, provided the prayers are performed in strict accordance with the laws governing these charms, the invalid can be completely cured.

Like charms, spells are of two kinds – *nooree*, and *naree* (*noor* in Arabic means 'celestial light', *nar* means 'fire'). The terms have their origin in the belief that God created the angels from light, Adam from earth, and Satan from fire. Hence any spells which take the form of Qur'anic words or passages are *nooree*, while any employed by the Jogees, in which they seek the aid of Satan's followers, are called *naree*. It is believed to be wrong for a Muslim to learn *naree*, though he is at liberty to use *nooree* for the gratification of his desires.

The exercise of spells is not, as in the case of charms, confined to the mullas or to those authorized by them, but may be practised by anyone who is a believer in Allah and Prophet Mohammed. They are chiefly passages from the Holy Book of the Muslims and their uses are quite as numerous as those of the charms. Nervous women recite them in order to give themselves confidence; warriors read them before going into battle. They are recited, or, rather, muttered, over an invalid; young children are never sent out without a spell being read over them by their fond mothers.

No dish of white pudding is ever eaten without *sura'la-ay-laf'* being read and puffed over the dish; this is done to avert the evil eye of the servants or anyone who may have looked at the food in such a way as to cause disease to those who eat it. If a party in a boat is overtaken in a storm, passages are read from the Qur'an to appease the fury of the water. On a dark night a woman who finds herself alone has only to mutter a passage from the Holy Book in order to shield herself from all evil, and with a sword in her hand and a *sura* on her lips she can travel any distance without the slightest fear of being harmed.

Some people, in order to ensure the safety of their jewel casket, read a spell over it and then deposit it in a cupboard where they leave it in perfect confidence that it is proof against theft. Some women go so far as to claim that the fertility of their gardens is due to the spells they puffed over each plant. Both charms and spells are tied into the hair as a cure for headache. *Sura' qulhowulla'* is also read over the head of the patient while the forehead is massaged with the thumb and index finger, both fingers being brought together at a point in the middle of the forehead just above the nose and the folds of skin thus gathered being pinched with a smart twitch.

Throughout the country there is a strong belief in divination, and every province has its own particular saint or local *mazar* to whom the people turn in time of need. The graves of *faqeers* who have lived a life of piety and self-mortification are believed to possess miraculous powers of granting the desires of those who honour and tend them. The most extraordinary stories are told of the graves of these saints, and even the trees which overshadow them are regarded by the populace as having curative properties. If a childless mother drinks a decoction made from the leaves of such a tree, she is sure to be blessed with a child. In certain of the quadrangles of the tombs masonry tanks are built, the water from which will relieve pain of almost any kind. Indeed, faith-healing superstitions cling to everything connected with the graves of these pious men. Not infrequently women tie little bits of rag on the trees near the shrine and wish for something, at the same time vowing that if their desire is granted they will cover the grave with a new blue covering called *chader*.

There are always a number of idlers who hang around these shrines, and earn their livelihood by fabricating stories regarding those who are buried there, investing them almost with the nature of a divinity and extracting fees from pilgrims and others who come to visit them. Many of the tombs in the Hazara districts have no roof, though the walls are high and the structure is frequently of stone. It is explained that the roof was pulled down by the saint himself, for during the first night it was intact, but on the second night the spirit of the saint wishing to ascend to heaven and finding itself entombed forced its way up through the roof so that the masonry fell. Since that time the passage has been left, and the saint's soul flows up during the night and returns during the day. It is said of one of these shrines that it lengthens two inches during the night and shrinks to its normal size with the return of daylight, though if the day is cloudy or wet it retains its abnormal length until the sun shines again.

Pilgrims or other visitors to the graves are given *taburruk*, or sacred presents, in the form of dates or other fruits or bread, or even some of the dust of the tomb or pieces of the masonry. These presents, which are regarded as having protective qualities, are carried about the person of the pilgrim. Not a few Kashmiri servants gather dust from the shrine of Mahmud of Ghaznee, which they sell by weight for a good price at Sarinagar.

In Badakhshan is the grave of a man of unknown nationality who is believed by some to have been a saint. It is said that he was fourteen feet in height and lived on the extreme edge of the earth. One night he dreamed that some people were digging a grave, and upon enquiry he was told that the grave was for him. The pious man ran to the other edge of the world, but once again he dreamed that his grave was being prepared. 'How,' asked the saint, 'am I going to meet my death?' In reply he was told that he would be stung by a scorpion. The *faqeer* ran to the middle of the earth, and then, in order to avoid putting his feet to the ground and so encountering a scorpion, rode on horseback until he reached the northern part of Afghanistan. Here he rested, and then, thinking to be safe from death's fatal fang, rode down the river in mid-stream. But his hour came, and a scorpion emerged from the hair of the horse's mane and stung him to death. Those who had heard his story, and had observed his virtuous way of living, buried him in Badakhshan, where his tomb affords relief to any who have been stung by a scorpion or bitten by snakes.

In certain districts, faith in the efficacy of the graves is carried so far as to amount almost to grave-worship. It is believed that it is only necessary to make a request at a *durgah* (tomb of a reputed pious person) in order to obtain whatever one desires. At certain times of the year, usually during the winter, great ceremonial gatherings take place at the graves, called *urs* or *julus* (literally, a procession, but in connection with the graves it means commemoration of the saint's pious doings).

On the occasion of the *urs*, a large number of adherents of the sect to which the *peer* (religious teacher) belongs gather together, and tents are pitched to accommodate the disciples for whom there is no room in the building. Religious songs are sung, and as the music reaches its climax the *darwash* work themselves into a state of frenzied ecstasy. The mullas and all those who know the real meaning of the Islamic teaching have placed a ban on the practice of divination, which they call *bidat* (an Arabic word meaning an 'introduction of ceremonies and rites which did not exist during the time of Mohammed, and hence are not permissible'). Yet, in face of strong denunciation by the priestly class, the faith in the supernatural power of the saints' graves remains unshaken, and men and women alike cling firmly to it. The cult is particularly common in the part of the country adjoining Persia, where the grave of practically anyone whose history is unknown, or to whom a virtuous life is attributed, is endowed with miraculous powers.

Many people will sit down in meditation before a grave, and, by holding their breath as long as possible, derive inspiration from the saint. Superstitious women select a particular grave to which to make their offerings, and every Thursday night they either take or send a female servant with an earthenware lamp with a cotton thread as a wick which they burn at the head of the grave. Often sweets or flowers are taken as offerings, or butter or *roghun* (ghee) is burnt in a lamp instead of oil; while some show their respect by having the grave sprayed with water during the summer months.

In wars between the clans the head of each visits the grave of a saint to obtain a blessing on the arms of his followers. Placing his rifle on the grave, he invokes the saint's aid to victory; then, taking it up again, he leads his men to battle.

A curious idea prevails among the women with regard to the white pudding impression, or *punja*, as it is called. During the day of Shubbarat a part of the floor is plastered with fine white clay and enclosed by curtains. A maiden lady makes a three-sided stage, on which is placed a big pot with a wide mouth. A pudding of rice is prepared in this pot, and when it is ready the lid of the pot is coated with a thick dough and the rice is allowed to cool. The lady of the house then presents the pudding as an offering to the Virgin Mary, Mother of Christ, and at the same time prays that she will grant the fulfilment of her request. During the ceremony no one of either sex is permitted to enter the room; if a man dared to step in, he would be blinded by the smoke of the cooking. The pudding remains there, and if the woman's wish is granted, it is accepted by the Mother of Christ making an impression on the smooth surface of the pudding with her left hand, so that a *punja* (impression of five fingers) appears. If the *punja* is seen, messengers are at once dispatched to summon the woman's friends and female relations to take part in the eating of the pudding, for whosoever eats a portion of it will be regarded with favour by her husband. The ceremony of the *punja* of Muryum (Virgin Mary) is confined exclusively to women.

From: *Afghanistan of the Afghans*
The Sirdar Ikbal Ali Shah

The Arabian Nights Adventures

SEIZED BY THE royal guard, the queen was dragged from the palace, and out to a bare patch of ground beyond the city walls...

...A patch of ground damp with blood.

The hood was jerked down into place.

A warrant bearing the king's coat of arms was presented to the executioner.

The prisoner was ordered to kneel.

Her delicate neck was forced against the wooden block, her nightdress flapping in the breeze.

Wheeling up into the dawn light, the axe fell.

Without ceremony or remorse, the queen's limp body was interred beside a thousand others.

As it was lowered into the grave, a desert wind tinged with dread tore through the capital.

Every young woman yet to be married was hidden away, for fear she'd be sent an invitation to her own wedding – a marriage to the cold-blooded King Shahriyar.

A marriage that invariably ended the same way – in a dawn appointment with the executioner's axe.

Yet another queen for a single night.

*

SHAH

A PALL OF terror hung over the land.

The king's spies were everywhere – searching for young women to be married at sunset, then executed at dawn. No one dared go out of their homes, in case an informant remembered they had a daughter, a sister, cousin, or niece.

Some families disguised their girls as boys, and smuggled them over the mountains to far-off lands. Most simply locked them away, refusing to allow them out, in fear theirs would be the next delicate neck on the executioner's block.

In the shadow of the palace, the king's vizier, Jafar, was sitting at the window of his home, pondering yet again how to put the bloodbath to an end. His wife blustered in, broke down in tears, and implored her husband to plead with the king.

'There's nothing I can do,' he answered. 'He's made up his mind. However hard I try, I can't talk sense into him. As you know, he's vowed to continue in this way – vengeance for the queen's infidelity.'

At that moment, the vizier's daughter entered. Her name was Scheherazade, and she was the apple of his eye. As keenly quick-witted as she was beautiful, she was blessed with a radiance that touched all who met her.

In her hand was a magnificent unopened envelope, her name inscribed beautifully on the front.

As soon as he saw it, the vizier choked back tears.

Unlike her father, Scheherazade didn't seem fearful so much as resolute.

'Dearest father,' she said, her tone reflective, 'I've made my decision.'

Her father stared deep into his daughter's eyes.

'I shall have a doctor swear that you're deranged!' he cried. 'Or have you smuggled over the border!'

'No, father,' Scheherazade answered. Opening the envelope, she read her name on the wedding invitation. 'I shall agree to his wishes, and be the king's next bride.'

Jafar leapt up.

'No no no!' he wailed, pulling his beloved daughter close, and scolding her at the same time. 'Put such senseless thoughts out of your head at once!'

But Scheherazade was adamant.

'If I don't wed him, another girl will be beheaded at dawn,' she said.

Bereft, the vizier replied:

'But at least it wouldn't be my daughter's head that falls.'

All morning, Scheherazade pleaded with her parents, and all morning they refused to let her be wed to the tyrannical king.

After what seemed like an eternity of argument, she motioned to the window. A splendid blue butterfly was flapping inside the glass, desperately trying to escape.

'See how it yearns to reach its destiny,' she said, opening the window.

Her father frowned as the insect flapped out into the sky.

'A pigeon could feast on it as soon as it's free.'

Scheherazade smiled.

'But, what if, by some strange quirk of fate, that little butterfly could prevent all the other butterflies from being trapped?'

SHAH

And so it was that, with much sorrow, the vizier and his wife agreed to allow their daughter to wed King Shahriyar.

*

As WORD OF the engagement was proclaimed throughout the kingdom, and a trousseau was prepared, Scheherazade took one last stroll alone through the market.

Covering herself with a simple cloak, she slipped out from the back door, promising to be back in time for the procession to the palace at dusk.

But rather than heading into the city, Scheherazade made her way in the opposite direction. Her feet moving as briskly as they could manage, she ventured over the river, across the floodplain, and into the forest.

Every parent warned their children to keep far away from that place, for fear that the witches living there would turn them into frogs. The ears of every child in the kingdom had heard stories of the dark arts, and had nightmares of the sorcery lurking there.

Every single child was terrified, that is, except the vizier's daughter.

While the other children followed their parents' advice, Scheherazade had always been the sort of girl who walked a path of her own.

And that was how she'd first met the kindly Blue Witch.

Over the years, since first straying into the forest and getting lost, Scheherazade had been taken in by the sorceress, and they had become firm friends. They told each other stories, laughed together, and confided in one another.

As always, the Blue Witch felt Scheherazade approaching, sensed her small feet pacing fast through the forest. Once she had greeted the girl and ushered her into the shack in which she lived, she said:

'You are as brave as you are beautiful, my dear, and equally foolish.'

A single tear welled up in Scheherazade's eye and rolled down her cheek.

'I must stop him,' she whispered. 'I must put an end to King Shahriyar's killing spree.'

The Blue Witch thought long and hard, her gaze tethered to the floor.

'If only he could be halted by magical means,' she said at length. 'But, alas, the king is protected by Yunan, a sorcerer whose wizardry overshadows my own. Unlike the black arts he wields, I cast white magic – spells spun for good.'

Scheherazade was about to say something, when the Blue Witch clapped her hands together.

The kingdom, and everything in it, paused by a spell of white magic, in which only good deeds could be done.

In the market, all the sellers and the buyers, the chickens and the goats, were unmoving. Up in the trees, the birds were still, too. And, in his palace, King Shahriyar was motionless, a forefinger raised above his head.

Even Scheherazade was frozen to the spot.

Taking advantage of the spell she'd cast, the Blue Witch set to work.

First, she hurried out into the forest and gathered ingredients.

Next, she prepared a fine powder – grinding up barks, crushing petals, and calling upon the Six Jinns to breathe life into her spell.

An hour after her hands had clapped, they did so once again, and the kingdom continued as though time and life were just as they had always been.

Filling a little embroidered pouch with the powder, the Blue Witch pressed it into Scheherazade's hand.

'Take this with you, and hide it with your trousseau,' she said. 'Follow the instructions I shall give you, and on no account reveal them to a living soul.'

*

As THE SUN slipped down below the city wall, Scheherazade was conveyed to the palace upon a litter.

Trumpets resounding, the shrill voices of the wedding party called out in joy. Beneath the semblance of merriment were sorrow, fear, and heavy hearts. The vizier, his wife, and second daughter accompanied the procession as it swept through the courtyards into the throne room.

There, dressed in regal finery, the king was waiting for his bride.

Within minutes, the ceremony was over, and Scheherazade was queen.

Trumpeters heralded the union.

The wedding party congratulated their daughter, and said their farewells.

In tears, the vizier hugged his daughter, breathing in her perfume one last time.

As they prepared to leave, Scheherazade asked a favour of her husband.

'Would you permit my little sister, Dunyazad, to unpack my trousseau?'

The king agreed, and the ground beneath the newlyweds' feet was sprinkled with rose petals as they made their way to the private quarters.

There was no one in the kingdom who hadn't heard talk of the monarch's extravagance and wealth. But it was not until Scheherazade set eyes on the royal apartment that she grasped the full extent of her husband's indulgence.

The walls were hung with the finest silks from distant lands, and the furniture was inset with precious gems. Exquisite mosaic fountains trickled with coloured water, solid-gold vases stood as tall as a man, and magnificent carpets from Samarkand were laid one over the next. Crystal chandeliers threw shadows over the scene plucked from a fairy-tale, the air scented with the fragrance of musk.

While Dunyazad set to work unpacking her sister's possessions, King Shahriyar paced over to a low table upon which an ornate hourglass was standing. He gazed at his new bride for a moment, his eyes burning like fire opals.

Then, grasping the hourglass in both hands, he turned it over.

A fine stream of sand from the deserts of Arabia began to fall.

'Dearest husband,' said Scheherazade, 'I'm cold. Might a brazier be brought so that I could warm myself?'

The king clapped his hands and roared an order. A fire was brought in, coals clicking and sparking as they warmed the air.

'Any other requests?' asked Shahriyar. Cocking his head to the hourglass, he added: 'Time is against us as you know.'

Having finished unpacking the trousseau, Dunyazad stepped over to where her sister was sitting, and whispered something in her ear.

The king narrowed his eyes.

'What does she want?'

'Oh, nothing, husband.'

'It was something, so it wasn't nothing.'

'Well, nothing of importance.'

'Speak it and I shall decide.'

Scheherazade blushed from embarrassment.

'Forgive her,' she replied. 'My sister merely asked whether I would tell her a story before she leaves. You see, it's a tradition in our home. I tell her a tale each night before she sleeps. As she can't be certain when she shall see me again, she hoped that I might oblige.'

King Shahriyar smiled, the first time his new bride had observed him do so. Seating himself on a jewel-encrusted divan, he motioned for her to continue.

Thanking her husband, Scheherazade stepped over to the brazier, warming her hands on the embers. In doing so, she cast a pinch of the powder given to her by the Blue Witch onto the coals.

For a moment, the room was perfumed with an aroma unlike any other – a scent of raw imagination and destiny.

Glancing over to the hourglass, the sands of time flowing fast, she began:

'There was once in far-off China a tailor's son named Aladdin, who lived with his mother in the dark years after his father's death. Theirs was an impoverished life without luxury, balanced on the margins of starvation.

'One day, a wealthy stranger arrived at their modest home. Greeting Aladdin, he declared he was the boy's long-lost uncle. As a member of the family, he showered the boy and his mother in affection, presenting them with finery from his travels…'

Pausing, Scheherazade peered into the brazier's embers.

'Is that it?!' bellowed the king.

'No, no, there's more. There is much more. But…'

'But?'

Uneasily, the young bride cast an eye over to the hourglass, a mound of sand having gathered in the lower sphere.

'But I don't imagine you would wish to hear of it on your wedding night.'

The king clapped his hands.

'Continue!' he boomed.

*

SHAH

ALL NIGHT LONG, Scheherazade spun the tale, summoning the sounds, sights, and smells so vividly that it was as though the story were taking place right there in the royal apartment.

No surprise of course, for the Blue Witch's spell had been to conjure the tale in all its fantastical detail, as the sands in the hourglass fell.

King Shahriyar listened to his bride's voice. Or, rather, he thought he listened to her. In actual fact, he was watching the story unfold in a scene conjured by the brazier's fire.

As the first strains of dawn light brought warmth to the sleeping city down below, Scheherazade paused, her gaze gliding onto the hourglass.

The last grain of sand slipped through its neck, signalling the time for execution. Right on cue, the royal guard marched through the palace to drag the new queen to meet her fate.

Tears welling in her eyes, Dunyazad looked at her sister.

'I am ready,' Scheherazade said in a low voice.

The king frowned.

'But I haven't heard the end of the story,' he said.

The chief vizier stood to attention at the door of the royal apartment.

'Your Majesty,' he spoke sombrely, setting eyes on his beloved daughter, 'the executioner is ready, his axe sharpened, and the grave freshly dug.'

The frown on the monarch's brow grew more furrowed.

'But I want to know how it ends,' he said vacantly.

Scheherazade and her sister swallowed hard.

The vizier exhaled.

Raising a forefinger above his head, the king pronounced:

'Today there will be no execution,' he said. 'This evening I shall hear the last segment of the tale. Once it's finished, the axe may swing and the grave be filled.'

*

ON THE SECOND evening, the hourglass was turned once again, grains of sand streaming through the slender neck of the magnificent device.

Dunyazad sat on the floor, the king on the low divan, and Scheherazade at the brazier, warming her hands. Although as quick-witted as she was lovely, the young queen's mastery in recounting the tale was inspired by the Blue Witch's enchantment.

Sprinkling a second pinch of the magic powder on the coals, Scheherazade continued the tale:

'And so it was that the boy born a tailor's son lived in luxury, with all the sweetmeats he could eat, and with a princess for his wife. All was well. Indeed, all was perfect. Then, one day, Aladdin quit the city on urgent business, leaving his wife to take care of their palatial home. With her husband gone, she was prone to boredom, and spent her days at the window, staring out at life on the street.

'On a particularly dull afternoon, she heard a tinker calling out as he pushed a cart. Unlike the usual assortment of worn-out pots and pans that tinkers tended to collect, this one was quite different. From what the princess could see, his cart was heaped with beautiful lamps made from the finest brass.

'"Old lamps for new!" he cried. "Come, quick, old lamps for new!"

'"That sounds like a wonderful bargain," the princess said to her maid. "Take that wretched old lamp of my husband's and see whether the tinker would exchange it for one of those lovely new lamps on his cart."

'Hurrying down with Aladdin's lamp, the maid returned in less time than it takes to tell, a shiny new lamp in her hands.'

All night Scheherazade spun the tale, the sands of the hourglass streaming through its neck towards the dawn. And all night long her sister and the king watched as the tale was enacted right there before them.

With only a handful of grains still to fall, the queen drew the story of The Wondrous Lamp to a close:

'Although Aladdin and the princess lived happily ever after,' she uttered, 'the same cannot be said for the tailor.'

King Shahriyar shrugged.

'Which tailor?'

'Aladdin's uncle.'

'The wretch of a man who tricked him?'

'No, Sire, the real uncle… the one who left his tailor shop to his sons. The first son, Ali Baba, was kindly but poor; and the second was rich. While Qasim enjoyed a life of privilege, having managed to trick a woman of high birth to marry him, the first brother, Ali Baba, was resigned to work as a woodcutter.

'While at rest one blistering afternoon in the forest, he heard the sound of horses' hooves galloping towards him.

Fearing it was the outriders of an army approaching, Ali Baba hid in a blasted tree. Peering through a slit in its side, he watched as forty thieves dismounted from their steeds, and strode up to a rock wall. "Open Sesame!" they cried. As the humble woodcutter watched, a great stone portal lifted upwards, revealing a secret cave, into which the thieves strode.

'A little time passed. The thieves exited, mounted their horses, and rode away as fast as they had come. When they were long gone, Ali Baba emerged from his hiding place, tramped timidly to the rock wall, and said the magic words. Instantly, the portal slid upwards, and Ali Baba entered the cave, filled as it was with the vast treasure of an empire.'

Scheherazade paused, as the last grain of sand slipped through the neck of the hourglass.

The sound of the royal guard approaching was followed once again by the voice of the chief vizier.

'Your Majesty, the executioner is waiting, and the grave freshly dug.'

Swallowing hard, the young queen glanced at her husband.

'There shall be no execution today!' he bellowed. 'It shall be postponed until tomorrow, once I have heard what happens to Ali Baba and the forty thieves.'

His eyes glazed over, the vizier bowed.

'At your service, Majesty,' he said.

From: *The Arabian Nights Adventures*
Tahir Shah

The Teaching-Story

I CAN THINK of no better way of beginning a consideration of stories than with a very short, true story, about the situation, the real intricacies, of dealing not only with stories, but with the talking and hearing process itself.

I was giving a lecture recently on the difficulty which people have in taking things in, especially at any speed, even if they do it sequentially; and how a story, or even a statement, might become a person's possession, as it were, so that it could be recalled to mind and considered from various points of view. 'It has been noticed,' I continued, 'that much information is not absorbed because many people cannot really absorb something when they have heard it only once...'

Immediately a hand went up, and someone sitting in the front row asked me: 'Would you mind saying that again?' I later enquired, and found out that he was neither hard of hearing nor a quick-witted humorist.

This time-lag, between the presentation of materials and their integration into the thinking and repertoire of action of the individual, has itself to be taught, we find, to quite a lot of people interested in stories. It is useful to other people, too, but we find it easy to observe and to test in the story-telling and story-hearing atmosphere. The holistic mode will obtain certain parts, and the more literal others. Neither will perceive many dimensions until a skill has been developed. This short Sufi tale is employed for the educational purpose of establishing in the mind the contention at least that one may need this time-lapse for this purpose, and it is not intended to make fun of any of the fictional figures appearing in it:

Time and Pomegranates

A disciple went to the house of a Sufi physician and asked to become an apprentice in the art of medicine.

'You are impatient,' said the doctor, 'and so you will fail to observe things which you will need to learn.'

But the young man pleaded, and the Sufi agreed to accept him.

After some years the youth felt that he could exercise some of the skills which he had learnt. One day a man was walking towards the house and the doctor – looking at him from a distance – said: 'That man is ill. He needs pomegranates.'

'You have made the diagnosis – let me prescribe for him, and I will have done half the work,' said the student.

'Very well,' said the teacher, 'providing that you remember that action should also be looked at as illustration.'

As soon as the patient arrived at the doorstep, the student brought him in and said: 'You are ill. Take pomegranates.'

'Pomegranates!' shouted the patient. 'Pomegranates to you – nonsense!' And he went away.

The young man asked his master what the meaning of the interchange had been.

'I will illustrate it the next time we get a similar case,' said the Sufi.

Shortly afterwards the two were sitting outside the house when the master looked up briefly and saw a man approaching.

'Here is an illustration for you – a man who needs pomegranates,' he said.

The patient was brought in, and the doctor said to him:

'You are a difficult and intricate case, I can see that. Let me see... yes, you need a special diet. This must be composed of something round, with small sacs inside it, naturally occurring. An orange... that would be of the wrong colour... lemons are too acidic... I have it: pomegranates!'

The patient went away, delighted and grateful.

'But Master,' said the student, 'why did you not say "pomegranates" straight away?'

'Because,' said the Sufi, 'he needed *time* as well as pomegranates.'[1]

Now, this tale usually produces some laughter, but sometimes, especially in cultures where people have acquired the habit of turning as many things as possible into wisecracks, we occasionally get such comments as 'that patient was a real idiot, wasn't he?'

---

1   Idries Shah, *The Dermis Probe*, London, Jonathan Cape, 1970, p. 72f; ISF Publishing, London, 2016, p. 79

Abolition of Impact

The abolition of the impact of a story or other stimulus is, of course, well known as a device, a way of avoiding the assimilation of its point, and this behaviour can frequently be seen in people who have the need, displayed, too, in other ways, of protecting themselves against outside influences. Other tales are used as a corrective to this, enabling people to laugh at themselves or to recognize that there is no sin in being prone to the same deficiencies as very many other people are.

I have come across very few reactions as dramatic as the one which followed my first publication, in 1969, of an ancient narrative about dramatic reactions. In something like 1500 words, well spaced out and occupying nine pages with plenty of white space, I retold the legend of the man who had a very big book with only a few words written in it, the words being concerned with how people judged by appearances and confused the container with the content, as it were, and were enraged when they found that this book has so few words in it. These nine pages were printed and published as a book, with some 300 other – blank – pages to bulk it out. The external shape, size and weight of this volume, which I entitled *The Book of the Book*,[2] presumably gave the impression that it had words right the way through, was filled with words. And the cover was gold-embossed.

---

2   Idries Shah, *The Book of the Book*, London 1969, 70, 73, 76; ISF Publishing, London, 2016

There was an immediate outcry. Reviewers, seeing that it had only nine pages of print, manifested their rage and disappointment at such a product. None of them, at first, noticed that it was a book about people who were seized by rage and disappointment when a book turned out to have nothing in it except something about people who were annoyed when they found that a book only warned about the container and the content. Presently, however, one by one, other reviewers started to see the point and to give it good reviews. It has now run through four editions: but not before an expert at the British Museum in London unhesitatingly declared that it was 'not a book at all', until we found a book which proved that it really did fulfil the criteria of a book laid down by UNESCO... Now and again I see references to it as 'causing a sensation' or as 'experimental and new', even in the London *Times*.

The confusion of the container and the content, of course, is a very common human tendency, causing the worship of externals and producing magic-wand type thinking, but for some reason called cargo-cultism only when it is found among under-developed peoples... The argument and illustration that there are these two modes – the inner and the outer shape – by means of stories such as this, makes it possible for the student to recall and replay, as it were, the model story and then to study his own behaviour to see whether, perhaps, he is developing a tendency towards superficiality, magical thinking or incomplete attention.

Analogical Teaching

Sufi analogical teaching has an interesting dimension which, as one becomes more familiar with it, can be observed almost everywhere. This is summed up in the statement that 'things which have a mental form also have a physical one: and also a form reflected in social happenings'. If the container is the human being, the content may be called the nature and quality of his inner self; whether you call this psychological, educational or spiritual. Sometimes you can see the literal disparity between container and content displayed, almost as a moral lesson or even as a social drama, in real life. This is what gives teaching-stories their reality, and also endows teaching narratives (accounts of contacts between teachers and learners) their vitality.

Here is an example of how the human neglectfulness of container and content in the inner sense can actually concretize itself in a real-life occurrence:

Last year the London *Times* reported[3] that one local authority in a British county had received a parcel on which they had to pay a heavy excess postage charge, since it bore no stamp. It was so badly packed that it had burst open in transit. Inside this interesting package, this container with such a disastrously negligent outwardness, what do you think there was? Nothing less than 200 leaflets from the Post Office Users' Council. They were entitled: 'Have you a complaint about the Post Office?'

---

3   *The Times,* London, 24 December 1975, p. 2, col. 6.

Here is another one, picked almost at random, which raises even deeper questions about container and content:

Nutrition from the Container
Four years ago it was stated that scientific tests had been carried out on the characteristics of various breakfast cereals and their containers. Rats were fed, in laboratory conditions, on diets of both the contents and the containers. The results indicate, and I quote, 'that the box cardboard is often more nutritious than the cereals inside'.[4]

I would draw a lesson from these instances to warn against assumptions about what one puts in, in imagined Sufi study, and what is really there, let alone what one puts it into.

When people have in fact become attached to externals, stories, often jokes, can be used to enable them to acquire a more constructive perspective. In Sufi circles it is not uncommon for a Sufi to prevent attachment to himself from the students, and to draw attention to the total phenomenon of the Sufi enterprise instead. We can take such a story as this one to impart the 'shock' which takes concentration *off* superficialities or irrelevancies, so that it may attach itself to something more fundamental, if less palpable:

'Innermost' Feelings
Now here is a Western story, but it will serve for this purpose. There was once a man who travelled to a far distant land

---

4 *The Observer* (magazine section), London, 31 March 1974, p. 41, col. 1.

to seek spiritual enlightenment. Finally he arrived at the dwelling of a sage who was reputed to be a master of secrets. At the precise moment that he was ushered into the presence of the great one, a strange agitation seized him, and he fell to the ground, feeling that the very earth might open up and swallow him.

'At last – at last,' he stammered, 'you have stirred my innermost being, Master of spiritual exaltation...'

'I am afraid I do not quite understand,' said the venerable teacher, 'how you can imagine that you can benefit from what was, in fact, only an earthquake. We have a lot of them around here, you know...'

It should be remembered that Sufi educational technique aims at removing, or helping to remove, superficial behaviour-pattern barriers to deeper understanding. This is because the concept of the exclusion of limiting factors is every bit as important among the Sufis as the inclusion of concepts and the use of special techniques for stimulating perceptions: indeed, the former must precede the latter.

Because most people will tend to adopt the outer practices of people and institutions which they respect or admire, many Sufi tales provide humorous or semi-humorous formats which can be recalled to mind to reduce this incrustation's effect in such cases. Most of the Sufi and other spiritual schools publicly known, whether here or elsewhere, are visibly, and for the Sufi effectively, disabled in their learning potential by exactly this accretion problem.

There is a tale which covers this; though it, like many other Sufi stories, also carries other dimensions which come to light when the consciousness is able to deal with them.

Stealing Advice

A man once applied to a Sufi to become his disciple, but was rejected as not being ready for this path. So he decided that he would learn what he could by direct methods. What could be wrong in adopting Sufi practice?

Finding out that a new disciple was being enrolled that evening, he climbed onto the roof of the Sufi meeting-place and listened to the first instructions being given by the Teacher:

'Do not walk on the left-hand side of a street; do not avoid a fortunate person; do not push yourself forward before others.' Well, that seemed easy enough to the eavesdropper, who, naturally, at once proceeded to apply these teachings to his own life.

But, as he was walking home along the right-hand side of a street, a plant pot fell on him from a balcony, and he was injured. Making friends with a prosperous merchant, all that happened was that the man swindled him. Finally, when he tried to apply for employment to feed himself (as he had lost all his money) he found that there were always other applicants there first, and without pushing he was unable even to obtain an interview.

Now, the tale continues, did he realize that the instructions were scripted, prescribed *only* for the man whom the Sufi had been talking to? Certainly not; he concluded that the

Sufi was a fraud, even an agent of the Devil. And, of course, it was because he was not yet ready for calculated, measured instructions that the Sufi had rejected his candidature in the first place.

These story-structures, in addition to displaying common features of human action, have two major functions. The first is to provide indications of the barriers to learning; the second is to place in the hands of the student the means to administer, to some degree, self-correction through feedback. These tales are used instead of community disciplines because Sufis do not organize into monastic or other 'orders' in which people are conditioned. The reason for this, of course, is that Sufis hold that such training may become another form of straitjacket, and tends to produce automatism and conditioned response behaviour, removing the element of choice in thought and action which is only available when the alternatives are known and the conditioning does not impose a certain so-called choice. The Sufi 'orders' known to history are late elaborations of the externals of schools.

(Although many of these so-called orders are named after their putative founders, they are later developments. Even historical research concurs in general with authentic contemporary Sufi teaching that there is neither proof nor reason for great teachers of the past actually organizing such restrictive institutions. Indeed, it would make nonsense of much of their teaching if they did.)

Like any other instruments, Sufi tales can be misused, and when – as is not infrequently true – both the supposed teacher (who tries to apply the stories from, say, books and is not himself a product of them) and the would-be learner are not operating within the real Sufi frame, nothing useful will happen at all. Unless you call propaganda or emotional stimulus useful, and you can get those anywhere.

The Symptoms

The following passage indicates one side of the situation which then obtains.

Someone asked a wise man, 'I have heard that humanity is suffering from an ailment which prevents men and women from seeing truth, from knowing themselves. What is the main symptom?'

He answered: 'The first symptom is to believe that one is *not* suffering from this illness at all. But when it *really* starts to take hold, the patient may *agree* that he is ill, but now insists that the disease is anything other than actually it is.'

This disordered perception is very marked in heroic but ill-considered attempts at obtaining esoteric knowledge, which really means 'simultaneous' knowledge, all over the world today.

Sufi teaching takes place within a system which is much more often than not indirect. It is sometimes unperceived at the moment of its operation, though not always in its externals. The thirteenth-century teacher Jalaludin Rumi refers to this indirect operational quality of stories which one often observes in action, through an actual tale – a tale explaining how a tale can work:

There was once a merchant who kept a parrot imprisoned in a cage. When about to visit India, on a business trip, he said to the bird:

'I am travelling to your homeland. Can I give any message to your relatives there?'

'Simply tell them,' said the parrot, 'that I am living here in a cage.'

When the merchant returned, he said to the parrot:

'I am sorry to have to tell you that when I found and informed your wild relatives in the jungle that you were caged, the shock was too much for one of them. As soon as he heard the news, he dropped from his branch, no doubt having died from grief.'

Immediately he had spoken, the parrot collapsed and lay inert on the floor of his cage.

Sorrowfully, the merchant took him and placed him outside in the garden. Then the parrot, having got the message, sat up and flew away, out of reach.

We must not think either that this exhausts the symbolism of this story, or that it will necessarily appeal to everyone. Rumi himself once said that counterfeit gold is only to be found because there is such a thing as *real* gold to be copied. And there is a true story, of something which took place in Britain not so long ago, which verifies our experience that many of our stories (and especially the events in them) appear on the surface to be so trivial to so many people that they reject them completely.

A jeweller in Birkenhead, Cheshire, in England, wanted to get people into his shop.[5] He handed out 3,000 stones to people in the street. They all looked like real diamonds, but all but four of them were glass. He explained, in a leaflet given to each recipient, that there were real diamonds among the give-away stones. Whoever got a stone of any kind was invited to visit the jewellery store, to find out if they had been lucky. Out of the 3,000 people getting the stones, only one – a woman – actually turned up at the shop. She was right: she had a genuine diamond. All the rest of the people, presumably, thought that they were *all* fakes. The real diamonds had been as quickly discarded as the spurious.

Now, if this kind of thing can happen with things as concrete as stones, and if people are in general as neglectful of possibilities as to provide only one individual in three thousand to have hope for success, you can see an instant analogy with our own experience.

The analogy includes the minus factors that people can call us fakes for peddling silly old stories and refuse to seek further. It also carries with it, however, the plus that enough people think that we are harmless peddlers of old stories to allow us to continue on our way…

Both the Qur'an in the seventh century and the writings of Rumi in the thirteenth (and many other books) have been opposed by wiseacres, and the 'wise', on exactly the grounds that they were just 'filled with old fables', which

---

5 *Daily Mail*, 'Giveaway Diamonds', by Tom Hendry, 20 July 1972, p. 3, col. 5.

could not possibly be of any use to anyone. So we remain in respectable company.

But even fables, stories of less deep outer messages than that of indirect teaching, can be used, and are widely used, to accustom even quite small children to the future realities of life in the Middle East and Central Asia, the heartland of my basic culture.

But you do not have to be a child to accept or to reject stories as vehicles for psychological action or knowledge...

When someone asked me on BBC Radio once why I used so many of other people's tales and did not make up any of my own, I said that nobody had asked me for my own. So the interviewer, of course, immediately asked me to tell an original one, which I did. A friend of mine had the radio on in his office at the time and asked his secretary what she thought of it. She said: 'No wonder nobody ever asks him – his stories are terrible...' But the main reason to adopt traditional tales is, of course, that you don't try to manufacture your own instrument if you already have a range of them, superbly made and totally effective, fashioned by master craftsmen.

From the Sufi understanding of human thinking, of course, the secretary could hardly be expected to rave about a story if she had other priorities on her mind. It is never easy to get publishers, for instance, to publish collections of Sufi tales if they first see the manuscript and judge that they are of what they call 'uneven quality'. Judging the tales for punch, humour, interest or whether they say anything to you at a given moment is using the stories in a way in which they are not intended to be used. An instrument is useful or not, according to whether circumstances are correct.

The Camelman and the Plastic

There is a true tale about this. I once showed a piece of clear plastic to a camelman. He looked at it and said: 'Interesting, but there is no future in it.'

I asked him why.

'Well,' he said, 'it is not sufficiently transparent to see through properly, it is probably very costly, you can't wear it, and it would not keep the glare out if I used it for a window in a tent…'

One great advantage of Sufi tales and narratives of encounters which I see – but which many others find irksome – is that they help to make real to the mind the fact that everything has its own, correct time. Now, this is a part of our daily experience (you cannot catch a train if it is not there, for instance, apart from all the other prerequisites needed to get on that train) but people tend to imagine that this sort of argument is always advanced to *stop* someone doing something, or to avoid having to do it. It is Sufi experience that people who can keep calm enough to realize that there might be a time and a place – and other requirements – for anything, are *more*, not less, able to benefit from that thing.

Here is a story which is almost always taken to mean that certain things are impossible, but which need not mean that at all:

A SON OF A SON I

Fish Out of Water

A would-be disciple begged a Sufi master to teach him exercises. The Sufi, however, said: 'I am going to tell you a *story* instead – then you won't *need* exercises.' He continued: 'There was once a man who agreed to train a fish who begged him to help, to live out of the water, being desperate to take up a life on land. Little by little, a few seconds and then a few minutes, then hours at a time, he managed to get it accustomed to the open air. In fact the fish went to live near him, with its own damp but open-air place in a flower-bed in the man's garden. It was delighted with its new life, and often used to say to him: "This is what I call real *living!*" Then, one day, there was a very heavy downpour of rain, which flooded the garden – and the fish was drowned.'

It makes a good laugh, and it can sound like a derisive tale. But the story only refers to *fish*, and as it is a story, 'fish' does not have to be an unalterable condition of the person being told it...

The usefulness of the teaching-story is boundless under the right conditions, though severely limited under two circumstances: the first of these, of course, is when people think of stories as trivial and only belonging to entertainment or for the inculcation of morals, and so on, as in the current versions of the fables of Aesop. Even if they are seen to show up amusing sides of human nature, this usage, this opinion about them, blunts their impact. So we can never be confident about their opportuneness until some context has been given about the traditional importance of the story, to enable our hearers to re-acquire flexibility of mental approach. The other limiting circumstance is when people have for some reason become so bemused by an attitude of awe and a desire for amazing secrets that they are, effectively, consuming that experience, the experience of awe, and get 'turned on', amazed and bemused by the story itself.

It is generally felt that these two attitudes are linked with the individual's desire to define exactly what the story phenomenon is, ahead of his willingness to have explained to him that it is a subtle and very sophisticated instrument. Such attitudes, incidentally, may betray the underlying motivation of the individual concerned as being a thirst for either order or excitement. Is it, we may ask, a desire for knowledge or self-development? We seldom find it wise to dissolve this 'fixation of choice', as it might be called, since the result usually is someone who may not now be fixated on an erroneous expectation from stories, but still has the desire for, say, explanations or emotional stimulus. The production of basic psychological balance is not the main job of the Sufi, who is always, moreover, aware of the significance of the saying: 'Before killing the cat, make arrangements about the mice.'

Teaching-stories *do* serve as correctives for various psychological conditions, though they are not primarily employed as a therapy, but rather as an illustration of what people are really like. The therapeutic effect, if any, would take place as a part of the entire operation of involvement in the tradition. This is seen as a harmonization, and not a treatment. The symptoms disappear, that is to say, when the ailment is not commanding a portion of the student's attention, which is extended for other purposes. The aim to provide the attention-capacity with fruitful objects of attention does not treat the symptoms, and does not treat the disease. The disease ceases to exist when the whole being is harmoniously balanced. It is not regarded as a therapeutic process, because the intention is not to cure and the procedures are not aimed at the ailment or to make the person feel better, or even to operate better on the ordinary psychological plane. The restoration of the harmony of the individual has, it is believed, higher aims than that, of which a *by-product* should be the vanishing of the disability.

When a *real* interest takes over, psychological troubles are remarkably often exorcised by it: a sort of reverse of the proverb: 'When the house catches fire, the toothache flies out of the window.'

This is more than a theory, seen from the Sufi perspective; for the learning-system, including the use of stories, is both primary and also the same element as has produced the Sufi exponent himself; the teaching is hence not exterior to the practice, and our kind of study is therefore participation activity. It is not objective in the sense that we can have, say, gardeners who never touch a plant, or experts on government who teach it but have never been near a government, let alone having discharged any functions connected therewith.

The motivation to study Sufism, or even to familiarize oneself with any of the system's procedures, will, according to the Sufis, only yield results to the extent to which the field as a whole has truly been entered into. Students-at-a-distance will always, of course, continue to obtain what they

SHAH

can from this and all other kinds of study. But the bits and pieces which can be obtained by this method will probably be produced by many other methods, including much more 'respectable' scientific ones, given enough time. There is a short tale which emphasizes the value of knowing what one is aiming for:

What He Was Trying to Do
A man went to a Sufi and said:

'My neighbour makes my life a misery by visiting me at all hours, hanging about the house and constantly asking questions.'

The Sufi advised:

'Nothing is easier than the cure for this. All you have to do is to ask the man for money every time you see him, and he will soon start to avoid you.'

'But supposing he then goes about the town telling everyone that I am a beggar?'

'Ah,' said the wise man, 'I see that you are hoping to control the thoughts of mankind, not trying to stop your neighbour annoying you. Do you *often* imagine that you want one thing when you really want another?'

The Sufi teaching-story, above all, does not require anyone to dress in comic clothes and adopt a peculiar attitude towards anyone or anything. It expects people to enlarge their horizons, but it has to have its own requirements fulfilled in order to operate to an appropriate degree. The introduction of this material into the West attracts all kinds of expectations, and some of them will undoubtedly produce hybrid results which could be absurd. Like all other forms of learning, it needs its own basic teaching institution – and that is not a do-it-yourself one. Someone engaged in self-study, runs the proverb, should not have a fool for a teacher. One story which is current in the West can be used to illustrate what I mean:

Doing Your Own Thing

A man once crossed a carrier pigeon with a parrot, so that its offspring could speak its message instead of having to carry a written one. But the bird which was produced by this experiment took hours instead of minutes to finish its journey.

'Why did you take so long?' the man asked it.

'Well, it was such a beautiful day,' said the superior bird, 'that I walked.'

This is why you have Aesop and wise saws instead of developmental instruments: you choose the inculcation of morals alone, or mainly so.

One can't help thinking of this story today, when people mix all sorts of techniques and exercises in trying for spiritual realization. Their results are as mixed up as the bird in the fable. The results of such hybridizing experiments can be long-lasting. Many are to be found in the East, and persist as circuses whose participants, generally, dislike stories and really do fear humour. They call themselves 'spiritual', however.

And, since we are talking about tales from the East, we can invoke a slightly different angle on the same subject: that this is an intact tradition with its own requirements. The stories belong to a whole spectrum of reality, they do not mix with cults and bits and pieces. Rather roughly, for the sensibilities of some of the delightful people who are perhaps accustomed to gentler treatment, I take the liberty of quoting a traditional saying often used by people less polished than you or I: 'If you have been asleep in a kennel, do not ask why you get up in the morning covered with fleas...'

It is important, at the very least, to familiarize oneself with the whole available range of stories put out in this manner, for they are to be considered the facets of a whole. And in addition, the individual story must be given close attention, so that it can yield its optimum value. To go from one to another choosing those which appeal, and giving no attention to those which do not stimulate us so much, however human a reaction, is a sign of a bad and unpromising student in this field. Our habits of lingering over the more desired or more pleasing things in life, when carried over into serious study can sometimes be barriers to progress in understanding. The difference between these two approaches was borne upon me one day recently in an entirely different connection.

Why Didn't You Say?
I was staying in the palace of a Middle Eastern potentate not very long ago, surrounded by every luxury. In the morning the major-domo arrived to take any orders, and I thought I would like to hear the radio, but there was not one in my apartments.

I asked him to arrange it. 'I would like to listen to the radio, please.'

'Of course. What programme?'

'The early-morning BBC World Service news.'

The following morning two men arrived, bearing the most advanced radio receiver I had ever seen. 'Where would you like it set up?'

'Right over here will do fine.'

One man sited the set, the other put on headphones and located the station. He looked at his watch. Very soon he gave a signal, and the radio amplifier was switched on. At full loudspeaker volume I heard the stirring march tune identifying London, Lillibulero... Then the news. When it was over, the two picked up their apparatus, and silently withdrew.

After breakfast, I went to pay my respects to the potentate, who asked me if all was to my liking.

'Yes, may your life be long! I did ask them to give me the London news, and they did, but I wish they had left the radio, so that I could listen to other programmes...'

'My dear fellow,' said the sovereign, for he had been educated in England and spoke like that, 'you must not blame us, but rather the fact that you are spending a little too much time in the West. Why on earth didn't you tell my chaps that you only wanted to twiddle? *Then* they would have left it...'

SO, IF PEOPLE INTERESTED IN EASTERN TALES ONLY WANT TO TWIDDLE, THEY SHOULD *SAY SO*... They can, on the other hand, look at the intact system, whether presented as Eastern or as a psychological and educational tool.

Having insisted that access to the whole range of the activity of Sufi study can only come through involvement in it, as with any other comprehensive operation, one can certainly enunciate other principles which may be of interest and of use to more generalized human areas: though I must stress that they are limited.

The zoologist Dr. Desmond Morris (who wrote *The Naked Ape* and other best-selling books on human behaviour) has noted the effect of Sufi stories on his daily life. Many of these, he states, were not appreciated by him at the time of reading, but their message and usefulness were understood when, subsequently, experiences corresponding to the structures laid down in the stories occurred in his dealings with other people. There was a *framework* for handling situations which he had not had before.

The Tales as Structures

Several scholars, both those specializing in the Middle East and others, have written recently that the tales – as *structures* which make possible the holding of certain concepts in a particular relationship – have an unusual value, sometimes in helping them to understand ranges of ideas which are not ordinarily linked in any other way. And, in the scientific field, for instance, the Mulla Nasrudin stories appear in, of all things, the Report of the Second Coral Gables Conference on Symmetry Principles at High Energy, to illustrate recondite concepts in physics. An interesting experiment is now going on showing that the usage of unfamiliar and even confusing stories and statements could be rendered in terms of one method of switching the brain's action from the sequential and logical to the simultaneous mode.

In this latter area, several Sufi tales in my *Tales of the Dervishes*[6] which have no obvious 'point' or which are susceptible to more than one interpretation, have been observed to work in this way. The bringing into greater action of the right-hemisphere functions and the attenuation of the left, may well be the reason for such disjointed injunctions as 'Think of the sound of no sound'.

I have myself been impressed to hear a small schoolboy, faced by the flow of words of an unusually lucid and logical youth, shout suddenly at him, 'Go knit yourself a slice of cake!' The effect was almost instantaneous, stopping the intellectual in his tracks. But it is hardly fair to use this knowledge deliberately to overcome someone else.

The holistic overall mode cannot of course compete in sequential activity, and seems to take over when the logical one is jammed by such statements as this. I once did this as a test when a Freudian psychiatrist was holding forth on something or other in highly respectful company, lucidly and persuasively. I said: 'Well, all Freudians are always saying things like "we must find out whether his grandmother bit him in the womb..."' The poor man gasped and stammered,

---

6   Idries Shah, *Tales of the Dervishes*, London 1967, etc., New York 1969, etc.; ISF Publishing, London, 2016

and all he could say was, rather weakly, 'But it is physically impossible for that to happen', and this drew such a roar of derision from the audience, whose brains were evidently sequentially operating, that he never regained his aplomb in their company.

The Secret Protecting Itself

The more recognizably 'Eastern mystical master' type of tale has an undeniable value in placing relationships into a new perspective, providing that it is employed within limits. If, for instance, these tales are read only as didactic and propagandist, designed to instil belief and create submission to the 'master's' wisdom, they cannot be used for *our* teaching purposes; consequently they get fed into indoctrination cults, or something which has turned or will turn into such a cult. If the message (that there are certain times and circumstances, certain arrangements of factors, which have to be observed in order to learn the things being taught by the tradition) is respected and not confused with one-upmanship, the tales can be extremely valuable. I sometimes ask myself, though, whether the phrase much used by Sufis, 'the secret protects itself', cannot be applied to such tales, as well as to other areas in Sufi experience – for a paranoid reaction to them effectively excludes the paranoid from that which they have to convey. Such stories are not, of course, the ingenuous attempts by crude esotericists from the East to impress and intimidate enquirers, or to bend them to their will: though some could be used for this by such people. Many an instrument can be used for cruder purposes than its original function. Indeed, one purpose of this exposition of mine is to put people on their guard.

Let us look at a sample of this kind of tale, with its built-in aversion-therapy element, likely to annoy and deflect anyone who thinks only that he is about to be deceived:

A Meaning of Silence
A Seeker-after-Truth who was anxious to find a true master saved up his money and made a long journey to the dwelling-place of a Sufi sage.

When he was admitted to the grounds of the house, the sage met him and talked for an hour or two about generalities. Since no mystical subject was mentioned, the visitor began to feel disappointed.

He stayed in the courtyard of the house, and some days later was admitted to the presence of the Sufi while he sat at his daily audience.

The visitor addressed the sage, saying: 'I have come from a great distance to enquire as to what might be the mark of a real master, so that I might adopt such a one, should I ever find him.'

The Sufi gave him no answer at all. When the assembly broke up at nightfall, the seeker went to his lodging. Here he found that another visitor was present, and he mentioned the matter to him.

'Your disappointment, which is with the sage, should be with yourself, for failing to understand him,' said the other. 'When he talked generalities to you, he was saying that you were still fit only for generalities, and should not try to converse on any higher subject until a master initiated such converse. When, in the assembly, you received only silence to your question, you were being shown that the mark of a real master is to be able *not* to answer questions put by people who are not able to make good use of an answer already given them.'

Since I started to publish these stories in 1964, and with an ever-increasing volume of letters, cablegrams and telephone calls which is quite astonishing, people have been showing the greatest possible interest in them. The most frequent question is: 'How can I *use* teaching-stories?', and a close second is the remark, 'I get no spiritual sensations from them.' Now, the answer to these questions is really very simple, and I have often been able to get people to produce the answer themselves, by throwing the question right back at them, asking them to question their assumptions. This technique, of course, is also advocated in dozens of the published tales themselves. Then, on reflection, they answer, of course, things like 'Perhaps I have to know *more* before I can use them', and 'Spirituality to me may mean something which gives me a certain kind of emotional sensation linked with specific images. So I may have to perceive what it really is.'

A Different Kind of Disciple

One of the specialities of the Sufis is to approach the same thing – the needs of the student – from many different directions, so that by what we call 'scatter' (a constellation of impacts), the picture ultimately comes together and he understands. Another story might make this versatility and undogmatic approach clearer:

There was once a Sufi teacher who dressed his disciples in robes of wool, had them carry begging bowls made of sea-coconuts, taught them to whirl in a mystic dance, and intone passages from certain classics.

A philosopher asked him: 'What would you do, as a Sufi teacher, if you went to a country where there were no sheep for the wool, where sea-coconuts were unknown, where dancing was considered immoral, and where you were not allowed to teach classics?'

He immediately answered: 'I would find, in such a place, a quite different kind of disciple.'

It is, in the Sufi area, the possibility of oneself becoming a quite different kind of disciple, learner or teacher, free from the tyranny of instruments, externals and dogma, which is predicated in the contention that all secondary ideas and things, among the Sufis, exist only to be dispensed with in higher ranges of education: and preferably as soon as possible.

Quite obviously, in any community there are many people who only obtain their sense of identity from such externals and appurtenances. They will not be attracted to the greater and most effective depths of teaching-stories – in fact, some are actually almost terrified by them.

Teaching-stories have been described to me, despairingly, as 'one long series of testing devices', which is only a little more useful than the phrase that 'life is only one damned thing after another'. However true it may be, is that all that can be seen by such an observer? Very possibly.

Teaching-stories, I am sure, annoy people because they will say, again and again, that you cannot treat measles by painting out the spots...

The Testing Function

And the testing function is certainly there. The chief feature of this testing, however, is to illustrate to the person himself what some of his major characteristics of thought are, so that he may modify them or be able to detach from them, instead of being their slave. Observing each other's reactions, too, can help a class to widen their perception of the tales.

One such story – *The Tale of the Sands* – sometimes shows people their own dependency situation, quite dramatically. In this tale the river, aware of its existence, runs towards the sea, but arrives before that at a stretch of sand, and starts to run away into nothingness, to become at best a marsh. Terrified of losing its identity, but with no real alternative, the river allows itself to be lifted up by the wind, though only after much debate and soul-searching. The wind carries it out of danger and allows it to fall, as water, safely as it precipitates against a mountain, at the other side.

Some people love this story. For others it has the awful quality of reminding them that they must die or that they may be being asked to choose someone or something, of whom or of which they know next to nothing, of a different kind from themselves, to submit to this and to be carried away to somewhere or something of which they have no knowledge or guarantee. Do these two reactions describe the story or the people who are commenting on it?

People exposed to this story can learn a lot about themselves just by testing its effect upon their feelings...

Rather, as it were, like a radioactive tracer in the bloodstream, you can observe the effect of these stories as they work their way through the culture. Human reactions to them are so varied and so indicative of the major preoccupations of those reacting that there is a great deal of useful instruction in how people behave to be gained just by monitoring what the stories' fate has been over a period of a decade.

Brainstorming sessions have been called to crack the codes of their meaning, papers have been written on their origins and derivatives. Middle Eastern publishers have been affronted that I could make what they imagine must be a good living by publishing 'futile tales from villagers in backward areas'. Some self-styled Sufis have claimed that they knew all about them all the time but wanted to use 'more effective means', while others of the same kidney have started to teach them themselves, saying to any enquirer that they had just been waiting to get around to them. And some, of course, have been setting them as exercises to their students, teasing out strange supposed 'meanings', or saying that one must not look for any meaning at all.

Nasrudin

The stories seem to have a magic which makes people reveal their true selves, one constantly feels. And they make a lot of things out of the academic world work. One scholar had told everyone who would listen that *I* had invented the esoteric qualities ascribed to the Mulla Nasrudin corpus. When he was told that there was an article about this by a Westerner who had studied these matters actually in the East, he instantly replied that I must have written the article myself. I am wondering what he will say when he learns that one of the earliest translations of Nasrudin in English, over a century old, speaks of this esoteric quality of what later became thought of merely as a joke-figure. He will no doubt think that I am a reincarnation of the translator of that time.

Putting In and Taking Out

What tends to make a fruitful approach to the tales difficult currently in the West is that the very tendencies which they are trying to describe are sometimes increased by the stories themselves. There is the same problem in the East, of course. I have heard at least twenty versions of one quip about this very subject which goes something like this:

An impatient student approached a Sufi and asked him: 'At what point will I be able to extract the meaning and make use of the content of the stories really effectively?'

The sage gave a great sigh and answered: 'At the exact point when you stop asking when you will get to that point, and put something *into* your study, instead of constantly trying to get something *out*.'

The legends which surround teaching-tales are, of course, numerous, even magical. It is widely believed, for instance, that people who repeat the Tale of Mushkil Gusha (which I have published in *Caravan of Dreams*[7]) will attract the help of the mysterious personage Mushkil Gusha, the Remover of All Difficulties. The Nasrudin tales are under a benevolent spell. It is said that whenever one of his tales is recited, seven more will have to be repeated, because as a schoolboy he was so addicted to stories and his teacher put this hex on him. My sister, Amina Shah, has recently republished the famous Sufi book *The Tale of the Four Dervishes*[8] in English. The legend which goes with this book is that a Sufi master placed the benediction upon it which makes its reciting a miraculous healing procedure. But for the most part, luckily, the story-form has made the tales most usually seen as entertainment, or to be understood on their lowest level, as moral warnings. This has prevented too much mumbo-jumbo from coalescing around them.

Minor advantages have also been spontaneously observed. When I did a documentary programme for British television, I told a group of children a tale which is familiar in Central Asia, and which we used in England as part of the teaching in the children's school at our house.

The Lion Who Saw His Face in the Water
There was once a lion who lived in a desert which was very windy; and because of this, the water in the holes from

---

7   Idries Shah, *Caravan of Dreams*, London 1968 etc., and Baltimore
      (Penguin) 1972; ISF Publishing, London, 2014
8   Amina Shah, *The Tale of the Four Dervishes*, London 1976, 1978.

which he usually drank was never still, for the wind riffled the surface and never reflected anything.

One day this lion wandered into a forest, where he hunted and played, until he felt rather tired and thirsty. Looking for water, he came across a pool of the coolest, most tempting, and most placid water that you could possibly imagine. Lions, like other wild animals, can smell water, and the scent of this water was like ambrosia to him.

So the lion approached the pool, and extended his neck to have a good drink. Suddenly, though, he saw his reflection – and imagined that it must be another lion.

'Oh dear,' he thought to himself, 'this must be water belonging to another lion – I had better be careful.'

He retreated, but then thirst drove him back again, and again he saw the head of a fearsome lion looking back at him from the surface of the pool.

This time our lion hoped that he might be able to frighten the 'other lion' away; and so he opened his mouth and gave a terrible roar. But no sooner had he bared his teeth than, of course, the mouth of the 'other' lion opened as well, and this seemed to our lion to be an awful and dangerous sight.

Again and again the lion retreated and then returned to the pool. Again and again he had the same experience.

After a long time, however, he was so thirsty and desperate that he decided to himself: 'Lion or no lion, I am going to drink from that pool!'

And, lo and behold, no sooner had he plunged his face into the water than the 'other lion' disappeared!

There was no special intention of spreading this story as a psychological support or therapeutic tool for parents with fearful children. But I got a good many letters after the TV film was shown, saying how parents had been able to use the story to reassure various youngsters who had fears of the unknown or of unfamiliar situations. It is true that these tales are told to children in the East, instead of the more gruesome ones which are often found in Hans Andersen and the Brothers Grimm, and no doubt there is a gap which could be filled here. They would be useful to children, and certainly entertain them, as we have found for many years. They are less attractive to many adults, as has been proved by the fact that the people who choose books for children, that is, adult publishers' readers, have universally turned them down as unsuitable or uninteresting, 'though,' as one has kindly said, 'admittedly curious'.

The stories have become something of a rage in schools and partly through BBC educational broadcasting, where they are constantly used and widely discussed, laying down a stratum of interest which results in constant enquiries and callers from all over the place.

*

No ACCOUNT OF teaching-stories can be really useful unless there has been a recital of some of these tales without any explanation at all. This is because some of the effect can be prevented by an interpretation, and the difference between an exposition and a teaching-event is precisely that in the latter nobody knows what his or her reaction is supposed to be (from any doctrinal standpoint) so that there can be a private reaction and a personal absorption of the materials. So let us look at one or two of the tales, now, under conditions of 'no explanation', so that we can observe our own reactions.

Panacea

There are colonies of dervishes (random and not well-informed seekers) who carry out rhythmic exercises which sometimes produce mental states that they regard (in the early stages of their experimentation) as divine illumination. Quite a lot of ordinary people, too, are attracted by this. They imagine, quite wrongly, that all dervishes are 'illuminated', and respect them.

One day, it is related, a well-meaning but ignorant Seeker-after-Truth arrived at the encampment of a group of these weirdly dressed dervishes, one of whose number was lying on the ground with his eyeballs rolled up, in an attitude of complete surrender, on his back, the very picture of total relaxation.

'I have come to share your life and experience your experiences,' said the man eagerly, to the chief of the dervishes.

'What would you like to share with us?' asked the chief.

'Allow me to share the condition and state of that recumbent dervish,' requested the visitor.

With their customary hospitality, the dervishes obliged. Forming a ring around their new friend, they helped a scorpion to sting him.

*

Admit One...

A dervish died, and was being questioned by the two angels who stand guard over the Gates of Paradise.

'Why should you be admitted here?'

'When I was on Earth, I was a follower of the Great Teacher Gilani...'

'Enter.'

His place was taken by the next man, who was asked the same question.

'*I* must certainly be allowed in – for I have heard what you said to the man in front of me, and *I* was the follower, at the very same time, of *three* of the Greatest Teachers.'

The angels barred his way: 'No, you will not be allowed to enter!'

'But why not?'

'Do you think that we admit people who don't know their own minds?'

*

Moths

A Sufi once established himself at a crossroads. At night he set up a very bright lamp. Not far away he lit a candle. Beside the candle he sat and read his books.

'There must be some secret wisdom in this,' the people of a nearby town said to one another. But they could not fathom the language of the demonstration, if such it was; nor could they penetrate the mystery of the teaching which was being offered them.

At last a group of curious citizens, unable to restrain themselves any longer, sent a deputation to ask why the Sufi had two forms of illumination, and why he had placed them in such a manner.

'Look,' he said, 'at the lamp. It is surrounded, every night, by thousands of moths. By providing that light for moths I am left in peace by them, to read by my candle. I please the moths – and keep them away from me.

'Thus it is with humanity. If everyone knew where real knowledge was, life would be chaos. As it is, people even become frenzied whenever they imagine, like the moths, that there is something which they should surround, especially if that thing is attractive to them.'

*

Reserved

There was once a pretended Sufi who had attracted a fair number of disciples, but he was nothing like as successful as a genuine teacher who lived in the next town.

He made up his mind to find out what the secret formula of the real Sufi was. Disguising himself, he asked for an audience and also to be enrolled as a disciple.

The Sufi took him in, and said: 'The one and only secret for you is that you make a mixture of sugar and water and lie out in the open air without moving, smeared with it, for several hours a day. Then you will attain to the adequate truth.'

The impostor went back to his own headquarters and told all his followers to use the sugar and water exercise. Insects descended in swarms on all of them, and all the disciples abandoned him.

Eventually, lonely and eaten up with curiosity, he returned to the Sufi. 'I came to you, I now confess, to learn your secret. But, when I gave your exercise to my disciples, they were plagued by hornets and they all deserted me,' he said.

'That's how it should have been,' said the Sufi. 'The idea was that your disciples should be driven away from the impostor, and that you would be driven to the stage of desperation and focus upon a single problem from which alone *you* can really learn.'

*

What to See

A party of pilgrims were sitting in the presence of a great spiritual teacher when he stood up and dramatically pointed at one of them. Immediately the man fell down in an ecstasy.

When they all got back to their resthouse, this man became impatient while they were excitedly discussing the miracle of the instant illumination.

'What about me?' he demanded. 'After all, it was me he did it to!' The leader of the group looked at him with disgust.

'You seem to forget,' he said, 'that we came to see *him*, the great man, doing the illuminating – not to see *you* being illuminated!'

Sure Remedy

A man went to visit his physician. 'My trouble is,' he told him, 'that I fall asleep during the very long lectures given by my spiritual guide.'

The doctor handed him a bottle of pills. 'One, three times a day,' he said.

'Thank you, doctor – do I take them with water?'

'No, *you* don't take them – in his food, you fool!'

*

Unanimous

Two would-be disciples met after having visited a certain sage.

'I have decided, after listening to that man,' said the first, 'that he lacks the spiritual insights which I previously hoped would characterize him…'

'Yes,' agreed the second Seeker-after-Truth, 'he wouldn't take me on, either!'

*

EDUCATING THROUGH THE teaching-story follows many of the patterns in other kinds of instruction. For example, there will always be *some* people – very few – in any community who will be able to understand the whole body of teaching material without any instruction, without the benefit of any specialized institution to impart this knowledge to people in measured and appropriate stages. You might guess how many people would be able to do this if you were to ask yourself, as a rough analogy, how many people in a country without, say, mathematics or poetry would be able to understand the whole of such an art or science just by immersing themselves in poetry or mathematics.

From our standpoint, therefore, the question is entirely hypothetical. Besides, it might be noted, why would anyone want to re-invent mathematics? Have you enough time, apart from capacity?

For what we call education, teaching and learning, there have to be teachers, materials and learners, and these have to be in a certain kind of alignment or relationship for the optimum results to be obtained.

We can prepare the climate, introduce ideas and indicate some usages of teaching-stories in an introduction such as this. Mentioning the unfamiliarity of the concept of stories, quoting some as illustrations of part of the process, referring to how people have reacted and continue to react to them, showing barriers to using them and contending that they are indeed highly sophisticated teaching-frames – this is what we have been doing, as a sort of gallop around some of the more easily noted relatively exterior features of this really intricate matter.

But there is no instant application of the stories as a sort of magic wand, or even as some kind of band-aid dressing.

The stories, as a body, and correctly used, offer a remarkable way into another way of thinking and of being. If they are considered only as individual items which can be adopted to add to a repertory, or for any other instantly obvious purpose, they are not much more useful than almost any other literary form intelligently used.

The whole, holistic if you like, body of material and its operation is being introduced now. I would ask you not to be satisfied with imitations. These, as I am sure you already know, are characterized by crypticism on the one hand and telling you what you want to hear on the other. No form of education I know about does that, but cults do. I can do no better than to quote at this point Rumi, one of our great masters: 'You may have a magic ring – but you must be a Solomon, master of invisible powers, to make it work.'

From: *A Perfumed Scorpion*
Idries Shah

Redtape-istan

WHEN I ROSE from the Turkoman rug which my Uzbek friend had spread for me in the rest-house, I walked towards the sea-shore, to be almost as deeply affected as I had been with the Central Asian story. It was past the time of the afternoon prayer, and the Chowpati beach was already getting crowded.

Parsi women in incredibly costly saris of wondrous hues and silken texture walked to and fro. Many sickly looking menfolk – said to be of too-inbred stock – with pinched cheeks, wearing black velvet pillbox caps, led children behind their ladies.

A hundred or more men and women clustered around a magician, who professed to swallow half a dozen razors at one gulp; the betel-nut seller smeared a lime paste on his leaves and handed them to a couple of north Indian youths.

The cool-drink seller was pouring out red and yellow and green sherbet from several bottles for those who could afford to pay a halfpenny for a glass. And, of course, there was a political lecturer with a fair number of listeners and interrupters.

Every one of the local beach trains which passed at seven-minute intervals brought more Parsi women, more children, more cool-drink sellers. There were more betel-nut sellers, more simpering youths with motorcycles and slicked hair, their 'European' suits too tight, their smiles too loose.

Well before sundown, the whole beach seemed one seething mass of humanity and a gigantic seaside fair. I was told that it was like this on every day of the year.

This was all very well, but there was still no progress towards a ticket for the pilgrim ship. Fate had not intervened, nor shown me any direction. 'Trust in Allah,' The Prophet said, 'but tie your camel first.' Very well.

I needed somewhere to stay for the night, even if I were casting myself upon divine mercy and provision.

I made my way to a forlorn caravanserai in the less aristocratic depths of the city, where the innkeeper told me that it would cost me more than a rupee and a half to secure a night's rest. I did not wish to waste that sum, equal to a whole day's wage for a labourer, and about nine-tenths of my total worth at the time.

It would have to be the House of God. So to an adjoining mosque I betook myself. A small tin box – one of those cheap and garishly decorated atrocities which you often see at rustic fairs – was my sole item of luggage.

However, it was late that night before the final resolution came to me regarding further travels. The previous day's meeting with the Nawab's courtier, and the story of the Uzbek, heightened my craving for Mecca. I would go, even though I did not know how.

Late though it was, and prompted by I know not what, I sallied forth to seek the residence of my Nawab friend. On no account could I ask the prince to pay my fare, yet I had no other ideas, either.

As the proverb says: 'In movement, there is blessing.'

The palatial mansion was a tremendous hike out of the city, in a remote and expensive suburb. With that tin box perched on my turbaned head in the approved fashion of the local wayfarer, I walked a mile, two miles, four, five, and then sat down to take a rest.

The horse-carriages, the perilous-looking tramway, even the rickshaws and the cars – all were at a standstill. The city was in deep slumber as I walked through bazaar after bazaar, passed the clock-tower, the railway station, the cricket grounds. Only the occasional night patrol passed me; and yet I walked. Could I, in disguise, perhaps swell the number of the Nawab's retainers? No: I had no passport. As soon as my real name were known, I would be unmasked. Loss of face, perhaps; suspicion of criminal intent – certain…

The party was due to sail for Arabia precisely at 11 a.m. the following morning.

At last, in the half-light of the dawn, I saw the nameplate of the road where the Nawab's dwelling, more of a palace than a house, was situated.

At the crossroads I made a longish stop to adjust my turban, dust my shoes, pull up my socks, and to tidy myself generally before appearing even before the night watchmen of my peer. If I could not accompany him to Mecca, I could at least say prayers with him the night before he set off, and wish him Godspeed.

I moved towards the house, the unsightly tin box under my arm. That box, which I had bought in a hurry earlier in the day, had, apart from its rustic floral design of lurid red and yellow, a picture of a heathen goddess with multifarious hands and feet.

This suddenly struck me as not entirely irrelevant. Fancy my possessing, flaunting, almost, that idolatrous kind of box – I, one of the Faithful, bound for the monotheistic shrine of Islam!

Thinking it over now, of course, it must have looked quite ridiculous when I stopped at the roadside at least twice, trying in the bright moonlight to rub off the figure of the pagan goddess from my Islamic luggage.

But, after all, I did have a prayer rug and a copy of the Holy Qur'an in it.

Now the stillness of the night was broken; the long-drawn-out chant of 'God is Greater, God is Greater' rose from the throat of the Caller, calling the faithful to the prayer of the dawn. 'Prayer is better than sleep!'

As I walked towards the minaret which marked the adjoining mosque, a small figure darted out of the darkness, pressed something into my hand, and whispered, in my own language, 'I entrust you to God' and then sped away.

Automatically I clutched the packet, which seemed like a melon-rind in paper, and put it into my tin box before hurrying into the mosque and standing in line with the Nawab's folk at prayer.

I was standing just beside His Highness in the mosque. I was expected to join his pilgrim band, of course. The Nawab was therefore not surprised to see me, as he said when our devotions were over.

'Have you made all your arrangements?' he asked. I just smiled and thanked him for his interest. Even if it meant, as seemed likely, no pilgrimage this year, that would be better than begging from a classmate. After all, a year's work as a labourer, if I lived in mosques, might get me enough. Or two years, even. Three? Perhaps. Some people walked for longer than that to reach Mecca.

The whole entourage, naturally, had already got their tickets to the Red Sea port of Jeddah. It was of course assumed that I, too, had provided myself with one, much before that morning. After all, within a few hours all would be on board the steamer.

Then I remembered the Dari-Persian whisper, the encounter near the mosque and, yes, the melon-rind.

Wrapped in a bag which had contained a melon was a large sum in paper-money. A note said, in a Central Asian scrawl: 'Friend, brother, compatriot: go to Holy Mecca as my substitute, in accordance with Islamic custom. Pray for me there. I am too sad, not in a spiritual state of mind, to go myself. I must return to Turkestan, until my sorrow is purged. I entrust thee to Allah!'

It was signed: 'Guljanev the Uzbek, melon-eater'.

The miracle had happened.

The next two hours were among the busiest in my life. I had to get a ticket, secure a passport, buy some medicine, the regulation sheet to be worn on the pilgrimage and some articles of clothing.

The difficulty was that not only were the various offices and shops where I had to go at very scattered points of the compass, but it was not at all probable that I would get accommodation on the ship. It was, of course, a pilgrim steamer in which they pack the travellers like pilchards in a tin. But the notice was, as people kept saying, 'absurdly short'. Nor could one get a passport by merely rushing into the Government Office. Indians themselves were known to call their country Redtape-istan.

It can therefore be imagined how I stumbled in my haste, running like a hunted thing. When I was so confused and jumpy that I could not tell them at the shipping company's office which class I wanted to travel, the booking clerk tapped me on the shoulder and took me aside: 'Take my tip…' and he stopped.

I took his tip, (which meant 'give me a tip', of course) and a number of rupees slipped from my hand into his.

Luckily I acquired the tipping skill early on in my frantic travels around Bombay; and so I soon realized that I needed a large part of the Uzbek's donation to bribe the police and passport office, the port authorities, the health people, and so on.

As one worthy put it to me: 'In India, *backsheesh* is democratic: everyone, large and small, takes it.' He wasn't lying, as the Kabulis put it.

I was travelling first-class, since nothing else was left: but I soon found that the pilgrim ships' first-class was worse than even tourist-third in most liners. The pilgrim traffic was one of the most lucrative and cynical of Bombay industries.

As I emerged from the booking-office like a veritable whirlwind, a typical oily local clerk noticed my tin box.

Eyeing it, he said, in that sibilant voice that portends, well, bribery, hereabouts: '*Sahib*, I note faint trace of Black Mother Goddess Kali picture painted on your case. She is the one I pray to daily in temple.'

He assumed a look of the greatest piety, his loincloth almost slipping off as he put his palms together in an attitude of the most profound prayer. I had already learnt that day that these types were the worst.

'And of course I need box just like that to remind me of her when I am not at temple. But I cannot afford one. Is that not too much sad? And also other sadness may come. For instance, I would not like it, *Sahib*, if it were found that your ticket had some irregularity. You wouldn't be able to catch ship, isn't it?' The prayer-rug under my arm was all I needed now; that and the Qur'an in its cotton bag slung over my shoulder. I pressed the box on the pious extortioner and, ignoring his heartfelt prayers that Holy Mother Kali would requite my spontaneous spiritual present, raced through an enveloping dust-cloud towards the Hajj ship.

Presently, what looked like thousands of people, a concourse of humanity, emptied itself from a train onto an adjoining jetty in front of me.

They were all making for a huge tin shed, the blazing sun of the tropics beating upon their shaven heads. All we pilgrims were to be vaccinated under that red-hot roof.

In row upon row we sat waiting for the doctor to arrive: Afghans, Persians, Javanese, Indians and Malays. There were Albanians and Yugoslavs, Chinese from Sinkiang, Chechens, Georgians, Siamese, Arabs, all staring at one another and often trying to follow languages few of us had ever heard before.

At last the vaccination was done. No sooner was the medical certificate grabbed and our fellow pilgrims free to move, than one could see some of them hurrying along a passage with the left shirt-sleeve still rolled up.

A moment later they were behind the shed, washing the scratch inflicted by the vaccinator. According to the rumour in many far-off villages of ancient Asia, the lymph used in its manufacture is considered to be 'an impurity of the cow', and such rumours in the East die hard.

At the quay lay the ship to Jeddah, and when the final word to depart was given by the medical authorities, there was a rush for the gangway.

Stalwart Pathans of the frontier, weak and ill-fed Bengalis, slant-eyed men of Bokhara, veiled women with children in their arms: all made one great rush.

They lugged their valuables along with them in sacks, crudely made boxes, or bulging baskets insecurely tied with ropes. The sacks, however, were in predominance; labelled as items of 'Portable Luggage', always 'Wanted on Voyage'.

We, the faithful, were excited, more truly excited than children before a party, for an emotional veil hung over the whole scene. We were bound for a city the thought of which had been with us since childhood; a city of holy dreams and devout yearning; almost in the blood of every Muslim – a part of a tradition thirteen centuries old.

And the noise and bustle blended with the sanctified air of the pilgrim ship. We rushed the gangway, people colliding with sacks; bundles and baskets pushing into people; a clay water-jar now peeping out of a sack, now pushed up by the jostling crowd, and then slipping out of the hands of its owner into the sea.

Thus the narrow pathway of the gangplank led the faithful to the deck and away down into the ship's enormous, cavernous depths.

Three shrill blasts, the thud of the engines, and slowly we moved away from the shore amid cries of 'God is Greater, God is Greater'.

Existence on the pilgrim ship, to one used to the ordinary comforts of life, was, to say the least, harassing. Although much had recently been done by the Saudi Government to provide better conditions, the devotees were appallingly jampacked, crowded together.

The worst phase of the voyage began on the third day, for practically every pilgrim was now in the throes of *mal-de-mer*. One of them, a cleric who only the day before had told me that he could never be seasick (due to his great piety), was in the very worst straits. Totally prostrated, he prayed loudly, earnestly and incessantly for God to send death to release him.

Then the shouting and the harrowing scenes came to a standstill, but morale was low. The sky was now grey, the wind swept the vessel, and the waves beat on the sides with more than ordinary force. The pilgrims, though more accustomed to the motion, still hated the sight of the waves.

Corpse-like figures lay on the deck, on their sacks of cooking-charcoal, on coiled ropes, everywhere, uttering not a word, hardly interested in existence and avoiding any food or drink. Many thought an evil spirit had come upon the boat.

But it takes more than a rough sea to suspend life altogether, for as soon as the waves subsided the corpselike ones rolled up their bedding, sat up and cooked their food. The Persians made tea, the Bengalis skinned fish, the Pathans were busy with their *pilau* rice of excellent flavour.

During the spell of seasickness, the pilgrims had lost all clear idea of their purpose; but on recovering they soon remembered the solemn idea that induced them to journey to the city of their childhood and lifelong prayers.

The atmosphere on the boat was suddenly thick with religion; prayer rugs and mats were spread, recitations of the Qur'an were chanted, doctors of theology were busy reading to the devotees those chapters of the Muslim Holy Book which related to that part of the journey of the pilgrimage.

In the afternoon, religious discussions took place, and even political ones: though both would usually end where they began. Thus the life of the pious on a pilgrim ship was spent, until one day, soon after dawn, the captain appeared on the deck and pointed out to us in the distance a dark blue line – the Holy Land of Islam! The Arabian coast! The port of Jeddah!

I could hardly speak for excitement, for was I not going to see that great unknown towards which I had stretched out my hands all my life?

Little by little it became clearer, as we stood watching it in our regulation pilgrim costume, until the white city of minarets and domes – Jeddah – lay as if cut in marble, when the boat dropped anchor some two miles from the shore.

From that point no ship could go nearer, as the reefs are very treacherous, and we crossed to the jetty in tiny sailing-boats, tossing like cockle-shells on the crest of the waves.

The first sight of Jeddah gripped me with a strange feeling of an end and a beginning. I gazed at it as a Muslim, with pleasure mingled with awe and reverence. Beyond that city, fifty miles or so away, lay Mecca, the goal of my hopes – the Holy of Holies of every Muslim.

Life's dream, I thought, had at last been realized. The tautness of the muscles of my face and those tears which dimmed my eyes were indications of my emotions.

The scene was strangely familiar, for had I not faced the Holy City, seeing it in my mind's eye five times every day in prayer? Absorbed in these thoughts, I remained in Jeddah for the night, and next day started towards Mecca.

Those of us who had more money than sense were bundled into a large motor-car, and were told that by this means we could best travel the fifty miles inland. We had not gone far when a halt was called at the reputed tomb of Eve. Curious as to the grave of my great ancestress, I alighted to examine it.

She must have been a lady of formidable proportions, for the original grave, I was told, was some eight feet long. But the plot had, by the time I arrived, mysteriously extended itself to altogether gigantic dimensions.

On payment of a fee, I learned that, during the old days, one could receive an oracular message from the buried progenitress of suffering humanity. This was, of course, supplied by a confederate of the tomb-keeper in an underground crypt, who, for a silver *thaler* or two, droned out a 'prophecy'. Fortunately, this evil practice was stopped by the advent of the Saudis, whose puritan Wahabi sect had swept down from Nejd in the north, onto this, the Hejaz region, when they conquered the peninsula.

As we trundled over the sandy tracts, we felt the grilling heat of the desert overpoweringly. I was dressed in the traditional 'sheet' which actually consists of two sheets, one for the upper part of the body, the other for the lower; knotted together, as pins or sewing are frowned on for pilgrim garb by Muslim law. In accordance with immemorial custom, too, my head was shaved and unprotected from the merciless sun.

At last, after twenty-five miles of the hottest journey that I have ever known, we halted at the half-way house of Bahra, where we were told there was a well. Thanks to the Wahabi King Abdul-Aziz, we found not only water, but even cool drinks – heaven-sent in the scorching heat of the desert.

Hardly had we journeyed three miles beyond the well when the rear wheels of our car sank deep in a sand-dune.

We alighted and strove to move the venerable and ancient vehicle, but to no purpose, and much to the contemptuous amusement of a passing Bedouin, who from the back of his swift-trotting camel jeered at us unmercifully.

'It serves you right for bringing that creation of Satan into the sacred land,' he yelled. 'Why can't you travel on camel-back, like other folk? See, I can make my camel stop when I want and go when I wish him to. Take that iron contraption back to the devil who made it.' He hauled us out, entirely by camel-power, now roaring with laughter at our red faces.

From the moment the pilgrim enters Mecca to the time of his departure, he is kept in a fever of excitement and pious frenzy. Ceremony after ceremony claims his constant and unfaltering attention. For hours, he is wedged in by swaying and seething crowds.

One of the rites is to pass seven times between the places called Safa and Marwa, the alleged tombs of Hagar and Ishmael, a distance of perhaps three hundred yards, which is known as the Sai ceremony, and from which one may acquire much merit. The road is not narrow, but is constantly crowded with pilgrims. Add to this, prayers five times a day, and there is not much time to see the sights of Mecca. Not that there is really much to see in the nonreligious sense of the term; the atmosphere of the town is austere – and so, indeed it should be. The Saudi Wahabis, the guardians of the Holy Shrines, had banned any action or even display which conflicted with the austerity of Islam.

Before the actual day of the pilgrimage and before attending the assembly of the Grand Muslim Conference, I had time to make occasional excursions in and around the city of Mecca. Walking right through it, the actual town cannot be more than two and a half miles long; beyond Babal Umra there are quite delightful houses of modern construction and with an adequate water supply. But the heart of Mecca is the Great Mosque, the Harem Sharif, in the centre of which stands the stone structure known as the Kaaba, the Cube. The Black Stone, which every pilgrim kisses, is built into one of its walls.

During my 40,000 miles or more of travelling by land and sea, both in the East and the West, I had not so far come upon a building with which I could compare the Great Mosque in Mecca. In design and style the structure has no parallel. Essentially, it is a great rectangular courtyard, about 250 yards long and a little less than this in width. Nineteen gateways give access to its interior; entering it a remarkable spectacle strikes upon the eyes. All around are colonnades crowned with rather low arch-shaped domes. Several minarets rise from the walls.

From various points along the outer colonnades, narrow pathways lead to the centre of the space where stands the Kaaba entirely draped in a thick black tapestry with gold-embroidered extracts from the Qur'an running in a band towards the top.

Nearby is the well of Zam Zam, reputed to have yielded water to Hagar. Then there are pulpits from which prayers are conducted, because pilgrims in prayer while actually inside the Great Mosque surround the stone structure of the Kaaba; and a great congregation of the Islamic world meets there five times a day.

The prayers take place at dawn, midday, afternoon, sunset and at night. All Muslims face towards Mecca in their devotions. When actually in Mecca, they face towards the

Great Mosque. When in the Mosque, they surround the Kaaba, facing any one of its four walls.

And now as to the spirit which grips one in Mecca. When I was on this journey, I had already lived in or had contact with the dazzling civilization of the West for about ten years. I loved comfort. While I could rough it on a journey, as most Orientals can, yet the lack of physical well-being in this city distressed me at first; that is, the veneer of Europe lay thick on me. I was not the most devout of Muslims, nor indeed was I over-conscious of the power of religion. There was a good deal of 'alloy in my heart', as the Sufis put it.

With this mental attitude I entered Mecca, expecting iced water, electric fans, sumptuously decorated apartments, good motor-cars and more.

Instead I found a temperature of over 133 degrees in the shade, no mechanical means of locomotion, strange food, very little ice, and apartments but poorly furnished. In fact, I met with every discomfort which one could fairly easily remedy outside Mecca.

But now a strange feeling came upon me. I found myself suddenly dropping into a sort of mental vacuum. Discomforts did not feel such. And if I did not pray, and pray in the grilling heat of the Great Mosque, I felt most wretched.

Everything else beyond Mecca, outside that quadrangle with its Kaaba, was lost to me – I literally forgot everything outside. All day long, all night too, I did nothing, cared to do nothing else but pray, bending and kneeling towards that mysterious and august stone building, standing as it did, draped in black. I slept on the stone floor of the Mosque, and used to get up and bathe for prayer at all sorts of odd hours of the night.

Nor was I alone in this practice; for every minute of the day and night people were reading the Qur'an, or bending low in prayer, or going around and around the Kaaba building, dazed as if by some indefinable influence.

But it is to be noted regretfully that the atmosphere changed when one went a little further away from the Great Mosque. One incident stands out clearly in my mind.

The Maulvi Mohammed Ah and his brother, Maulvi Shaukat Ah – at the time giants of Indian politics – were staying in Mecca, awaiting the opening of the World Muslim Conference which the Wahabi king had convened. They were delegates and I was an observer.

My visit to their lodgings to inquire after the health of the Mohammed Ah – who had been ill – and my reception there may prove how true is the saying that even in Mecca people may behave in an unholy manner. It is widely beheved, incidentally, that the influence of the Holy City corresponds to the reverence in which one truly holds it.

When I arrived at the apartment of the Maulvis, I found them lolling about on cushions, and engaged in a fierce argument with the Palestinian delegates about the alleged atrocities of the Wahabi king.

That they were the guests of that king in Mecca may not be beside the point. Upon my taking my seat at the end of the room, a silence fell upon the company. A silence which menaced, for I knew that these mullas had never favoured my line of policy. In spite of my youth, they were well aware of it, and spared no opportunity to denounce me. It should be observed that they spared nobody whose opinion differed from theirs in the least degree. They looked upon each other as venerable authorities and sat brooding over vanished glories, when an insignificant man like me dared to challenge their opinion. At last, grimacing like an ogre, the younger brother spoke – to the Grand Mufti of Jerusalem:

'This man,' he said, pointing to me, 'this youth, is one of our most brilliant men of Islam, but he likes the British and,' he sneered, 'whether he loves Islam or the British more, I do not know.'

I could not control my temper, and in a spirited reply reminded him that he had misunderstood me all along, and that he was a little too concerned about losing his self-fashioned crown at the hands of younger people, whilst at no time would I sell myself for anybody's friendship.

The other brother took the words out of the mouth of one, Sulaiman Nadir, and taunted me for taking a wife from a different clan than my own, as if that were a matter of Islamic importance.

It is strange, though, how both taunts came home to roost. The younger Maulvi, in public and before witnesses, in London and in tears, begged the British during the Indian Round Table Conference, to bury him in their own country – in the land for the lifeblood of whose people he had thirsted until only a year or two before.

His brother was later married to a young and virtuous English girl; hardly a member of his clan.

I did not mention, did I, that when I returned to my accustomed place on the floor of the Grand Mosque, I recounted what had passed to two Sufi sages, who sat by the Bab Ibrahim?

One said: 'As they regard it a sin to be friends with the British, and appear to hate them, it may well be that at least one of them may one day be compelled to seek British mercy.'

The other Sufi then said: 'It could well happen that an Indian Muslim might abhor the mixing of blood, infected as he is with the accursed racial superiority feelings of that country. And so it may come to pass that an Indian might even marry an English lady, after once thinking that such an act would demean him.'

From: *Alone in Arabian Nights*
The Sirdar Ikbal Ali Shah

The Princess of Zilzilam

THERE WAS ONCE a green jinn who, tricked by a magician, had lain trapped inside an ugly lead urn for a thousand years and a day.

As he languished there, the jinn vowed that he would wreak havoc on humankind if he were ever to get free.

He waited. And he waited.

And he vowed and he vowed.

But the urn in which the jinn was imprisoned had been thrown by the magician into the deepest stretch of the Red Sea.

And there it lay for an eternity.

Until, one dark night, it was moved by a rogue current, and then swept up in a fisherman's net as it raked across the sea floor.

The net was hauled up onto the decks, and the urn was discovered.

Hopeful of finding treasure, the captain wasted no time in breaking the lead seal.

Within an instant, the green jinn had surged from the container, slain the captain and his men, and drunk all the blood in their veins.

Soaring up and up into the night, his form billowed outwards and upwards, until he became the sky and the heavens.

'I vow to slaughter every living thing on this earth!' he declared. 'And shall not rest until every heart – human or animal – has been extinguished, and until I have devoured every last drop of blood!'

With that, the green jinn opened his mouth and bore down on the city of Alexandria.

Believing that an eclipse was taking place, the people ran into the twisting streets of the old city and gazed up at the sky.

What they saw in its place was more terrifying than any far-fetched nightmare.

The green jinn's mouth was leering down towards them, a kaleidoscope of carnage: fifty rows of blood-stained teeth, the rotting, festering cadavers of unknown dead.

The diseased.

The putrefying stench of death.

Blood, blood, blood.

The people of Alexandria charged about in all directions, fleeing for their lives. Some hid under their beds. Others dived into empty barrels. More still threw themselves into the sea.

Standing in the middle of the main street was a young man called Adam. Unlike the other people panicking around him, he was not fearful of the sight.

Rather, he was intrigued.

A fraction of a second before the jinn's mouth claimed its prey, Adam raised an index finger high above his head, and called out:

'Whatever depraved creature you are, desist for a moment, until you have heard what I have to say! Not to allow me to speak would be an act of despicable cowardice!'

It just so happened that the green jinn was troubled by almost nothing at all. But the thought of being regarded as a coward vexed him greatly.

So he paused, his mouth in mid-attack, his eyes rolling with rage.

'How could you consume us,' shouted Adam as loudly as he was able, 'without informing us why you are doing so?'

The green jinn shook with rage. And as he shook, the heavens shook, and the world shook as well.

'Your pitiable race entrapped me in an urn for a thousand years and a day,' he roared, 'and you, and all other living things, shall now pay the price of my wrath!'

With the people of the city hastening about in terror around him, Adam touched a fingertip to his chin.

He thought for a moment, then he said:

'Well, O mighty creature, surely you would wish to talk to me before you snuff out my life?'

The jinn drew breath to speak. And, as he did so, the palm trees on the coast were sucked back, as if a storm was about to make landfall.

'I have no time to waste in meeting my victims one by one!' he spat.

But just before the monster could utter another syllable, Adam held up his finger again.

'I feel embarrassed to tell you this,' he said slowly, 'but everyone is gossiping about you in the lanes of the old city.'

'No doubt they are declaring how fearsome I am!' cried the monster.

'Alas, they are not, O great one,' Adam replied.

The jinn narrowed his eyes, each one the size of the moon.

'I shall slay you first for uttering lies!'

Adam held his ground, his head cocked back as he took in the creature's immense form.

'They are saying that you're attacking us out of fear,' he said, 'and out of sheer cowardice. They say that you couldn't harm an ant let alone a great city such as Alexandria!'

'Pah!' exclaimed the green jinn. 'I could swallow the entire city whole! And I will!'

Swelling in size until even larger than before, the monster once again bore down.

But Adam laughed at the sight.

'Your cowardice is surely proven by your size,' he said. 'Any creature so enormous could destroy an entire city. The challenge would be to cause the same harm when smaller in scale.'

The green jinn emitted a crazed shriek of fury. So loud and violent was it, that the ground buckled as though struck by an earthquake.

'I could slay you all if I were half the size!' he boasted, before instantly reducing his form to the size of a mountain.

Adam held up a finger.

'You are still very big,' he said, 'and it is making conversing with you challenging. Could you not make yourself a little smaller?'

The green jinn shrank again, from the size of a mountain, until he was the height of a giant, a giant in human form. His mouth packed with sharp yellow teeth, each one framed in red, he loomed down over Adam.

'Speak your last words O mortal!' he bellowed.

Adam touched a finger to his chin once again.

'Surely even a giant could exact terrible damage on a place like this,' he said. 'But that's not what the people of Alexandria think. As I told you, they say that you couldn't harm an ant!'

The green jinn turned purple with wrath, his mouth dripping with blood.

'Show me an ant, and I shall smite it!' he exclaimed.

Adam leant down, and pretended to pick a speck from the ground.

'Here is an ant,' he said.

Filling his lungs with air, the jinn was about to blow a jet of fire down at the ant, when Adam said:

'As everyone knows, the people of Alexandria are very hard to impress. They take any opportunity to make fun of people from outside the city. And if they see a giant killing an ant – well, that's not going to impress them at all.'

The green jinn released his breath. He frowned.

'Well, what would impress them?' he asked. 'And tell me swiftly, or I shall snuff you out as soon as look at you.'

Adam thought for a moment, and replied:

'Well, surely, what would impress them would be an ant to be dispatched by something even smaller than it, like a flea.'

The green jinn spat blood.

'I have dignity, you know!' he exclaimed. 'I am a great jinn, and am not going to transform myself into a flea.'

'A pity,' said Adam. 'Then the people will gossip about you all the more.'

'But I am just about to kill every last one of them!' bawled the green jinn. 'So I really don't care what they say!'

Adam sighed.

'But surely as a creature of such dignity and poise, you would feel all the more satisfied were you to prove your strength by such an insignificant act as killing an ant.'

Spitting more blood and then fire, the green jinn reduced his size from that of a giant to that of a flea.

'Show me the ant,' said a faint voice, 'so that I may smite it at once!'

But Adam wasn't listening. Instead, he stepped forwards and ground the sole of his sandal into the dirt, until the green jinn was quite definitely dead.

Word of his bravery and cunning spread through Alexandria, and Adam was hailed as the city's saviour. Gifts and titles were lavished upon him, and the wealthiest members of society sought to marry him to their most beautiful daughters.

But, courteously, Adam refused all the awards, the gifts, and the invitations to wed.

Packing a simple leather satchel, he set out into the desert, hoping to have a little time and space to think.

With the stars glinting in the heavens above, he sat beside his campfire. Staring into the flames, his mind thought about the frailty of jinn and of men.

Suddenly, Adam heard a voice.

'Adam, dear Adam,' it said. 'My name is Leila, and I am the daughter of the King of Zilzilam. I am trapped beneath the very sands on which you are camped. Rescue me and I promise to fill your heart with joy.'

Adam twisted round to the left, then the right. The enveloping darkness was empty of any life.

'I can't see you,' Adam whispered. 'Am I imagining you?'

The voice came again, a little louder than before, running on the breeze.

'I am trapped beneath the sands. Walk ten paces south of the fire. Dig down with your hands, and you will find a stone slab. Pull it back and descend.'

Half-wondering whether he was dreaming, Adam glanced back at the fire. The embers were glowing now, fanned by the wind.

He was about to curl up on his blanket and sleep, but the voice came a third time:

'Please come and save me, dear Adam, I beg you...'

Adam got to his feet, and counted ten paces south of the campfire. Then, kneeling, he dug down through the cool sand with his hands. He was about to give up, when his fingertips touched something hard.

Stone.

Digging faster, he unearthed a granite slab, a great iron ring set squarely in the middle. Without giving it any thought, he yanked the ring with all his strength, and the slab slid easily away.

Adam peered down the hole into a dawn realm.

Squinting, he made out a kind of tropical jungle: a profusion of trees and luxuriant vines, of insects and suffocating heat. Climbing down through the boughs of a colossal tree, he made his way onto the forest floor.

As he stood there, taking in a scene from a dreamscape, the first light broke through.

A pair of suns rose both at once – one in the east, the other in the west.

Shading his eyes, Adam watched as the jungle came to life.

Animals he had never seen before swung from one vine to the next, or prowled between the trees, hunting their morning prey.

There were sloths with two heads, zebra in rainbow stripes, and cheetahs weighed down with mighty ibex horns. And there were giant anteaters as well, and mice with human-like hands and feet, and spiders the size of antelopes.

Through the jungle wafted the voice once again:

'Clear your mind of everything you know, Adam,' it cautioned, 'and place one foot before the next. Whatever you do, do not glance down at your feet.'

'How do I know that I can trust you?' Adam thought.

Reading his mind, the voice answered:

'You do not, and that's why you can.'

Doing as he was told, Adam trod a path through the trees, taking care not to look down. As he paced along, he smelled the aroma of roasting meat, and the tart scent of bitter oranges. Then he felt a strange sensation... a sensation of something crawling over his feet and legs.

Straining to obey the voice, he forced himself to refrain from looking down. But the smell and the tingling became too great. Unable to withstand a moment more, Adam lowered his gaze.

Horror is too feeble a word to describe his distress.

His feet and legs were sheathed in squirming worms, glowing red as they gnawed at his flesh. And, as they did so, they emitted a coating of waxy oil, a kind of anaesthetic.

Fearfully, Adam swished the worms away.

But as he did so more appeared, until his hands were covered in them as well.

As he fought in a frenzy to rid himself of the scourge, the voice came once again. Soothing and calm, it drifted effortlessly through the trees.

'Rip off your shirt,' it said, 'and allow the worms to feast on your chest.'

'But they're killing me!' Adam shouted out loud.

'Trust me,' said the voice.

Without any other choice, Adam tore off his shirt. The worms slithered all over his chest, glowing red as they got to work on it.

But, quite suddenly, they began to turn purple-blue and fall away as scabs.

Adam tramped on through the suffocation of trees, following the voice.

The undergrowth became increasingly dense, until it was a struggle to make any headway at all.

Progressing inch by inch, Adam began to sense grave danger.

Something deep inside was cautioning him to turn back, to flee. But, as before, the voice soothed him, luring him forwards.

All of a sudden, the trees gave way to a wide clearing. The ground there was infested with orange beetles, armed with crab claws.

In the middle of the glade was a primitive machine.

The sides consisted of three pairs of multiple scimitars, each one attached to a flywheel. The central unit was a mass of cogs and levers, with a large pair of scales at the front. But the base of the creation was not mechanical at all.

It was alive.

Avocado-green and scaly, it was the colour and consistency of an alligator's back, and was moving slowly, as if rearranging itself.

Approaching cautiously, crunching a path through the orange beetles, Adam took in the details of the outlandish contraption. As he drew close, he noticed something – something that caused his feet to root themselves in the ground.

A woman was encased in the central unit.

Strapped down, she was unable to move. The scimitars were angled in such a way as to carve her up if she tried to escape. Without being told, Adam knew that the woman was Princess Leila.

'I shall disarm this thing and release you!' he exclaimed, quite overcome with sorrow.

The princess did not reply.

Not at first.

She just blinked, the rest of her body held rigid. Then, telepathically, she said:

'Dear Adam, I am indebted for your bravery. But there is only one way to rescue me. In the pans of the scales you will need to place two objects. The first is Hope, and the other – Fear. Attempt to disentangle me, and I shall be chopped to pieces.'

'But Hope and Fear have no form,' Adam said. 'They are invisible, intangible.'

The princess blinked once again.

'It is for you to find them,' she replied, a tear running down her cheek.

'Where shall I search?'

'In your heart.'

Adam reached forwards, until his hand was no more than an inch from the machine. He could feel the princess's warmth.

'I will save you,' he said. 'If I have to scour the universe for Hope and for Fear…'

With that, he was gone.

Retracing his path once again to the surface, Adam found himself at the campfire, the embers still crackling and spitting in the breeze. Leaning back on his haunches, he pondered how and where to find the qualities needed for the scales.

'I shall set out at dawn, and travel the world,' he whispered, 'and will not give up until I have captured Hope and Fear.'

Before the sun had broken over the horizon, Adam's footsteps stretched in a line to eternity.

He walked through days and nights, seeking out anyone who could help him with his quest.

In the next kingdom, he met a hermit who listened to his tale. When he had heard it, the recluse instructed him to search out the Blue Mountains. Because only there, the hermit insisted, could the riddle be solved.

At the Blue Mountains, Adam was informed by a diviner that the only way to find Fear and Hope was not to search for them at all.

Undeterred, he kept searching.

He walked and he walked, and he walked and he walked, until he had crossed half the known world. Each person he asked pointed him in the direction of another, until he was despondent and almost broken. His health suffering from worry, he realized how deeply he had fallen in love with Princess Leila.

After many months of adventure, he found himself in the middle of nowhere – at the desert campfire where his journey had begun.

'I have failed you, dearest Leila,' he said in a whisper, his words carried away on the breeze.

'No, no, you have not, Adam,' came the voice. 'Look into your heart and you will know what to place on the scales.'

Plunging his head in his hands, he struggled to reach a decision.

But he could not.

And so, unable to carry on, he paced over to the stone slab, and descended back into the jungle world in which the King of Zilzilam's daughter was kept prisoner.

Although months and years had passed on the surface, it seemed as if the sands of the hourglass fell far more slowly in the jungle realm than they did above. Hardly a day had gone by since he had embarked on his quest.

Wending his way through the trees, Adam retraced his path towards the glade in which the princess was imprisoned. As he walked fitfully between the vines, he noticed a mango tree, its ripe fruit hanging down in great quantities.

Overcome with hunger, he picked one of the mangoes and ate it.

Within a few feet of the tree, he reached the glade in which the machine was still standing. As before, the scimitars were razor-sharp, glinting in the blinding light.

While he watched, they began to move as if his arrival had triggered them. The scimitars scythed alarmingly through the air and, as they did so, the machine's reptilian underbelly coursed back and forth, surging to life.

'Please hurry!' whispered the princess. 'Precious time is running out. In moments, I fear I shall be dead!'

Adam stood before the machine, his blood fortified with adrenalin. Although desperate to rescue the princess, he felt helpless. With her certain death a moment away, Adam knew he had to try something.

As he conjured up the courage to overcome his fear and destroy the machine, he felt his face and hands running with perspiration.

'Fear,' he thought, wiping his forehead dry. 'This is Fear!'

Rinsing a hand over his brow once again, he collected a few drops of sweat, and dripped them into the left pan of the scale.

But what about Hope?

Drawing a deep breath, Adam was about to resign himself to failure, when he remembered the mango seed, still clutched in his hand.

'This is Hope,' he said. 'The Hope of a mango tree.'

In a quick movement, he dropped the seed into the second pan.

The machine whirred and grunted, the scimitars flashing in the jungle light.

And all of a sudden, the straps and bindings disintegrated.

Princess Leila was free.

Adam and the princess returned to the surface, and to the Land of Zilzilam.

Forty days of celebration were held, so overjoyed was Leila's father that his favourite daughter had been saved.

When the festivities were at an end, Adam and the princess were married in a tumultuous marriage ceremony.

Another forty days of festivities followed.

And, with time, Adam ascended to the throne of Zilzilam, reigning as its king for many years. His wisdom and courage are still spoken of today, and his acts of kindness are the stuff of legend far beyond the ancient walls of Zilzilam.

As the years passed, King Adam devoted more and more of his time to improving the kingdom, and the living standards of its people. He made sure that everyone had enough food and a good education, and that every citizen had the opportunity to come to him directly with their problems. The gates to the palace were always open, and everyone knew that King Adam would see them if they needed his help.

One evening, when he had ruled for seventeen years, Adam was sitting in the durbar attending to some official papers. As he pressed his signet ring into a wax seal, a wizened old man staggered in. The man had a long white beard that reached down to his knees, and was wearing a jet-black cloak that covered his form in its entirety.

Rising from his throne, King Adam went to greet the stranger.

When they were both seated, and once tea had been served, the old man spoke:

'O great King Adam of Zilzilam,' he said, his words muffled with age, 'I have waited seventy years to bring you a message, a message that will save your kingdom and your life.'

Adam looked into the old man's dull eyes, and wondered whether he was unhinged. But before he could say a word, the stranger went on:

'When I was a young man,' he said, 'I was a shepherd on a remote hillside a great distance from here. From dawn until dusk each day, I tended the family flocks. And each night, I would bed down on the hay in a little stone barn, and I would sleep like the dead.

'One night, while deep asleep, I walked from the barn, over the hills, until I came to a jagged rock face. There, in a cleft between the crags, an oracle spoke to me. It said that I was to be a messenger and that, one day many years hence, a good king would be saved by the message I was to impart.'

'What was the message?' asked Adam gently.

The old man held out a withered hand.

'I shall tell you,' he said. 'Each night I would return to the crag as a dream-walker. And I would listen to the message of the oracle. And, little by little, the oracle passed on details of the message in a most unusual way. Only when the entire message had been entrusted to me did I awake to understand that I had been the confidant to an oracle.

'As the messenger, I was instructed to keep the message with me at all times in a certain way, and to bring it to you on this day. The oracle said that you, King Adam, would understand the secret wisdom held within it, and that by doing so, your kingdom would endure until eternity.'

'Could I have the message?' asked Adam, growing a little impatient.

Again, the old man held out a hand.

'I shall give it to you,' he said solemnly.

A SON OF A SON I

Standing slowly to his feet, he unfastened the buttons of his jet-black cloak, and the robe fell to the floor. Beneath it, the ancient was naked.

Every square inch of his skin was tattooed with words.

'This is the message,' he said.

And, with that, he expired.

From: *Scorpion Soup*
Tahir Shah

The Fakirs and Their Doctrines

THE WEST, WHICH prides itself with some justification upon having rescued from oblivion many aspects of Oriental culture and learning, has been profoundly influenced by *Tasawwuf*: the doctrine of the Fakirs. Yet how many people, apart from a handful of Orientalists, can say what this is?

Yoga, Shinto, Buddhism, Taoism and Confucianism, all have their devotees in Europe and America. Yet Sufism – the ultimate mystical sanction of the Arabs, Persians, Turks and the rest of the Muslim World – remains the last closed book of the mysterious East.

Is Sufism a religion? An occult cult? A way of life? It is, in part, all of these things – and none of them. Among the four hundred million followers of Islam, *Tasawwuf* commands a power such as no political, social or economic creed does here or elsewhere.

Organized in a semi-monastic, semi-military fashion, this amazing philosophy was shared by elements as diverse as the ancient Arab alchemists – the Brethren of Purity – the Mahdist warriors of the Sudan and the greatest classical poets of Persia. Under the banner of the Fakirs (literally 'the humble ones'), the Turkish Empire's dervishes stormed Vienna. Urged on by Sufi mystical poetry (and, it is claimed, supernatural power) the Afghans conquered India.

Then, on the other side of the coin, Sufi literature and culture were responsible for some of the outstanding architecture and art of Asia.

What are the origins of this strange cult, which even modern researchers acknowledge to be still the strongest single force in the Middle East today? In spite of the fact that a considerable literature on the subject exists in Oriental languages, nothing is known with complete certainty as to the very beginnings of the cult.

Sufi historians trace their foundation to Mohammad himself, but it has been stated that this esoteric cult stems from man's earliest strivings to liberate his ego from material things. This, in fact, is the main aim of the movement. Sufism is a distinct and very complete way of life, setting as its goal the realization of man's (and woman's) believed role in life.

Man, argue the Sufi saints, is part of the Eternal Whole, from which everything is derived, and to which all must return. His mission is in preparing himself for that return. This can only be achieved through purification. When the human soul is correctly harnessed to the body, and has obtained complete control over it, then man appears in his perfect form: the Perfect Man, in fact, emerges as closely resembling the superman, possessed of amazing powers, who figures in the aspirations of Eastern and Western occultism alike.

There are distinct steps by which a 'seeker' progresses towards this end. Organized in Orders resembling the monastic orders of the Middle Ages (alleged by some to have been modelled on Sufism), the first condition of enrolment is that the recruit must be 'in the world but not of it'. This is the first important respect in which the cult differs from almost every other mystical philosophy. For it is fundamental that every Sufi must devote his life to some useful occupation. His aim being to become an ideal member of society, it naturally follows that he cannot cut himself off from the world. In the words of one authority:[9]

> Man is destined to live a social life. His part is to be with other men. In serving Sufism he is serving the Infinite, serving himself, and serving society. He cannot cut himself off from any one of these obligations and become or remain a Sufi. The only discipline worthwhile is that which is achieved in the midst of temptation. A man who, like the anchorite, abandons the world and cuts himself off from temptations and distractions cannot achieve power. For power is that which is won through being wrested from the midst of weakness and uncertainty. The ascetic living a wholly monastic life is deluding himself!

Though the word 'Fakir' has come to be used in the West as denoting a kind of itinerant juggler or wonder-worker, its real meaning is merely 'a humble man'. Humility of the Seeker is the first requirement. He must renounce his struggle for mere worldly aims until he gets the reason for life into the

---

9   Akbar Khan, *Tasawwuf-i-Azim*. Persian MS., seventeenth century.

correct perspective. This is not, in fact, contradictory. For a man may legitimately enjoy the things of the world, provided that he has learnt humility in their application.

What has given Sufis – in their role of fakirs or dervishes – that halo of invulnerability, infallibility and superiority is the application of this doctrine. There is no doubt at all that the concentration of mind achieved by Sufis is responsible for what could be classed as truly supernatural manifestations. There are instances, recorded with as much historical accuracy as one may expect anywhere, of the strange power of some of these men. Approaching the question in as scientific a manner as possible, many are the instances of bogus Sufis merely playing upon the gullibility of the masses. On the other hand, tens of thousands of unbiased people are convinced of the fact that *Tasawwuf* can bring power of an unheard-of degree to some of its practitioners.

It is necessary to point out here, as in other parts of this book, that such manifestations may, if true, merely be the application of secrets of nature which are as yet imperfectly understood by orthodox science.

What are the miracles and powers attributed to the Sufi saints? While there is almost no thaumaturgic phenomenon which has not been claimed by some authority as performed by dervishes, some miracles are more characteristic of the cult than others. The first one (in conformity with the belief that time is non-existent) is the annihilation of conventional time. Stories – some of them on the authority of meticulously accurate historians – covering this phenomenon are many and varied.

Perhaps the most famous is the case of the Sheikh Shahab-el-Din. He was able to induce, it is said, the appearance of fruits, people and objects absolutely at will. It is related of him that he once asked the Sultan of Egypt to place his head in a vessel of water. Instantly the sultan found himself transformed into a shipwrecked mariner, cast ashore in some totally unknown land.

He was rescued by woodmen, entered the nearest town (vowing vengeance against the sheikh whose magic had placed him in this plight) and started work there as a slave. After a number of years he gained his freedom, started a business, married and settled down. Eventually, becoming impoverished again, he became a freelance porter, in an attempt to support his wife and seven children.

One day, chancing to be by the seashore again, he dived into the water for a bathe.

Immediately he found himself back in the palace at Cairo, again the king, surrounded by courtiers, with the grave-faced sheikh before him. The whole experience, though it had seemed like years, had taken only a few seconds.

This application of the doctrine that 'time has no meaning to the Sufi' is reflected in a famous instance of the life of Muhammad. It is related that The Prophet, when setting out on his miraculous 'Night Journey', was taken by the angel Gabriel to heaven, to hell and to Jerusalem. After four score and ten conferences with God, he returned to earth, just in time to catch a pot of water that had been overturned when the angel took him away.

In addition to the non-existence of time, space plays little part in preventing the Sufi adept from travelling where he will. Transportation of many of the most famous Sufi teachers is said to have been a common event. Sufis have been seen at the same time in places many thousands of miles apart. Sheikh Abdul-Qadir Gelani – one of the most celebrated saints of Sufism – was believed to have travelled thousands of miles 'in a flash', in order to be present at the funeral of some fellow adept.

Walking upon the surface of water, and flying enormous distances in the full view of people on the ground, are other wonders said to be regularly performed by the initiates.

Miracles, as such, are thought to be possible only to prophets. But wonders (*karámát*) are held to be possible to a great number of Sufis. The activities of magicians – which are generally a form of deception worked upon gullible people – are classed as *istidraaj*, signifying mere conjuring tricks and works of stealth. Magic proper, by which is meant thaumaturgy through the aid of spirits, is an entirely different branch of occult science.

Organization of the Orders
Mystical Orders of this type lay down rigid rules in a set pattern for aspirants to Sufi power. Apart from those who pursue the cult alone, all new recruits must be accepted according to a formula by a *Pir*, or teacher. Sons follow in their fathers' footsteps in entering the Order to which their parent belonged; and only those who have been

recommended by certain sponsors may be accepted as disciples into the first degree of '*Sálik*': Seeker.

Orders, which are named after their founder (Naqshbandíyya, Chishtíyya, Qádriyya, etc.) are organized in groups studying under acknowledged masters. Promotion from one degree to the next is through a patent or declaration by the master of the group to which the acolyte belongs. In order to study a particular branch of the art, students may travel from Morocco to Java, or from as far afield as China to Libya, to join the *halka* (circle) of a celebrated teacher. Then, if the latter agrees, the candidate will be placed on probation for some months. Living a life of poverty, dressed perhaps in saffron robes and performing menial tasks, the seeker during the period of his studies must remain attached to his master with a devotion which far exceeds even the most rigorous discipline of any military force.

He must take part in the ritual recitations of certain holy and secret scripts, must observe the Five Ritual Prayers and ablutions, the annual month of fasting from dawn to sunset, and read the works of the masters.

The Orders

Several distinct Orders or *Tariqas* ('Pathways') of Sufism are known. All trace their origins to Muhammad himself, and also to his companions. It has been asserted that they originated in a mystical fraternity among The Prophet's immediate followers – the *Asháb-Us-Safá*, or Companions of the Bench. These men, about whom very little is definitely known, immersed themselves in good works, contemplation, fasting and prayer. Even the derivation of their name is shrouded in mystery. The widest held theories, however, state that they are either named after their woollen robes (*souf*, wool, in Arabic), or from '*saf*', purity.

The main orders today are the Naqshbandíyya, Chishtíyya, Qádriyya and Suharwardíyya. Each is self-contained in itself; none is inimical to the others: saints and practices are sometimes held in common; the objectives of mankind, and particularly of the Sufis, are almost identical in each.

There are a number of other Orders, scattered from Morocco to Java, through India, Afghanistan – anywhere, in fact, that Islam has spread. In all cases, rites and writings are highly symbolistic.

In every case admission to an Order depends upon sponsorship and initiation.

Sufis traditionally hold an important, if undefined, place in both society and history. The Dervishes of the Sudan were – and still are – a Sufi Order, organized as a militant and nowadays philanthropic entity. In the days of the Ottoman Empire, the greatly feared Jannissary shock-troops were a military Sufi fraternity, connected with what are today known as the Naqshbandíyya. The present King of Libya, Sayed Idris, is the Chief of a Sufi order, and most, if not all, of his subjects consider themselves Sufis. The Fakir of Ipi – that 'Firebrand of the North-West Frontier of India' – is a Sufi leader. These brief facts may tend to give the impression that there is much militarism in the different Orders: perhaps the explanation may be that other aspects of the cult are less well known in the West; reference to them out of context would serve only to confuse the reader.

Objects of Sufism

The theory of Sufism is that man, in his ordinary state as part-animal, part-spirit, is incomplete. All Sufi doctrine and ritual is dedicated towards making the Seeker (*Sálik*) pure, and therefore *Insán-i-Kámil* – a Perfect Man, or Complete Man. It is envisaged that a person may be able to achieve this state of Completeness by himself, or even through means other than Sufism. Yet it is contended that Sufism is the established way, with its prescribed method and the guidance of the Masters who have already trod the Path.

When the aspirant has attained the state of completeness which is the goal of the cult, he is then in tune with the Infinite; and those strivings and uncertainties to which he, as a mere imperfect mortal, has been subjected, are no more. This ultimate stage of achievement is known as *Wasl*, 'Union'.

The monastic life, however, is strongly eschewed by all Sufi thinkers. They reason that if a man deprives society of his service and activity, he is being anti-social. Being anti-social is against the Divine Plan. Hence he must, in the words of the First Principle of Sufism, 'Be *in* the world but not *of* the world!'

The hierarchy of Muslim Sufi saints, therefore, are known by their occupations as well as by their titles. Hence, one (Attar) was a chemist; another (Hadrat Baháuddin Naqshband) was a painter, and so on. Certain kings of

India and Persia, upon becoming Sufis, took up some extra occupation to pay for their own upkeep, while still remaining rulers and taking nothing from the treasury on their own account.

The Invisible Rulership of Sufism

Chief of the entire Sufi system is the *Qutub*: he is the most enlightened of all Sufis, has attained the degree of *Wasl* (Union with the Infinite) and holds power over, according to some, the entire Sufi organism. Others say that the *Qutub* has considerable political or temporal power as well. In any case, his identity is known to very few. He maintains communication only with the Leaders of the Orders.

Conferences are held telepathically, or else by means of 'time and space annihilation'. The latter phenomenon is said to mean that Sufis of the degree of *Wasl* are able to transport themselves anywhere instantaneously, in physical form, by a process of decorporealization.

The *Qutub* is attended by four deputies – the *Awtád*, or Pillars, whose function is to maintain knowledge of, and power over, the four corners of the earth, and to report to him constantly the state of affairs in every country. Subservient to the *Awtád* are the forty *Abdal* ('those who have become spiritually changed'), and under them, in turn, seventy Nobles, who in their turn command three hundred Lords. Sufi saints who do not hold an actual office in this hierarchy are termed Saint: *Wali*.

Entry and Initiation

Entry into an Order is made through one of the many hundreds of branches (*halka*) – also known as Circles – which flourish throughout the East. Although explanations of the more esoteric aspects of the cult are not forthcoming to any but initiates, it is important to note that his membership of an Order is usually not kept a secret by an initiate.

In some places men take their young sons to be present at the rites of the Order; hence many grow up with a curiosity about Sufism, and it may be said to be unusual for the son of a Sufi not to join the Order himself.

When a candidate for the lowest degree (that of *Sálik* – Seeker) is presented, he may be allowed to attend meetings for some time before being presented formally by his sponsors for enrolment. Acceptance by a Chief, or *Pir*, does not necessarily mean that promotion is likely to follow. This is one of the truly extraordinary facets of Sufism, as opposed to other mystical or secret fraternities. Promotion or elevation in the Order, or even the passing of secret knowledge, come to a person automatically as soon as he is ready for it.

Unless the aspirant is 'Mature' (*Pukhta*) for enlightenment, he will never progress. Once he has been initiated, however, he will most probably be on the Road to Success, and if he adheres rigidly to the rites and practices of the Order, he will be able to benefit from them. In other words, if – as sometimes happens – a person other than an initiated Sufi attends a Sufi *halka*, he may hear all that is being said, he may take part in all the repetitions of sacred formulae, he may even join in the ritual circumambulations: but he will derive no enlightenment, no benefit, no understanding therefrom.

A striking example of this is the Monastery of the Maulavi Order in Cyprus, where anyone at all may attend the strange ceremonies of the 'Dancing Dervishes' – and the latter are in no way put out by the presence of infidels, uninitiates or even detractors. It is their unshakeable belief that their ceremonies and repetitions of formulae (*dhikr*) are efficacious only for those who are initiated.

Newcomers, having been introduced into the circle of Sufis, generally attend for several sessions of recitation, repetition of holy phrases, singing or dancing, depending upon the Order in question. In relation to music, some Orders employ music, others do not even permit recitations, except *sotto voce*.

At a convenient moment in the proceedings, the candidate is presented to the Chief of the Circle. He may then be asked certain questions to determine his suitability. If he is accepted, the Chief takes him by the hands and whispers to this effect in his ears. The recruit is then known as a Seeker, and the only remaining rite to be performed to complete his enrolment in the Order is the Great Oath. In this the *Sálik* undertakes to obey his *Pir*, absolutely and without reservation.

While nearly every Sufi following the Path is a properly coached and entered Member of his Order, one other form of Sufism is known. This, called *Uwaysi*, is practised by those who, while following established Sufi patterns of discipline and thought, are yet affiliated to no Order. The name is derived from one Uways ul Qarani, of Yaman, a contemporary of Muhammad, who is said to have been in spiritual contact with The Prophet in spite of never having met him.

Two important facts about Sufism are exemplified in this *Uwaysi* doctrine. First, it shows the spiritual or telepathic link which forms a significant part of the cult. Just as time has no established meaning to the Sufi, so it is possible for one of their number to be in communication with another who may be far away – or may even be dead. Hence we find important Sufi saints claiming inspiration and co-operation with others whom they may never have met; or else from the spirit of one long dead. Secondly, it is acknowledged by Sufism that progress may be made in the Path by one who is not under direct or constant instruction from his *Pir* or master. At the same time it is emphasized that such cases are rare.

The Sufi Path

Following his acceptance by the Chief of the *halka*, the Seeker gains the title of *Murid*: disciple, and must then embark upon the rigorous preparation which will lead him to Stage Two: that of *Tariqat*, or potentiality. This latter forms the first real degree of Sufism, and denotes spiritual progress.

Between the First and Second Degrees, in addition to obeying every instruction of the Master, the disciple must not omit any point of the ritual observance of formal Islam.

In addition to reading certain prescribed books, he spends as much time as he can on the recitation of *dhikrs*. These formulae are designed to remedy any defect in belief or ability that may have been discerned by the *Pir*. This is considered to be the period of rededication to the theme of 'Be *in* the world, yet not *of* the world'. The intention and aim of every Seeker at this stage is to concentrate upon the thoughts and personality of the *Pir*. In his turn, the *Pir* turns his thoughts regularly towards those of the disciple, sending him vital spiritual energy, to fortify him in the battle against the 'Self'. By the Self is meant the things of the flesh which detract from true spiritual progress.

In the stage of *Muridi*, too, the Seeker may take part in the nightly meetings of the Dervishes (Sufis), in their *halka*, or monastery. Present at such meetings, and repeating the same *dhikrs*, may be Sufis in several different stages of advancement. But this will not affect the potency of the *dhikrs* or the progress of individuals, because it is held that the same *dhikr* may be of great value in any one of the stages. This is, of course, determined by the *Pir*.

When the disciple merits the title of *Tariqat* – either because his *Pir* decides so or because he himself has reached the stage of knowing that he has progressed – he transfers his attention from the thoughts of his Leader to those of the actual Founder of the particular Order. At this time, however, the Leader keeps his own thoughts focused upon the disciple, to reinforce his spiritual powers.

It is at this stage that the disciple may be allowed to pursue certain thaumaturgic practices, if his *Pir* decides that it be permissible. His abilities in occult knowledge and actual magical phenomena are great, but he may employ them only with consent.

These Sufis are now in the Stage of *Safar-ullah*: the Journey to Knowledge. They must concentrate upon the achievement of one-ness with the spirit of the Founder of the Order, whom they now call *Pir*, in place of the Leader whose disciple they are. The Leader himself is now known as *Sheikh*, or *Murshid*.

They travel, often to far countries, at the behest of the *Murshid*. Preaching the cult is not allowed, unless they are asked about it, and unless they feel that their questioners may be able to profit by such knowledge. Pilgrimages to Mecca, Medina, Jerusalem and to other shrines are undertaken. This stage generally takes far longer of attainment than the previous one.

It is known and recorded, however, that promotions from a low stage to one of the highest may take place without the intervention of the *Murshid*.

After *Tariqat* comes Stage Three: *Arif*, the Knower. At this point the Seeker dedicates himself to the attainment of unity with the thoughts of Muhammad, and has graduated beyond the mind of the founder of the Order. This part of the road is known as *Safar li-Allah*: the Journey Away from Neglectfulness.

Occult and all supernatural powers are very marked in the Stage of *Arif*. The spirit has been all but purged of the detrimental physical aspects and lusts. The 'Self' is well under control. All that remains is the Summit – the Degree of *Fana*, or Annihilation. This means the total destruction of all thoughts which separate the Seeker from the full knowledge of all things. Farther than this he cannot go – except to Stage Five, which involves a return to the baser life, in order to purify others.

Miracles of the Sufis

Kamáluddin, one of the most important of the Sufi historians, gives a typical example of raising of the dead, as familiar to students of the Naqshbandi Order.

Qaiyúm, a Naqshbandi leader, is stated to have revived his granddaughter, even though her death had been certified three days before. The saint maintained that she was still alive. It was only when the body was actually showing signs of decomposition (of rapid onset in the Indian climate) that he simply called to her... and she is claimed to have sat up immediately.

A large number of miracles are reported of the best-known woman Sufi, Rabii'a al-Adawiya, in the eighth century.

Her main teaching, as expounded to the few who know her well, was that prayer and the recitation of formulae were the Gateway to Knowledge and hence to power. She was disinclined to concentrate upon the generally accepted use of prayer as a means towards forgiveness and salvation.

Using the formula *Lá-illáhá-illa-alláh* ('There is no God save Allah, the One'), she is reputed to have made fires without wood, obtained food without leaving her house, and been supernaturally supplied with sufficient gold for her needs.

She was sold as a slave early in her life. One day her master said that he once noticed that a lamp seemed suspended above her, yet without support of any kind. This experience so troubled him that he immediately set her free, without saying anything to anyone.

Sufi miracle-workers, in addition to the observance of the ritual prayers and ablutions, employ several principal *dhikrs* which induce the concentration of mind that enables occult phenomena of almost every type to be produced. Among these achievements are the ability to relieve pain and destroy disease, transportation anywhere in the twinkling of an eye, knowledge of future events and also of what anyone is thinking, even though that person may not be present.

Dhikrs of the Sufis

All recitations are performed in a state of ritual purity. The face, arms, feet and mouth are washed. If the Seeker has slept since his last *dhikr*, he must have a bath. Any other pollution must also be removed by complete immersion.

Dhikrs are generally said during the hours of darkness. When a supernatural result is desired, the *dhikr* must dwell upon some facet of the Divine power allied to the effect to be accomplished. Thus, when a Sufi wishes to cure illness, he prepares himself by repeating a *dhikr* consisting of the Name of God which denotes healing. By this means the Sufi intends to collect in his mind a tremendous potential of mental force associated with healing. This he projects towards the object of his attentions, at the same time concentrating upon the desired result.

When a Sufi's aid is invoked to ensure, for example, success in any venture, he will purify himself and spend three nights, culminating on a Thursday, reciting the simple formula *Ya Fátih* ('O Victor') – one of the Attributes of the All-Powerful. On Thursday (the 'powerful' night of the week) the full quota of power will have been built up in his mind: this, at any event, is the theory. He may also give the person a talisman or amulet with the *dhikr* written on it, to wear on his arm. Even today, these *dhikr* amulets are widely worn among all classes in the Muslim East. It is not uncommon for Sufis to receive a visitation from some important member of the Order – perhaps long dead – advising them as to the best course to take in any matter upon which they are uncertain.

At the outset of his training the more esoteric aspects of Sufism are of less concern to the Seeker than the attainment of progress through implicit obedience to the formulae of the cult. The root of all such progress is *dhikr*. Having either been given a set *dhikr* to repeat (if he is under the direct guidance of a sheikh), or having selected one himself (if he is an *Uwaysi* working towards the goal alone), his task is to repeat it with meticulous regard for the times and frequency of its saying.

If the formula is said under the breath ('*dhikr khafi*'), a rosary with ninety-nine beads is used, one bead being told after each repetition. In the case of the '*dhikr jali*' (loud repetition) the rosary is often not used. When not attending an actual *halka* ('circle') meeting, the Seeker generally goes to some quiet place, or spends his contemplation-time in a room set aside for the purpose.

There is, too, the exercise known as *fikr*, which consists of meditation: concentration upon some power that is desired, or upon the immensity of the Universe. When *dhikr* and *fikr* have been indulged in to such an extent that they become second nature, the Superior Form of *dhikr* becomes necessary. This is the control and concentration of breath: the mind is concentrated upon a single idea, and the original *dhikr* formula or another one is recited, this time in set rhythm corresponding to the breathing.

When the *dhikr* has so sunk into the mind that it is being automatically repeated without conscious effort – then the 'Superior Form' is used. According to Sufi doctrine, mastery of the thought processes and their linking with the body have been achieved.

The purpose of this Superior Form is the production of the next – and highly important – phenomenon: ecstasy. While it is conceded that ecstasy can come without the *dhikrs*, it is claimed that it cannot be induced so readily by other means. In the state of ecstasy, which may be followed by unconsciousness, the mind undergoes a transformation whose nature is not described. True ecstasy is known by the technical term *wajd*, and paves the way to *Khatrat* – illumination. Here the mind and soul are liberated from the body, and knowledge and power take the place of the base thoughts of which the mind has been purified. In the Chishti Order, music is used to induce the ecstatic state; some orders claim that their members fall into a trance after looking into the eyes of their sheikh. The so-called Dancing Dervishes accomplish trance and ecstatic phenomena through monotonous circumambulations, and this is most marked in the Maulavi Order, most popular in Turkey. In the ecstatic state Sufis are believed to be able to overcome all barriers of time, space and thought. They are able to cause apparently impossible things to happen merely because they no are longer confined by the barriers which exist for more ordinary people. Certain it is that some of their supernatural activities are difficult, at the present stage of knowledge, to account for. It will be observed that the general principles to be found in very many systems of religious and occult practice are strangely similar. The principles of leadership, discipleship and discipline, contemplation and monoideism can be found in the secret and not so secret rites of nearly every people.

If the wonder-workings of the Sufis and Hindu gurus, the African witch-doctors and the Amazonian medicine-men are to be investigated in a spirit of true science, there can be no question of belief or disbelief. We must admit that we have not conclusively shown that secret esoteric lore does not exist. Neither can we explain the similarities on a basis of psychology: that these rites are only symbolic of man's limited and natural strivings for superiority alone. The scope for investigation is extraordinarily wide.

From: *Oriental Magic*
Idries Shah

Desert Ways

As I BENT down to unstrap my camel load, someone tugged at the hem of my long, flowing robe. Then the wet nose of the camel touched my bared arm, and I thought that the tail of my loose shirt must have been caught under the bag which I had unloaded. Once again I felt – yes, this time it was certain: a pull at my clothes.

'In the Name of Allah! In the Name of Almighty God!' and the voice of a prostrate form, gurgling from a hoarse throat, was drowned by the sound of the bubbling camels in the quadrangle of our desert rest-house.

With more than ordinary curiosity, I bent down towards the one who had pulled at my garments, and whose words of supplication had been almost swallowed up in the general din of shouting drivers as they unloaded their beasts of burden.

I flashed my torch at the man. He lay, face downwards now, holding his side, apparently in great pain. His eyes – Oh those eyes! I can't forget them – they had a haunted look. And his face – well, you have heard of the fantastic hawklike features of the desert sheikh? He could have beaten most, if not all, of his film counterparts, for the aristocracy of the desert was writ large on his visage.

Now a change seemed to come over him, as if he was summoning his last reserves of strength for some action…

Suddenly, he leaped up like a wounded panther and snatched the flashlight from my hand.

'Thinkest thou that in the heart of the desert people will spare thy life if they see thee making light without a fire?'

A long memory came back to me, for had I not been shot at, once, in a Bedouin encampment as a magician for 'making light out of nothing, like the one cast down from Allah's Palace'?

The man now squatted down beside me. Our backs rested against my sitting camel. From his cummerbund he produced a paper, shading the light of the torch with the skirt of his long robe whilst I read the epistle.

It was a letter from one of my oldest friends in these parts, begging help for this hunted man!

'Peace be to thee, my brother!' I shook him by the hand. 'What a great honour has fallen upon me. It shall, indeed, be my pride to escort thee, the friend of Murad; for Murad once saved mine life's blood.'

'Sh-hhh!' he placed his hand on my lips.

I took the tip, for the camel may not understand a conversation, but Allah only can tell who hides behind the camel; and although my new friend knew that I, as Murad's seasoned commercial agent, could smuggle him even to heaven, yet even here and now, he said there were eighteen men in the rest-house who would almost literally drink his blood.

169

With what care I could bestow, the sheikh's wounds were attended to by me. His enemies had only half-buried the point of their blades in his thigh, and he had slain three before he got to where I was unloading my mount.

It is true that as trading goes in Arabia, I was not an ordinary merchant, but the roving commission given me by Murad, the merchant prince of Damascus, had made it possible for me to travel safely for many months into the most covetously guarded parts of inner Arabia where inter-clan fighting is so dangerous that they shoot first and ask later. But, indebted though I was to Murad, I would have hesitated a little before agreeing to smuggle his friend to safety had I known then what I was to learn of the facts of the case.

That night I had intended to rest before taking the long sandy stretch that lay before me from the banks of the River Jordan eastwards. But Murad's letter and the plight of the young sheikh compelled my departure.

A haze floated over the distant sand dunes, as the silvery moon, like a blazing scimitar, rose higher and higher above the horizon. The sleepy gate-keeper rubbed his eyes as my camel lumbered out.

'Thou goest at an evil hour!' he shouted. 'For, beyond the ridge, thy life will be in the palm of thy hand!'

It was fortunate, however, that he did not plunge his spear into the sack that hung by the side of my camel. For a good reason I had accommodated the wounded sheikh in it, and, stuffing hay in another sack, I had placed it at my back to look like someone sitting behind me.

For three hours my speedy camel did gallop. She was the best trotter in Murad's stables, and the sheikh felt fairly safe, because not until dawn could any man fire on us during those days of the month of fasting, when all the faithful must remain peaceful to one another during the hours of night.

Then the face of the moon began to tarnish and the sand now showed curious strands of colour in that half-light which betokens the approaching dawn. Then a streak shot up, all along the rim of the desert: the sheikh wriggled in his suspended cradle, but lay still again when I announced the approaching light of day.

With a sense which comes to desert travellers, the sheikh and I had a presentiment that we were being followed at a discreet distance. Only of the aircraft or armoured cars searching for the fugitive sheikh did we have fear.

These were the times of the French Mandate over Syria, and the sheikh was what today would be called a freedom-fighter.

But maybe the French will spare him, I thought, and have just placed a price on his head only to set the Bedouins of the desert on his trail.

If that were the case, I thought, then we were more than a match for the Bedouins. A smuggled machine-gun provided by Murad, and which equalled the balance of my camel's load, would see to that.

Just as I was rounding the bend of Bin Khiza, I could have yelled with delight at the sight of the tent-dwellers not too far below where French territory ceased. But it was still a good three miles. Hard hoofs hit on rock; presently an Arab climbed up the ridge on our right and then ducked down. We were spotted.

Almost immediately, a bullet sang past me. There was no time to lose. The sheikh crouched behind a boulder, and in a trice I saw the sack which rode behind me rent to bits by bullets. I was now manning my machine-gun. Knowing that they would not shoot down the camel, I let her run towards the friendly encampments.

Our attackers were spread out fanwise, skirmishing fashion. But our superior arms were playing havoc with their ranks. Muffled faces jumped up and fell before the flailing of the machine-gun fire. Presently their leader steeled himself and stood up with a long-barrelled musket and took aim in the most heroic but foolhardy manner imaginable. A shot from the sheikh's rifle made him whirl in a frenzied circle, and he dropped on his face.

Now they were closing upon us, now retreating. The automatic weapon barked unceasingly. Then it jammed, as these devil's contraptions seem to love to do.

I appealed to even my game leg to do its best, as I scrambled down, yard by yard, towards the land of friendly Bin Khiza. It was, after all, the nephew of the sheikh of that tribe who was with me, blazing away for his life. As such he had been introduced in the letter which he had taken from his girdle.

Another attack was launched against us; amazingly, the machine-gun unjammed itself and this attack, too, was repelled. We were crawling to safety as we turned and fired, again and again. Forms of our enemies rose only to be mown down by the devil's own weapon.

Then the burring and whirring sound of aero-engines struck upon our ears. 'What in the Name of Allah…!' I shouted.

They swept down; one could see clearly from their wing insignia that they were the French desert patrol. Within a few moments they had landed a small, armed group. But by then we were already arriving at the outpost of Bin Khiza's tents. Free men, in the territory of the free, in Independent Arabia.

A dozen horsemen, led by the sheikh of the tribe himself, rode towards us, firing a welcoming salute into the air. The leader embraced me with a mighty bear-hug.

News had reached him, by relay courier, mounted on the country's fastest mares, that Murad was having the sheikh's nephew escorted to him, it was hoped, by me. He anticipated trouble, but not a pitched battle like the one that we had just been through.

'And let mine eyes that have dimmed with waiting alight upon my dearest nephew's lustrous features!' He pulled the cloak from my ward's face.

A murderous gleam stole into the old man's eyes, as he started back from the sight. The one whom I had smuggled made a wry face.

'*Aman – Aman* – in the Name of Allah I seek peace, and sanctuary!' he said.

'In His Name I give it' stammered the sheikh.

173

Then the stranger spoke, in perfect Arabic: 'Aye, it is true that thy nephew wanted to escape, and he confided in me. Him I had drugged and dressed him with mine own uniform, stole his papers and in his guise I have reached safely here out of the hands of my regiment. As to me, my name is Krutz,' and the German renegade hung his head in shame.

I saw the Arab chieftain's thumb curl over the hammer of the carbine. Then he tarried.

'In the Name of Allah thou hast asked peace and sanctuary,' he said, red mounting to his cheeks. 'In His Name I have given it; but go thee back to thy regiment before sundown, for let infidel kill infidel; I shall not pollute my blade by slaying dogs.'

The deserter's eyes shot with blood.

'I shall not go back to the hell from which I have escaped,' he shouted, and as the old sheikh turned, there was a sharp report. Smoke floated from the mouth of the deserter. In his teeth was the end of the barrel of his rifle. So that, if your way should be one day to the Wadi of Bin Khiza, see a rudely erected tombstone with 'Al Almani…' (the German…) on it.

One lesson which the incident has left with me is that of one thing you can be absolutely sure in desert travel, it is that you can be sure of nothing, least of all your fellow travellers.

I lost my way more than once over the devious tracks of the desert when I trekked back to the south, and I discovered to my amazement that the Arabs of Jordan have hardly any sense of direction outside the area over which they graze their animals.

Fortunately for me, twenty miles to the east of Deraa is Bosrah, a great conical peak which projects prominently from the hills in the background. This landmark proved essential in my final journeyings in Jordan and it allowed me more than once to correct the failings of so-called Arab guides whom I sometimes recruited from encampments.

If weak in geography, they were always strong in encouragement. Whenever asked where anywhere was, they invariably answered, '*Qarib* – it is near!'

Beyond Deraa, one moves into the country of the Druses – a race about whom not a great deal is known and who had a bad reputation with the French for their warlike proclivities, as well as for insisting also that they are originally French and good Catholics. The French constantly complained that the Turks said that, during the days of the Ottoman Empire, the Druses had always sworn they were Turks by origin and good Sunni Muslims.

Personally, however, I found the Druses to be quite pleasant people and not sparing in their hospitality.

The men, especially, are of magnificent physique and they are great horsemen. They have, however, one curious practice: they blacken all around their eyes. I discovered that this was not out of any desire to adorn the manly face. The substance which is used for this treatment is held to keep away the flies – of which there are positive clouds in some areas – and to safeguard the eyes from the glare of the blazing sun.

The men certainly have magnificent eyesight, rivalling in this respect the tribesmen of the Pashtun lands in Central Asia. They can observe even the slightest movement over incredible distances and they are natural and splendid shots.

Life in the Druse mountains can be exciting for the unaccompanied wayfarer, for the tracks over the mountains are littered with boulders which have been precipitated down from above.

Journeying along these paths, every now and again one hears an ominous rumble and looks up at the hillside with no little apprehension. Quite often, miniature landslides obliterate the tracks and bring down with them rocks and boulders which fly at unexpected angles. Many of these boulders would be sufficient to crush a man or a mule.

I had several narrow escapes from this kind of unpleasant death, but these were the only occasions when I suffered perturbation. The Druses, as far as I was concerned, belied their generally fierce reputation and I found them almost shy, rather than an aggressive people.

All the time, however, one could sense a certain atmosphere. Here were a people who would remain quiet and law-abiding if they were left to their own devices. Quite obviously, they were resentful of intrusion and suspicious of any interference from an outside power.

The Turks, during their regime, evidently realized this. In any case, their suzerainty was quite nominal.

One thing that makes the Druses a rather difficult people to make conform to modern ideas of administration is the nature of their religion. Its secrets are zealously guarded and no man is initiated into the mystic rites until he has more than reached the age of discretion. And when he is admitted into his church, he has to make the most terrible and binding vows never to disclose to any who is not a full initiate, any of the secrets of his faith.

Consequently, the Druses never speak of their religion and little is known about it beyond the fact that it resembles a somewhat curious mixture of Christianity and Islam, and uses secret signs and passwords.

They have one outstanding belief and that is in regard to transmigration. They believe that, at the time of death, the soul passes into whatever is born on their land at that moment – no matter whether the new-born one is human or an animal. Should death take place at a moment when no living thing is born, then they believe that the soul passes away to China; and the people of the Jebel Druse believe that there are many of their race in China.

These people do not worship in churches, mosques or temples, as do those who have other faiths. They are careful to perform their religious ceremonies in some chamber carefully hidden away from the eyes of the curious.

Most carefully guarded also is their sacred book upon which, they say, nobody who has not been initiated with the full rites of the faith has ever been allowed to gaze.

This secrecy which attends the religious observances of the Druses also extends, in some measure, to their relations with people of other races. Many of the troubles of the past have undoubtedly been due to a disregard of this trait.

Farther on northward, when working toward the Iraqi frontier with the Jebel (mountain) Druses left behind, I had the misfortune one night to stay in a small house where a man became sick. Apparently he was taken seriously ill in the middle of the night, for my sleep was disturbed by the shuffling of many feet.

Those who have been taught to respect the sickroom and to enter it only when bidden or by permission of the doctor, would view with amazement that which transpires in this part of the Near East when a man is unfortunate enough to be ill.

The noise in this house was such that sleep was impossible. When I rose to investigate the cause of the confusion I found the place filled with friends and curious neighbours who had been hastily summoned to render aid. This motley crowd was busily engaged in prescribing all manner of incredible remedies and charms, mostly at the tops of their voices.

The man's bed, a hard pallet on the floor, was literally surrounded by those anxious to try their medical skill. It was quite obvious that the patient was seriously ill, for already two freshly killed chickens had been applied warm to his feet.

Every few minutes the unfortunate was dosed with an evil-smelling concoction, declared, by the old lady who had apparently dispensed it, to be capable of restoring any but one who was actually dead.

It was in my heart to believe her, too. I should have had to have been on the verge of coma not to have arisen and hurriedly fled from that noxious smell.

Others who assisted plied the patient with charms made of earth, and yet others were deliberating whether or not one should be dispatched for a lamb which could be sacrificed for the good of the patient.

The wife of the man demurred and suggested that the company should at least await the morn before embarking on such desperate measures.

It was easy to understand her concern. Chickens, charms and potions cost money or its equivalent, and already she had mortgaged a goodly part of her household goods in acquiring remedies for her man.

Whether or not it became necessary to slaughter a lamb I shall never know, because I thought it expedient to change my quarters. I could do little more. I could not possibly have intruded into the circle around the sick man, even though I was aware that the treatment he was receiving was probably hastening him to his death.

Indeed, his friends and neighbours evidently worked with thoroughness, for I was told, early the next morning, that the man was dead.

Going to collect the belongings which I had left in the house the previous night, I found that this was indeed so. The poor widow was bewailing her lot. I could only attempt to console her by contributing to the burial fund.

A long strip of muslin had been resurrected from somewhere, and from the smell of camphor which it gave off it was reasonable to assume that it had been used at more than one burial already. The body of the man was wrapped in this shroud and it would be little more than this which he would require.

Later that day I saw the remains being carried away in a rough wooden box – for the dead have to be interred quickly in the East.

The box was carried from the house by the friends who had done so much to expedite the man's end; they performed this service not from any sense of remorse, but because those who act as pall-bearers acquire great merit.

As the cortege proceeds, the first person of the same religion who is met is expected to relieve one of the mourners and thus the burden is shifted from shoulder to shoulder until the burial place is reached.

The coffin or box, with the shawl which is placed over it, are not interred. These are hired for the occasion by the poorer people and returned to the hirer after the body has been placed in a deep grave with only the muslin shroud as a cover. A priest was hurriedly summoned to recite from the New Testament in Arabic.

At yet another village I came across an occurrence which was more pleasing – nothing less than a wedding. The ceremonies attaching to marriages differ from country to country, sometimes in vital respects, sometimes in lesser. Invariably, however, they are of interest to onlookers, if not always for the principal participants.

Here the wedding is divided into two distinct ceremonies – the actual betrothal and the wedding ceremony proper.

In Muslim law, both ceremonies are legal and binding. Consequently, there is more involved in the initial function than the light-hearted bestowal of a ring which may, or may not, already have adorned the finger of some earlier fiancée.

The ceremony of betrothal is a very serious one, into the preliminaries of which the families of both contracting parties have entered with zest, for it is one requiring the exercise of much business acumen.

Quite often betrothals are arranged by marriage brokers, many of whom are old women. They receive a commission from the two parties for their services. Much the same practice is observed by many of the Jewish fraternity, even in London, and it has not been unknown, I was told there on good authority, for Mayfair hostesses to receive a valuable 'present' for arranging a match between some wealthy social aspirant and a member of the peerage. The arrangement in every instance is mainly commercial.

The peoples of this part of the East, however, have one practice which may or may not commend itself to brides of other nations.

In the betrothal ceremony which I witnessed, the bridegroom-to-be was the sheikh of the village and the girl the daughter of a neighbouring chief. They were not wanting in worldly goods, especially as the bridegroom's father was also a merchant who had journeyed to England and had taken to himself a *Feranghi*, a Frankish wife. But of that more presently.

The bride, her mother and other feminine friends were accommodated in one room while the bridegroom and his friends occupied one adjoining.

The presiding elder (he is not a priest: marriages are civil contracts) took up a position in the doorway between the two rooms and read from a list detailing the property of the bride.

It had not been prepared merely to impress the neighbours and the friends of the family, or from any sense of false pride. There was a real purpose to this part of the proceedings.

All the articles named by the elder were to give her a sense of security. In later years, should the man desire to divorce the bride, he would be unable to send her away penniless. He would have to provide her with all the goods and chattels mentioned in the list.

This practice may seem curious to some Western minds; nevertheless, it has its counterpart in Western marriage settlements. In Germany especially, it is frequently the practice for the groom to cite in his marriage settlement the cars, the houses and other items which one day might come into his possession. There is a close association between the two forms of contract.

I remained in this village long enough to witness the second part of the ceremony, since this took place only a few days after the first.

The bride lived in a flat-roofed single storey house and, in common with half a dozen other such structures, it looked out upon a courtyard. In Europe you would say that it was but one of a collection of cottages which shared a common backyard.

All the neighbours came to the assistance of the bride and freely loaned carpets which were laid over the stone slabs of the court. These loans were augmented with gifts of flowers with which the court was further decorated.

A huge tea-urn had been obtained and this was kept bubbling the whole day. It was greatly in demand; its only rivals being long pipes of sweet sherbet which were passed from hand to hand. The court, by the way, was given over entirely to the women.

The bride was attired in a new silk robe and her neck was adorned with a string of glass beads amongst which were interspersed a few gold and silver coins.

This trousseau was the gift of the groom – another pleasing practice, some fathers-in-law will say.

The bride had not disdained cosmetics. Her cheeks were rouged, her eyes had been blacked with *kohl* and her garments had been plentifully besprinkled with scent.

The hostess of the occasion – quite an old woman – seemed to be serving in a professional capacity. Obviously she augmented her income by providing her services in this way. No mere amateur could have carried off the role as did she.

As the guests entered the courtyard they peered around for this woman and then advanced upon her, enunciating the words: 'May this wedding be blessed.'

And the hostess, with supreme gravity, would respond: 'In the Name of God enter; your kindness in coming to assist us is indeed great.'

In the adjoining house, where the guests of the sheikh were assembled, a somewhat similar scene was being enacted. Here, however, the masculine temperament made for a little more verve and vigour.

A wandering minstrel had been imported to amuse the guests and he sang songs in a shrill, minor key, the words of which were improvised to meet the needs of the occasion.

Masculine humour, at such events as weddings, is cruder and much more direct than the feminine, and judging from the roars of laughter which the minstrel produced from the guests and the obvious discomfiture of the groom on sundry occasions, the man was well worth his fee.

The entertainer's voice was shrill and piercing, and I could not but notice with amusement that, when he introduced some sally at the expense of the bridegroom, the feminine chatter from the nearby courtyard suddenly ceased, and the hidden audience there was patently listening to the words with appreciation.

Once even, the fair ones so far forgot themselves as to echo the boisterous laughter of the men when the minstrel had been particularly audacious.

The formal part of the ceremony – a brief affair – had taken place earlier in the day and the singing and the laughter and the drinking of tea, coffee and sherbet proceeded until a late hour. At dusk, candles and lamps were produced and the whole assembly was served with a repast consisting of coloured rice, mutton, pomegranates and sweets.

Later, as the party showed signs of breaking up, a medley of particularly efficient bandsmen appeared as if by magic, and the surrounding roofs of the nearby houses became crowded with those anxious to witness the final phase of the ceremony.

The male guests assembled around the groom as an escort and a procession was formed which made its way slowly to the home of the bride.

As the groom reached the threshold of his bride's abode a lamb was sacrificed, and then the bride was led to the doorway and given over to the bridegroom amidst the plaudits of the spectators and the raucous blowing of trumpets.

In all these proceedings, Sheikh Abdullah, the bridegroom's father, was, I felt, taking but a half-hearted interest. His mind, it would seem, was flying back to some distant scenes, some former experiences. At first, I thought that a man past middle age could hardly be expected to raise enough enthusiasm about an affair which warms young hearts, but the reason was different. He was recollecting his own former (*Feranghi*) wife: the mother of the boy whose wedding he was celebrating.

Until late that night I sat with him. Then he became reminiscent. During the Great War, when European countries were at each other's throats, he found a chance of selling the wares of his land at a hundred per cent profit. To make more money he went to England. He lived the part, and began his story in the present tense; and I will let him relate it in his own way.

From: *Alone in Arabian Nights*
The Sirdar Ikbal Ali Shah

Children of the Devil

DUSK FALLS SWIFTLY in southern Ethiopia, casting a cape of blackness over the gold mines.

The air gradually cools and then comes alive with tremendous bats. Noah said they were the spirits of the miners killed in cave-ins. Enraged at being cheated by death, they were desperate to bite their companions who still worked in the mines.

Soon after dusk the strong young men slunk up from the mine shafts and returned to the village. Even for them it was far too dangerous to stay out after dark. Who knew what a shaft miner had swallowed? Given the right circumstances there were plenty of would-be murderers eager to find out.

'They slit your throat with a razor-blade or a sharpened belt buckle,' Samson explained. 'Then they cut open your intestines and sometimes even your bowels.'

'Very messy,' added Noah.

'How does the murderer get away with it if he's covered in blood?'

'That's not the problem,' said Noah. 'If he's found gold he'll buy some *araki* and everyone will forgive him. The problem is if he *doesn't* find anything and he can't afford a few rounds of drinks.'

There was no church at the encampment, a fact which made Samson increasingly restless. He said he could smell depravity in the air. Noah, also a staunch Christian, had proposed erecting a house of worship, but the other miners had scoffed at the idea.

They said a church was a waste of money, and proposed instead that a team of them should be sent up to the northern state of Tigray to bring back new prostitutes. The ones at the mines were, by all accounts, riddled with venereal disease. Tigrayan women have angelic features and copper skin, and are considered by many people to be the most beautiful women in Africa. A large number of the prostitutes I'd seen at the mining village, not to mention in the bars in Kebra Mengist and Shakiso, were Tigrayan. Samson told me that prostitutes usually work in another region, for fear of bringing shame on their families.

Without a church to pray in, Samson and Noah sat on a bench in the bar and talked about Jesus. They swapped stories of his life and drew morals from his teachings. A pressure lamp lit up the room like daylight, causing the huddle of miners to blink nervously. They preferred the shadows. An empty glass was sitting before every one of them. Bizarrely, the walls of the bar were papered with *The Straits Times*, the Singapore daily. Beside my head was an interesting feature about black magic rites performed by Dayak headhunters in Malaysia. I pointed it out, but no one was interested. They had only two things on their mind – *araki*, and how to get some more of it.

Noah said that little gold had been found that day, so I bought a round of drinks. The *araki* was served warm, straight from the still. Quite often a batch is so strong it turns to a crude form of poison, knocking out everyone who drinks it. Quality control is non-existent.

Samson and Noah shunned the *araki* and pulled out their Bibles. I respected them for staying faithful to their religion in what were testing circumstances. They were like missionaries in a foreign land. But they knew as well as I that saving souls and spreading God's Word was a sure-fire way of getting themselves killed. What surprised me most was that Samson had managed to wrench himself from the debauched spiral of life at the mine.

'Gold mining is like a drug,' he said. 'The more gold you get, the more you need to excite you. Your closest friends are dying around you, but you don't give them a second thought. All you can think about is *araki*, Tigrayan whores and the meaningless knick-knacks you're going to buy.'

Samson's father had stressed the value of education to his sons.

Studying, he'd told Samson as a youngster, was the key which could open the doors to life. I was struck by the clear goals Samson had set himself, now that he had escaped from the world of prospecting. In his spare time, he was learning computer programming, a skill which he had heard would be useful if and when he got to America.

'For years I wasted every moment working at a mine like this,' he said, pressing his Bible to his stomach. 'I turned my back on my parents and my true friends, accusing them of jealousy. But worst of all I turned my back on God. If I'd not got away, I'd have been dead long ago. Yes, I may be much poorer – but driving a taxi is more honourable than this!'

He motioned to the pack of thirsty miners who were ready for more free drinks. Then he begged Noah to leave the mines. But his friend said he was wedded to the profession, addicted to the thrill of danger and the financial rewards.

When I had doled out as much charity as I could afford, a string of tall Tigrayan women trooped into the bar, each wearing yellow vinyl shoes and a transparent top. Their hair was braided tightly and their mouths shone with fuchsia-pink lipstick. None of the miners had any money, but the girls took credit. Samson said some of the men, the older ones at least, had wives. But they liked the prostitutes, whom they considered to be sophisticated. One of the women, plumper than the rest, sat down beside me. Her name was Hannah. When I asked what she thought of the miners, she rolled her eyes and blew me a kiss.

'You go America, tomorrow?' she replied.

I didn't understand.

'No, no, I'll be staying here at the mine for a few days.'

'Not America… tomorrow?'

'No,' I said.

She sneered at me and turned her attention to a hulking creature with a fresh gash down one cheek. Again, I heard her asking about America. I doubted if the man even had a passport, let alone a visa to the United States. But as he massaged her thighs, he whispered: 'America, America.'

The evening dragged on, with Samson and Noah discussing the Psalms, and the miners racking up huge bills on credit with the working women and the bar's one-eyed owner. As the hours passed, it seemed that everyone was talking about America, and any man who merely uttered the magic word was assured the Tigrayan girls' attention.

As I settled down to sleep in Noah's hut that night, I wondered how an entire population could have become so desperate to get to a place of which they knew so little. Samson rarely stopped going on about the life he'd lead in that far-off land. Even as he read the Bible or discussed the lives of the Apostles, I could sense him thinking of America.

To him and others, America was a place full of opportunities where Ethiopians were given prospects and a future. Samson had applied to the US Embassy for a visa but had been refused. He knew the chances of gaining entry were slim, and he was turning his mind to more subversive tactics. Someone had told him that you could go to Mexico and cross the border by swimming the Río Grande. Another had suggested he find a rich American woman and persuade her to marry him.

The following morning, three more women asked me if I was going to America. Then a gang of children selling maize and roasted barley came over to tell me that it was nearly time for America. They would be going over there to have a look.

'When? When are you going?'

'Oh,' one replied dreamily, 'any minute now.'

191

By the time the first rays of sunlight spilled over into the mine, two thousand workers were busy digging the ground or lugging ore up to the panning pools. As the sun rose it baked the ground, making the business of digging far harder. The miners toiled away like convicts.

A few years before, I'd seen Sebastião Salgado's extraordinary black-and-white photographs of the enormous Serra Pelada gold mine in Brazil. I remembered images of mud-drenched men, tens of thousands of them, climbing rickety ladders up the sides of the pit. They carried sacks on their backs, filled with soil to pan. The mine near Shakiso didn't have ladders. Rather, the workers would take their positions and stay in them. In some ways their system was more efficient. Hurling pans of earth up in a giant relay was much speedier and far less tiring.

The miners were working together because they had to, but I never got the feeling that they did so willingly. Given half a chance, they would happily have killed the man or woman next to them for the smallest nugget of gold. Noah pointed out three or four characters to keep away from.

'That's Josiah,' he said, pointing to an elderly miner with a limp. 'He killed his own wife after suspecting she'd stolen a pouch of gold from him. He's already asking why you have come here.'

Noah tapped one finger on his nose meaningfully.

'And that's Yohannes over there. He's got AIDS, but he still rapes the Tigrayan girls.'

Later that morning I left the mine and walked back through the village. Samson had been complaining that his shoes were being ruined by the ankle-deep mud and I'd offered to buy him a pair of rubber boots. We headed for the market area and had a good look through the heaps of old clothes on offer. The only boots were parrot green and four sizes too big. He took them anyway.

There was a commotion at the far end of the market. In the distance I made out a throng of Tigrayan girls mobbing a stall. They were admiring its stock of impressive merchandise. There were lipsticks and handbags, blankets and bed sheets, leather footballs and French aftershave, silk shirts, Swatch watches and cartons of 555-brand cigarettes. Some of the girls sidled up to me and implored me to buy them luxuries.

Samson said it was all contraband, brought from Djibouti once a week by a travelling salesman.

'He goes from mine to mine selling this rubbish. Who needs aftershave in a place like this? Instead of saving their money these foolish people come here, to America!'

'America?' I exclaimed.

Samson pointed to a crude, hand-drawn board hanging above the stall.

Scrawled upon it, in Amharic, was the word 'America'.

As we wandered back towards the crater I found myself questioning man's obsession with gold.

How could a simple, relatively useless yellow metal have been so important for so long? Was it the colour, the weight, or the warmth of it in one's hand? Or was it the fact that gold stays brilliant and clear of rust in even the wettest climate?

Whatever the reason, gold has been hoarded and worked since the days of the ancient Egyptians, though man discovered the metal long before Pharaonic times. Fragments of natural gold have been found in Spanish caves, apparently put there forty thousand years ago by Palaeolithic man. And the lure of gold has been responsible for some truly terrible episodes in history, not least the Spanish conquest of the Americas that brought the Aztec and the Incan empires to a swift and brutal end.

With the sun beating down on our heads, we clambered down the slalom of trails leading towards the floor of the crater. The first thing I noticed as I descended was a sharp rise in temperature. Fifty feet down and I was gasping for breath, asphyxiated by the press of hot air. Another fifty feet and my pores began to run with sweat. The miners tossed up their weighty pans higher and higher in their well-rehearsed relay. They too were sweating, but I never saw one of them pause for water. When they needed to pee, they did it where they stood.

We squatted in the deep glutinous mud at the bottom of the crater, catching our breath and wishing we'd brought a supply of drinking water. Around us were dozens of women and children, all shovelling earth on to the round wooden pans. Up above, the children had been thrilled at the spectacle of a foreigner and eager to cluster around and get a good look. But on the floor of the pit there was no such interest.

The children worked like slaves.

Indeed, they were slaves, for I doubt they got any share of the money they earned. Working alongside them, their mothers were brawny and well built, with strong backs and muscular hands. Several of them were obviously pregnant.

One of the boys, aged about ten, slipped me an affecting smile. Samson told me that the children start young.

'They work down here in the pit,' he said, 'but they're more useful to bore the tunnels which run along the actual gold seams. You can send a child down a hole just a few inches wide.'

'Don't they ever get stuck?'

Samson nodded.

'Yes. Then they suffocate. Or else they're killed in cave-ins.'

Our timing couldn't have been worse. As Samson finished his sentence, we heard shouts from beyond the pit. The area echoed with sound at the best of times, but these yells rose above the usual noise. Many of the miners dropped their pans and scrambled to the surface. Others were running round the periphery of the crater.

'Cave-in,' said Samson coldly. 'Someone's trapped, probably a child.'

We left the women and children and hurried up the steep banks and over to the maze of tunnels. A crowd of miners were digging furiously with pikes and spades, and one man was shouting out, calling a single name: 'Adi! Adi! Adi!' But there was no response.

A woman came running, tearing barefoot down the track from the village. She was weeping hysterically. I found out later that no one had called her, she had simply known that her son, her eldest boy, was trapped. We listened, all quiet, desperate for a sound. But there was silence, a terrible, haunting silence.

The woman ran from one hole to the next, crying down each tunnel. All the other children had scurried to the surface. They said that Adi had been digging in a separate tunnel, away from the others, when the earth above had collapsed. The mother screamed, her features locked in an ecstasy of pain. Nothing is so agonizing as to see the face of a mother who has lost her child. I couldn't bear to watch. The miners crowded round, comforting her. I wanted someone to reassure the woman that there was hope, that children have been pulled from rubble days after an earthquake.

But like everyone else, she knew that her son was already dead.

Adi's body was eventually found a few minutes before sunset.

The time that it took to dig the boy out was testimony to the depth at which he had been working. The camp's wild, carefree atmosphere had evaporated. That evening none of the miners joked or boasted, and there was no talk of Tigrayan whores. Instead they banded together like brothers, and for the first time I felt respect for them. One of their own had died. He may have been a child of nine or ten, but he was a miner who'd perished in the line of duty. In silence the corpse was carried at shoulder height down the muddy track into the village. The mother walked beside her son, resting her hand gently on his head. Her eyes were swollen with grief.

The sordid carnival of the previous night was nothing but a memory. No one drank in the bar. The few clients who couldn't stay away simply sat there staring into space, consoling each other. In the back room, the fire under the still was starved of fuel. The drip, drip, drip of transparent liquid had ceased. The whores sat about plaiting their hair, ready for a night without trade.

Adi's crushed body was wrapped in a clean white shawl and laid out in his parents' home. Samson and I stopped there to pay our respects. The hut was already filled with people.

Samson recited Psalm 23 as softly as I've ever heard it spoken:

The Lord is my shepherd; I shall not want.
He maketh me lie down in green pastures:
he leadeth me beside the still waters.
He restoreth my soul...

Samson's eyes were closed as he spoke.

Perhaps he was remembering past friends and enemies whose lives had ended under the ground. When we left the hut, he looked up to heaven and rebuked God.

Then he held his Bible to his face and wept.

Next morning, long before the mining had begun, the villagers rose and filed from the camp.

Most were wrapped against the early chill in their *shammas*. Their heads were bent towards the ground, their faces long and drawn. Noah led the procession which snaked for a mile or so south of the mine. We walked near him. Behind us Adi's body was carried at waist height, with his mother and father, and their closest friends following behind.

A grave had been carved out of the brick-red soil in an area away from the gold seam. The body was placed in the hole and, with little ceremony, it was covered over. Then the first light of dawn turned the sky steel blue.

By seven o'clock the mine was burgeoning with activity again. The pans of golden earth were wending their way up from the bottom of the pit, and the dark, cramped network of tunnels was busy with infant workers. A young miner had been lost, but hardly anyone stopped to reflect. Contemplation is a luxury, requiring time and alternatives.

In the late afternoon a vehicle could be seen negotiating the jagged track leading to the mining community.

We could hear its engine revving for a mile or more before it arrived. The miners didn't have to look: they knew the car. It was the property of a local government bureaucrat. Somehow he'd heard that there had been a death and he had come to get the details down on paper.

Noah told me to go into his thatched hut as quickly as I could. The only thing the bureaucrat would like more than a dead miner was a foreigner to torment. So I hid in Noah's shack while Samson hastened back and forth, filling me in on what was happening. The administrator, he said, was questioning Adi's parents, telling them to go to Shakiso to help with an official report. That was the last thing they intended to do.

'If the government knows about this and other illegal mines,' I asked, 'then why don't they close them down?'

Samson winked.

'They're in it for the money,' he said. 'They buy most of the gold, and they sell it at a big profit. Unless they send the army down here they're never going to be able to stop all the mining, and this way at least they get the lion's share of the profits.'

Despite this, I found that the miners had a pretty accurate idea of international gold prices. For this reason they only sold part of their haul to the officials.

'If they let on just how much gold's coming from this seam,' said Samson, 'then the government would have no choice but to nationalize the place. Then they might have a rebellion on their hands.'

There was already insurrection in the air. Samson reported that hundreds of miners had left the pit and were massing around the official. I could make out loud voices, then shouting, and finally the rumble of an engine as it sparked to life.

'How did he find out that someone had died?' I asked Noah later when he returned from the shaft.

'There are spies, lots of them,' he replied. 'In fact it is strange that they haven't handed you in.'

Now that he mentioned it, I realized that the miners had been friendly towards me. They had welcomed me as courteously as they knew how, and some had offered to show me the surrounding area at night or to feed me.

'You'd better watch out,' said Noah, 'they're probably planning to rob you or kill you.'

'America,' added Samson.

'The market stall?'

Noah frowned.

'No, the country America,' he said. 'They see you as their way out of here and over there.'

Like all Ethiopians, the miners had a grand plan which culminated with their arrival in the United States. No other country was good enough – none had the cachet of America. I hadn't been in Ethiopia long, but dozens of people had already asked me how to get a visa for America. I'd even heard of agents who, for a steep fee, could prescribe the best route across the Atlantic.

Noah pointed to a man outside one of the huts lolling back on a home-made chair.

'That man there,' he said, 'he's an expert on America.'

Dawit's head was round, like a small watermelon, and it appeared to balance on his wide shoulders without any trace of a neck. His palms were as soft as a beauty queen's cheeks. They'd obviously never been down the mines. Dawit laughed riotously at the slightest opportunity, and I asked him why he was always so cheerful.

'We Amhara are very happy people,' he replied.

'What's the best way to get to America then?'

Dawit stopped laughing and lowered his head. The only thing he never joked about was business.

'These days it's harder to get an asylum visa,' he said, 'but there are lots of other ways in. You can go through another country, like Germany, France or Britain. You can say you're a priest and get a Christian foundation to sponsor you, or pretend to be a Jew and go via Israel. Or, if you can get to Mexico, you can jump across the river…' He paused for a moment, trying to remember its name. 'The Río Grande, they call it the Río Grande, and the water's very low at the moment. But the best way to get to America,' he said, flexing his shoulders, 'is to get yourself a foreigner's passport.'

I was struck by how much Dawit knew and the more we spoke, the more impressed I became. There were very few questions he could not answer. At last I asked him which was his favourite American city.

Dawit looked blank and then burst out laughing, and Noah and Samson collapsed in hysterics. When eventually they stopped, the three of them stared at me as if I were mad.

'He's never been to America,' said Noah.

After meeting Dawit, I tiptoed around the village, gripped by paranoia.

If I disappeared and my passport was taken by a swarthy young Ethiopian, it could be months or years before the crime was discovered. I told Samson of my worry and forbade him to leave my side even when I was asleep – in fact especially when I was asleep. That night my dreams were filled with gangs of miners creeping into the hut, snatching my passport and slitting my throat. Then they fought with each other to see who would win my passport for the journey to America.

The next morning I awoke to find Dawit at the foot of my sleeping bag. He'd had an idea in the night, he said. I was to give a short informal talk about America to the miners. As someone who'd passed through US Immigration several times I had inside knowledge that I could pass on. It sounded like an easy way to please the community, so I agreed to talk in the open space that evening.

Life at the gold mine was pleasant so long as you didn't have to do any mining. There was a perpetual sense of risk, balanced by the lure of instant wealth. The place was like a grand casino. Money raised by communal mining was shared out, but anyone who found a large nugget was permitted by the others to keep it. Whether anyone realized it or not, the system encouraged industriousness. The big problem though was that all of them were unable to stop mining, regardless of how much gold they found.

Everyone I spoke to said they would leave if they found a big enough nugget, but I knew that that was a lie. The miners had become addicted to the gambler's lifestyle. Nothing, except possibly religion, could prize them away. And in any case, anyone cashing in on a big find had debts to pay, and what was left would be blown in an instant.

'If you look at this place,' said Samson as we sat together in the late morning sun, 'you'd think there wouldn't be much in the way of expense. But you'd be wrong. Miners make good money, much more than any other Ethiopians. But they have to pay back the money they owe to other miners, they have to buy clothes and food, and they have to send money home to their families. Then there are illegitimate children to care for, there's *araki* to buy, and Tigrayan girls to employ.' Samson stared at the baked earth as he remembered the corrosive existence. 'The most expensive thing of all,' he added, 'is treating others to luxuries – women and drink.'

'But why pay for others if you can't afford to?'

Samson smiled from the corner of his mouth.

'Just in case one of them finds a big nugget,' he said. 'If you don't help them when they're poor, they won't remember you when they're rich.'

Life must have been much the same for prospectors working in the Klondike, in California, or in Australia in the mid-nineteenth century. The first great gold rush took place near the Sacramento River in northern California in 1848. A carpenter working at a sawmill there found a sizeable gold nugget. Try as he might to keep his find quiet, word soon got out. Within days there were tens of thousands of would-be miners camped out nearby, and within four years more than 250,000 miners had descended on California. Living in the most terrible conditions and blinded by greed, they were risking everything for the sake of gold.

I recently encountered an Italian whose great-great-grandfather had set out from his native Milan in search of a fortune in California. He saw the prospectors living like dogs, eating rotten supplies and using lousy equipment. The Italian had intended to search for gold like the rest of them. But as soon as he saw the conditions in which they lived, he changed tack. Instead of thinking about gold, he turned his hand to bringing in supplies. Within weeks he'd made a fortune selling saddles and clothes, pans, chemicals, tents and food.

Look at the map and you can see traces of those pioneering days in the names – Bonanza Creek, Gold Hill, Gold Creek, Eureka. But the name which crops up again and again is Ophir. Christian miners were certain that they'd discovered the Old Testament land. In Bedakaysa no one apart from Samson and Noah had ever heard of Ophir. They had no interest in Bible readings. They had been residents of hell for far too long. Samson called them 'The Children of the Devil'.

We often discussed the idea of Ophir. Samson felt sure that Solomon's gold had come from ancient Ethiopian mines. He pointed out that the Israelites had probably acquired the metal from many mines in one region rather than from a single glorious pit. He said that a giant mine only existed in the minds of novelists and Hollywood, and he reminded me that an entire region, or country, can get mined out, especially where the gold veins are close to the surface, as they are in Ethiopia. Modern industrial mining processes can sift through thousands of tonnes of ore each day. But mining was no less thorough before the days of heavy machinery. Hundreds of thousands of prospectors at the Klondike River did the work of the machines, as they do today in mines like Bedakaysa.

In London I had managed to find a handful of books written at the end of the 1800s that told of Great Zimbabwe, the ruins which the Victorians thought were once Ophir.

One of the volumes had been published in 1899 and was written by an eccentric German professor called Carl Peters. The book was entitled *King Solomon's Golden Ophir: A Research into the Most Ancient Gold Production in History*. Peters tackled the subject with Teutonic thoroughness and came up with an interesting theory. The Old Testament writers were usually very precise in giving details. Why then did they give no indication as to the whereabouts of Ophir? They seemed to assume, says Peters, that everyone knew where it might be found. If Ophir was remote there would have been a need to supply the curious with details. Africa was a land known to the ancients, though they appreciated little of its interior, a vast realm they referred to as *Ubi Leones*, meaning 'Here Are Lions'.

Might not Africa and Ophir have been one and the same?

In support of his theory, he looked at the etymology of the word 'Africa'. The original root of the name, according to him, was *Afer*, probably meaning 'Red' or 'Red Land', as in the common colour of the continent's soil. *Afri* were its people, and *African*, the adjective describing them.

In the century since Peters's book was published, it has been proved that the Great Zimbabwe ruins are not connected with the ancient Israelite kingdom, the land of Solomon. Even so, Peters's theory seems plausible. Ophir might well have been Africa, and Solomon's gold might well have come from a region of the continent that lay close to his kingdom, the mountainous hinterland of Ethiopia.

Through the afternoon the miners worked hard, ferrying great pans of earth from the bottom of the crater, up to the water where they were panned.

Young children darted about selling sticks of roasted maize, sugar cubes and knitted hats. From time to time women and the older kids came up from the mine where they'd been digging and swapped places with the panners. Theirs was back-breaking work, but at least they could wade in the thigh-deep water and keep cool.

The male miners were proud of their profession and keen for their sons to follow them. Noah told me that mining gold was considered the most macho thing a man could do. Miners scoffed at farmers and laughed uncontrollably if one mentioned people who did office work. They rated the value of a job by the thickness of the callouses it gave their hands.

Noah was an exception. He had two young sons but he shuddered at the thought of them entering the mine.

'They're having an education,' he said. 'The only way I can pay for it, though, is by mining. I pray that I'll find a big nugget. Why do you think I spend such long hours in the tunnels risking my life?'

'Where is your family?'

'Back in Kebra Mengist,' he replied. 'I won't let them even come to the mine. I'm not ashamed of the work, but I don't want my wife or my two boys to see the savage people I live with.'

Dawit came over and said it was time for my talk. He'd spread the word through his network of contacts and he expected a bumper audience. We made our way to a flat patch of land to the west of the main mine. Young men would sometimes play football there. Others used it for their ablutions, and the place was running with rats and stank of human excrement. Despite the stench, dozens of miners had already arrived.

More were turning up every minute.

Most of them knew that a foreigner had been staying in the village, but until that moment they had regarded me as of little use. That was about to change. Dawit had billed me as the man who could put an end to all their problems – he had declared somewhat fictitiously that I was the missing link between them and America.

Samson grew nervous when he saw the extent of the crowd. He said there was a danger of the local official closing the event down and arresting us. Having been in big gatherings in India and Africa before, I was more worried by another danger. At a right-wing rally in Nigeria, given by a fanatical Christian preacher from Germany, I'd seen dozens of people trampled to death. The pastor claimed to have the power to heal the sick. He told hundreds of cripples to make a pyre from their crutches and wheelchairs.

When they'd done this, the preacher claimed to have healed everyone, and with that he drove off in his stretch Mercedes. Of course no one was cured. Instead, tempers boiled over and the crowd stampeded. The saddest thing was to see all the disabled left lying on the ground without their crutches and wheelchairs, unable to get home.

Dawit assured me that there would be no stampede. Everyone present, he said, had paid one *birr* entrance fee, or at least had promised to pay later. The children sat at the front, wriggling in the dirt, a little unsure of why they had been coaxed to attend. Their parents and the general population of miners stood behind them. There must have been about five hundred people. The Tigrayan girls had donned their best dresses and vinyl high heels, and were sitting with the children. The entire congregation was united by their interest in the title of my talk, 'Getting to America'.

When they were quiet, and we were sure that there were no stragglers still to come, Dawit introduced me, speaking in Amharic, while Samson translated.

'Mr. Tahir has come from faraway America,' said Dawit, 'to tell you about his wonderful country and how to get there.'

After a prolonged greeting, I began my talk. Whenever I said the word 'America', the gathering drew a deep breath.

'America is an amazing country,' I said, waiting for Dawit to finish translating my words. 'It's sometimes known as "The Land of the Free" because everyone has rights.'

One of the young men began to heckle me, demanding to know what people in America thought of Ethiopians there.

'People like Ethiopians in America,' I said, reassuringly. 'I've met many Ethiopians there who have a good wage, but they were not frightened of starting in a simple job.'

'Like gold mining in a pit?' called another.

'Not exactly… more like working in a restaurant. But it's important to study hard and to learn English. If you have a qualification you can earn a lot of money.'

The audience looked worried. None of them had any qualifications.

'Tell them the best way to get into America,' prompted Dawit.

I thought for a moment.

'It's a big country,' I said, 'with many ports of entry. Some people cross over from Mexico, but that's getting harder; and others come in by sea. But the best way is to get a friend or a relative to sponsor you, or to have a job waiting for you. You see, if you're "uniquely qualified", they can easily bring you from overseas to do the job.'

Dawit struggled to translate the concept into Amharic.

One of the Tigrayan girls had a question. She rose to her feet, thrust her chest out towards me and asked: 'Do American men need us?'

I was taken aback by this question, but rather than discourage her, I replied with enthusiasm.

'Yes, I'm sure they do!'

I carried on, padding the talk out with information about life in America, saying it wasn't all like the movies, and that the streets weren't paved with gold. Some of my metaphors must have suffered in translation.

Then, winding up, I said jokingly that they could push me down one of the mine shafts and steal my passport. That would give one of them at least an easy entry into America.

The miners looked at me and then at each other.

Then they stared at the ground and giggled nervously.

From: *In Search of King Solomon's Mines*
Tahir Shah

Maruf the Cobbler

ONCE UPON A time in the city of Cairo lived a cobbler named Maruf and his wife Fatima. This hag treated him so badly, repaying every good action with a bad one, that Maruf began to look upon her as the embodiment of the inexplicable contrariness of the world.

Bowed down with a sense of real injustice, driven to the last extremity of despair, he fled to a ruined monastery near the city where he plunged himself in prayer and supplication, calling out incessantly: 'Lord, I beg of thee to send me a means of release, so that I may travel an immense distance from this place, to find safety and hope.'

This he continued to do for several hours when an amazing thing happened. A being of great height and strange appearance seemed to pass straight through the wall in front of him, after the manner attributed to the powers of the *Abdal*, the 'Changed Ones', who are human beings who have attained powers far beyond those of ordinary men.

'I am the Abdel-Makan, the Servant of this Place,' said the apparition. 'What do you ask from me?'

Maruf told him all his problems. The Changed One had Maruf mount his back, and they flew through the air for several hours at an unparalleled speed. Maruf found himself as daylight dawned in a far city on the borders of China, a rich and beautiful place.

One of the citizens stopped him in the street and asked him who he was. When Maruf told him, and tried to explain the manner of his coming, a crowd of jeering louts collected; throwing sticks and stones, they accused him of being mad or else an impostor of some kind.

The mob was still handling the unfortunate cobbler roughly when a merchant rode up and dispersed them, saying, 'Have shame! A stranger is a guest, bound to us by the sacred bonds of hospitality and worthy of our protection.' His name was Ali.

Ali explained to his friend how he had progressed from rags to riches in this strange city of Ikhtiyar. The merchants there, it seemed, were generally more inclined than other folk to take a man at his word. If he was poor, they would not give him much of a chance in life, because they considered that man was poor because he had to be so. If, on the other hand, a man was said to be rich, they would give him consideration, credit and honour.

Ali had discovered this fact. He had therefore gone to several rich merchants of the town and asked them for loans, saying that a caravan of his had not yet arrived. The loans were made, Ali multiplied the money by trading in the great bazaars, and he had been able to return the original capital and actually make himself rich.

He advised Maruf to do the same.

Thus it was that Maruf, dressed by his friend in a sumptuous robe, went and borrowed from one merchant after another. The only difference was that, because of his charitable disposition, Maruf gave the money away to beggars. His caravan, after months of waiting, showed no signs of arriving, and Maruf was doing no business, but his charity increased, for people vied with each other to give money on loan to a man who immediately spent it on charity. In this way, they thought, they would both get their loans back when the caravan arrived and also participate, at one remove, in the blessing inseparable from acts of benevolence.

As time passed, however, the merchants began to wonder whether Maruf was, after all, an impostor. They went to the king of the city to complain. The king called Maruf before him.

The king was in two minds about Maruf and resolved to test him. He had a valuable jewel, which he decided to present to the merchant Maruf, to see whether he realized its value or not. If he did, the king – who was a greedy man – would give his daughter in marriage to Maruf. If he did not, he would be thrown in jail.

Maruf presented himself at Court, and the jewel was placed in his hands. 'This is for you, good Maruf,' said the king. 'But tell me, why do you not pay your debts?'

'Because, Your Majesty, my caravan of priceless things has still not arrived. As for this jewel, I think it better for Your Majesty to keep it, for it is worthless compared to the really valuable jewels which I have in my caravan.'

Overcome by greed the king dismissed Maruf and sent a message to the representative of the merchants to hold their peace. He resolved to marry the princess to the merchant, in spite of the grand wazir's opposition. The wazir said that Maruf was a manifest liar. The king, however, remembered that the wazir had been asking for the princess's hand for years, and attributed his advice to prejudice.

Maruf, when he was told that the king would bestow his daughter upon him, merely said to the wazir, 'Tell His Majesty that until my caravan arrives, loaded with priceless jewels and the like, I cannot make due provision for a princess-wife, and hence I suggest the marriage be postponed.'

Told of this attitude, the king immediately opened his treasury to Maruf, so that he could choose whatever he needed for the setting up of a suitable way of life and for gifts consonant with the rank of a royal son-in-law.

Never was such a marriage seen in that or any other country. Not only were alms distributed by the handful of jewels, but everyone who even heard of the wedding was given a lavish present. The celebrations lasted for forty days in unprecedented magnificence.

When they were at last alone, Maruf said to his bride: 'I have already taken so much from your father that I am troubled,' because he had to account for his being somewhat sore at heart.

'Think nothing of it,' said the princess, 'for when your caravan arrives, all will be well.'

Meanwhile the wazir renewed his agitation with the king to investigate Maruf's real position. They decided to seek the princess's help, and she agreed to find out, at an opportune moment, the real truth of the matter.

As they lay in one another's arms, the princess that night asked her husband to explain the mystery of the missing caravan. Maruf had just that very day told his friend Ali that he indeed did have a caravan of priceless worth. But now he decided to speak the truth. 'There is no caravan,' he said, 'and although the wazir is right, his words are due to his greed. Your father, too, gave you to me because of his own greed. Why did you yourself consent to marry me?'

'You are my husband,' replied the princess, 'and I will never disgrace you. Take these fifty thousand gold pieces, flee the country, send me a message from safety, where I will join you in due course. Meanwhile, leave me to attend to the Court situation.' Dressed as a slave, Maruf fled in the dead of night.

Now, when the king and the wazir called the Princess Dunia to them for her report, she said:

'Respected Father and Most Worthy Wazir, I was about to broach the question with my husband Maruf last night, when a strange thing happened.'

'What was that?' they exclaimed together.

'Ten Mamelukes, dressed most magnificently, arrived beneath the palace window, carrying a letter from the chief of Maruf's caravan. The letter said that they had been delayed because of an attack by numerous Bedouins, fifty of the guards out of the five hundred were killed, and a quantity of the merchandise, two hundred camel-loads, was carried off.'

'And what did Maruf say?'

'He said very little. Two hundred loads and fifty lives were nothing, he thought. But he at once rode off to meet the caravan and bring it back to us.'

Thus the princess bought time.

As for Maruf, he rode hard, not knowing where, until he came to a peasant ploughing a small strip of land. To him he gave greeting, and the peasant said, out of the goodness of his heart:

'Be a guest of mine, Great Slave of the King's Majesty. I will bring you some food to share with me.'

He hurried off, and Maruf, touched by his kindness, decided to continue with the man's ploughing, as a contribution to his welfare. He had not made many furrows when the plough struck a stone. When he pulled it away, a flight of steps leading into the ground was revealed. Below was a huge chamber, filled with in numerable treasures.

In a crystal box was a ring, which Maruf picked out and rubbed. Instantly a strange apparition materialized, crying: 'Here am I, thy servant, my Lord.'

Maruf discovered that this jinn was known as Father of Happiness, and that he was one of the most powerful commanders of the jinn, and that the treasure had belonged to the ancient King Shaddad, son of Aad. The Father of Happiness was now the slave of Maruf.

The cobbler ordered the treasure to be taken to the surface of the ground. Then it was loaded on camels and mules and horses, materialized by the jinn. Every kind of precious material was also produced by the other jinns who

served the Father of Happiness, and the caravan was soon
ready to depart.

The peasant returned with a little barley and pulse. Now
that he saw Maruf and his treasures he imagined that this
must be a king. Maruf gave him some gold and told him
to claim a greater reward later. Accepting the peasant's
hospitality, he ate only pulse and barley.

Maruf sent the jinns (for such were the men and animals
in disguise) ahead to the city of his father-in-law. When
they arrived, the king attacked the wazir for his having ever
suggested that Maruf was a pauper. When the princess heard
that a resplendent caravan had arrived, belonging to Maruf,
she did not know what the truth was. She suspected that
Maruf had said that he had lied in order to test her loyalty.

Maruf's friend Ali, for his part, assumed that this great
caravan was the work of the princess, who must surely in
some way have contrived to save her husband's name and
life.

All the merchants who had lent money to Maruf, and
had wondered at his generosity with it, were now even more
amazed at the amount of gold, jewels and gifts which he was
distributing to the poor and needy.

But the wazir was still suspicious. No merchant was ever
known to act in this way, he told the king, and he proposed
a plot. He lured Maruf into a garden, plied him with music
and wine, and in his drunkenness Maruf confessed the
truth. The wazir then borrowed the magical ring from the
unresisting Maruf, made the jinn appear, and ordered him to
spirit Maruf away into the farthest desert. Reviling him for

revealing the precious secret, the jinn willingly snatched up Maruf and threw him down in the Hadhramaut wilderness. Now the wazir commanded the jinn to take his master the king and hurl him down together with Maruf. The wazir seized power and even tried to seduce the princess.

The princess, however, when the wazir came to her, got possession of the ring from his finger, rubbed it and had the jinn take the minister away in chains. In one hour the jinn had brought back the king and Maruf to the palace. The wazir was put to death for his treachery, and Maruf became the prime minister in his stead.

They lived happily together thereafter. The king died and Maruf succeeded him. He now had a son. The princess retained possession of the ring. Now she became ill and, handing over the care of the child and the ring to Maruf, she died, warning him to take equal care of each.

Not long afterwards, King Maruf was lying in bed when he awoke with a start. Beside him was none other than his first wife, the hideous Fatima, transported there by magical means. She explained what had befallen her.

When Maruf disappeared she repented and became a beggar. Life was hard, and she was reduced to the utmost extremity of suffering. One day while she was lying down trying to sleep, she cried out in her distress, when a jinn appeared and told her about the adventures of Maruf since they had last met. She asked him to take her to Ikhtiyar, and she had been brought there with the speed of light.

She was now most contrite, and Maruf agreed to take her back as his wife, warning her that he was now a king and master of a magical ring, whose servitor was the great jinn, Father of Happiness. Humbly, she thanked him, and took her place as the queen. But she hated the little prince.

Now, at night, Maruf used to take off his magical ring. Fatima knew this, and before long crept into his bedroom and stole it. The little boy, however, had followed her, and when he saw her steal the ring, he drew his tiny sword and killed the hag, fearful of the exercise of her new power.

Thus did the false Fatima find her grave at the place of her greatest honour. Now Maruf called the honest peasant who had been the instrument of his salvation and made him prime minister. He married the peasant's daughter. And thereafter all lived in happiness and success.

Like various other dervish tales, this one appears in the *Arabian Nights*. Unlike most Sufi allegories, it is not found in poetic form. Again, unlike most except for the Mulla Nasrudin cycle, it is sometimes performed in *chaikhanas* (tea houses) as a drama.

It has no moral, as people in the West are accustomed to them, but it stresses certain cause-and-effect relationships which are a marked feature of some Sufi literature.

From: *Tales of the Dervishes*
Idries Shah

In Arabia

Previous chapters of Arabian geography must have prepared my readers into believing that an Arab is a nomad by necessity. There are no vast stretches of cultivable fields, water is scarce, and both heat and cold are intense. The life in the desert, therefore, according to the European's idea, is one of the most primitive fashions. Where there are oases, a few hundred acres of land are sown there; there a small agricultural community lives, tilling the boulder-strewn land with the wooden plough which has seen little change since Adam's time. Amongst the palm groves low-roofed mud houses ramble into the distance, and an unpretentious walled courtyard in the centre of the village is all by which you could recognize a sheikh's residence.

The town Arab resembles his kinsmen only in the manner of dress. In almost all other traits he differs from the desert dweller as might a man of a different race. The unwritten Bedouin law is enforced in the desert, while the town Arabs are considered to have 'grown soft' in the more advanced legal code of foreign nations, and are therefore regarded as scarcely fit associates of the warriors in the sandy stretches of Central Arabia.

The various portions of inner Arabia – which alone merits the name of true Arabia – afford habitation to numerous clans and tribes, and as often as not clan is at war against clan and tribe against tribe even amongst its own clan. The stable wealth of these people is invested in camels, goats, and horses; and where there is no history of blood-feud due to the infringement of some moral code, the raids are generally undertaken for precisely the same 'love of the game' as was sheep stealing in old Scotland, or cattle lifting is today in the American wild west.

The real colour of the desert you do not see till you leave the western fringes of it quite fifty miles behind you. The ordinary traveller, of course, takes a seat in an enormous motor-lorry, and moves with the motor caravan to Baghdad twice a week. He is protected part of the way by the French and on the eastern side by the British armed cars, and after a more or less comfortable journey of over forty-eight hours reaches safety on the shores of the Persian Gulf from the Mediterranean Sea. But that is not the way to see Arabia.

Grey dawn was paling before the rising sun beyond Damascus when I left that city for the interior of the Arab land. Qasim wore his headgear low because, as he explained to me later, he was a marked man with the French authorities. But it was the gay prancing of his bay mare that entranced me as we journeyed on and on to the little-known oasis of Bani-Othman, many scores of miles from Western civilization.

True to his word, the sheikh had sent Qasim to escort me to his desert fastness, at the request of an important Arab chief in Jerusalem. For fully four hours we rode on vast stretches of hard and soft sand alternately, over the dry riverbeds and rocks of grey and reddish stone, till a rounding of a bend brought us on the edge of a wadi stretching as far down as the eye could see. 'You see those black spots?' asked Qasim, with something of the triumph of the returned exile in his tone. 'That is where our territory begins,' he grinned under the folds of his headgear. 'You see those black spots?' he asked again. 'They are the tents of our desert guards.' The importance of those dwellers in the black tents was not appreciated by me till there was a raid upon the encampment of my host, and when those outposts had slain practically a quarter of the retreating forces of the attackers.

Things in the distance as you see them in the desert give a very peculiar visual impression. When we were on slightly higher ground than the black tents of the Bedouins, those spots looked extremely small – so small, indeed, that without field-glasses you could scarcely distinguish them from the adjoining stunted shrubs or even boulders; but when we descended to their level they stood in bold relief, even larger in size than they actually were.

I was comparing these impressions when suddenly my eye alighted upon little clouds of yellow sand in the adjoining valley. In no time they grew in size, and presently the grey-brown robes of the riders were plainly visible. There were eight of them, and they rode towards us like a very whirlwind. The youngest, jumping from his horse, approached Qasim, and on being assured that I was the guest of the sheikh, exchanged salutations of Islam. The sheikh was anxious about me, he said, because I was expected at his capital for the last two days. They had apparently made some mistake in the calendar, for the Christian calendar and that of Islam differ by some days, as theirs are the lunar months.

The sheikh met us some two hundred yards outside his encampment. His 'capital' lay some three miles eastward in the oasis below, but he preferred to live in the open air with his clan in the black tents. The preliminary salutations and giving and blessing each other with the peace of Allah having been gone through, I went to the reception tent. It was hardly a tent in the Western sense, it was more truly an awning, or a large piece of black felt which is stretched over a wooden tent skeleton and made fast with camel-hair ropes. A tall man might touch its roof, and although there are side curtains to it, they are used only when the intense heat of the sun is to be shut out during the middle of the day. At night all curtains are rolled up to give access to the welcome air.

On the hard sand, under this tent of some seventy feet in length, I sat on the right-hand side of the sheikh as his principal guest. Others, according to their ranks, sat cross-legged on large bolsters stuffed with hay and covered by rich Oriental carpets. The black slave poured out the coffee, first to me and then to his master, who, as a token of friendship, exchanged cups with me. The coffee was passed and repassed for quite two hours, and the only saving grace was that at no one time they give you more than a mere large sip in your cup. It is generally sugarless, unless you especially ask for Turkish coffee, and aromatics are added to it.

The priest began to call the faithful to prayer. 'Allah is great, Allah is great!' he shouted, keeping his fingers in his ears as he stood facing the desert air Mecca-wards. Everyone stood behind him for the prayer, during which the stillness of the wide, wide sandy stretches was intense. Then a lantern was lighted and fastened to the tent pole, droves of camels lumbered their way to the rear portion of the encampment, torches were lit, someone in the distance began to play on a stringed instrument, for the hour of supper was drawing nigh, and then the deep sleep for the weary of the desert!

Presently there was a hurry and bustle, and I saw from the adjoining tent a dozen men, carrying an enormous cauldron. They swayed with its weight. It was deposited before the sheikh's tent, and as we sat around it, what did I see but a whole roasted goat, floating in the gravy! Two more cauldrons followed this one, in which there was boiled rice. My host rolled up his sleeves, as he tore bits of meat for me from the roast with his fingers. I am sure he must have heaped quite eight pounds of it before me. Then we got down to the business of eating it. Pot after pot was brought, men feasted, and having had their fill, made room for the fresh arrivals, till the ceremony lasted a whole hour. Sour camel's milk was passed round as the only substitute for water; and I, for one, felt that I had eaten too well and not too wisely. It was a right royal feast of the desert king.

Coffee was passed round once again, and then after a short prayer the sheikh went to the tent of his ladies to see how they were faring. He was soon amongst us again, when, unlike the Wahabis, we all smoked cigarettes, and then stories of long ago in the golden age of the wild Arabians were told.

Giving his best tent accommodation to me, the sheikh bade me goodnight to see to the posting of guards around the encampment, for night prowlers are many and varied in that area. I lay quite a while awake, on the hard sand, on which two thick woollen mattresses had been placed, with a rug thrown over. The night was perfectly calm and silent, and stars hung from the pitch-dark night sky like radiant bunches of giant grapes. Was it the mystery of a star-lit desert sky or my fatigue that kept me awake to the middle of the night? I tossed upon my bed. It was all quiet, nothing but the guard moved in the distance. In and out of the dim glow of the dying fire he came out to look around, had a peep at me and then went to his post again. I think his companion must have noticed my restlessness, when he came to ask me whether all was well with me. And then, by the way of apology or merely good fellowship of Arabian hospitality, he began to tell me of his earlier life. He startled me by telling me right away that he was a brigand, a brigand born, and that life he had enjoyed for the sheer sport of it. He meant no one any harm, he merely did it because he found that there was not much else to do in his younger days. And then he went to Mecca, since when he had reformed and was now only a warrior with the sheikh. This is the story he told me. I give it in his own colourful description.

I will call my brigand Suleiman, though that is not his real name, but I might have occasion to return to his particular locality, and it would scarcely be healthy for me there did he know that I had been writing about him thus – he is a touchy person, Suleiman. I soon found that he had once been a nobleman of the desert, but that bad fortune had dogged his footsteps almost from the first. I think it was because I was a man of his own rank that he attempted to justify himself to me, and thus acquainted me with passages in his life which he did not originally intend to allude to, telling me very much more than he had meant to do in the first instance.

Suleiman 'commenced business' as a brigand about the age of sixteen, when the last break in his civil fortunes took place, and he had been engaged in his treacherous occupation for more than a quarter of a century at the time I encountered him. He was particularly proud of the fact that not one of the large number of prisoners he had taken had ever failed to be ransomed. Several had certainly lost their ears or had their noses split because of their friends' delay, but none had forfeited their lives.

But others who had resisted capture had not been so happy. Of these quite a number had bitten the dust. 'But it was in fair fight,' maintained Suleiman, 'and had they realized how small my ransoms actually were, they would not have considered it worthwhile to resist.' It was, indeed, because of the lightness of his ransoms that he invariably received them. 'Small profits and quick returns' was evidently his motto.

Yet he had tales harrowing enough. That of the young bridegroom was, perhaps, the most human. A young merchant of means had been travelling from Aleppo through Suleiman's 'territory', as he called it, and had been captured by him. A message was at once dispatched to the capital to demand quite a reasonable ransom from the young man's mother. But the lady absolutely refused to pay it unless the young merchant gave up the girl to whom he was betrothed, and to whom she had taken a dislike. All representations seemed to be of no avail, and at last Suleiman, who sympathized with the merchant, allowed him to go free, on the understanding that he pledged himself to remit the amount of the ransom on his return home.

He duly returned, to find his mother dead. Smitten with remorse at having, as he thought, gone contrary to the wishes of his deceased parent, he gave up the lady to whom he had been affianced. Now comes the strange part of this history. The lady, heartbroken, escaped from her father's house, meaning to seek her lover and plead with him. In doing so she was captured by Suleiman's agents and brought to him. A letter was at once sent to the young merchant, requesting a ransom, and it brought him in person. In the end Suleiman refused the ransom, and so employed his good endeavours that he brought the two lovers together again, finally escorting them back to Aleppo, where they were happily married.

But some of Suleiman's reminiscences were not without a spice of humour. Perhaps that which dealt with the fat widow was the most amusing of all. The lady, the widow of a French Army officer, had been captured near Suleiman's fastness, and as she was as poor as she was stout, she refused to pay a penny of ransom, or even to have her relations apprised of her capture. In vain the brigand assured her that, unless she gave him the name of some responsible relation, he would be forced to take extreme measures. The lady absolutely refused.

But, to his horror, she at last intimated that she did not desire to be ransomed. She had taken a fancy to Suleiman, and would remain with him as his wife. I can recall the comical expression of the brigand's face as he narrated the awful circumstances to me. Horror-stricken, he at once proposed to release her, but go she would not, repeating deliberately that they were twin souls, and that Allah had undoubtedly brought them together in so romantic a manner because they were destined for each other. At last, protests being of no avail, Suleiman was forced to have the lady tied on a horse and conducted back to the borders of civilization. But, horror of horrors! she actually returned, and made matters so unpleasant that at last she had to be bought off. So were the tables turned, and as Suleiman narrated the dreadful story the perspiration ran in trickles down the deep furrows of his expressive face.

Not a little horrible were some of the tales which Suleiman recounted to me with a naturalness which seemed to add a touch of the gruesome to them. There was, for example, that dreadful story, a story which seemed to make the night darker, of the fruit merchant who had no relations to whom to apply for ransom. Terrified and in despair, he had taken his own life and that of his wife and brother rather than face the tortures to which he believed Suleiman would put him.

These and many another yarn, comic and tragic, Suleiman told me as we sat beside his camp-fire. Indeed, they would fill a good-sized volume, the romances of this Arab Rob Roy

SHAH

who warred on the rich, but certainly had a soft side for the poor and needy, whom he frequently assisted with food and money.

From: *Arabia*
The Sirdar Ikbal Ali Shah

Insider Information

IRRITATED BY PEBBLES, potent emetics and coal-tar soap, the delicate lining of my stomach finally began to give.

The magician's latest wheeze had played havoc with my body's finely tuned homeostatic system. Mine was a case in which the scientist had lost control of his experiment. Decreasing the temperature of 104 degrees Fahrenheit had called for drastic action. Gokul had been instructed to find a *barafwalla*, an ice seller. He ran out into the tree-lined streets of Alipore and commandeered two blocks of ice which were being lugged on the back of a cart to the nearby Zoological Gardens. Taking charge, Feroze pointed his bull's pizzle riding crop at the servant's bathtub, then at the ice and, lastly, at me. The *barafwallas* heaved their load into the bath and threw me on top.

Solace, at last.

The *barafwallas*, the Master, Rublu, and a gaggle of snorting servants gathered round to enjoy the spectacle. Each watched transfixed as I shuddered with cold and heat at the same time. First they observed the sea of soapy sweat surging like tainted spring water from my pores. Then they gawked as my steaming perspiration melted the ice – revealing an entombed frozen sewer rat.

Like an amateur mammoth hunter, Gokul chipped away at the ice with the end of a spoon to excavate the rodent.

'Good work, Gokul,' said Feroze, who was having a whale of a time at my expense. 'It's a big one, even for Kolkata. When you've extracted it, put it in the fridge… we'll do a dissection later.'

Three days passed before I could ingest any soft foods.

Even then I limited myself to a diet of soupy *daal* and mashed bananas, washed down with warm water. Ever courteous, Gokul attempted to nurse my digestive tract back to its original condition. But the damage had been done. Abdominal pain, loss of appetite and severe vomiting followed: classic symptoms of a peptic ulcer. My malady would have alarmed the most hardened of surgeons.

Fortunately, despite the grave nature of my condition, I had an incentive to recover – the prospect of revenge.

On the afternoon of the third day after the trial by temperature, Gokul stuck a hand down his *lungi* and fished something out. It was a neat bunch of *neem* sticks. He blew on them lightly, apologizing that they had become dampened by his private parts. His loins were the only place hidden from the magician's continual scrutiny. I snatched the bundle to my chest and examined it. The *neem* sticks were fastened together with three turquoise elastic bands. I hurried the contraband to my room, and hid it beneath the inner sole of my left shoe. Ready for action… All I needed now was the right moment to attack.

When I informed him of my deteriorating gastric condition, Feroze regarded the office calendar on the wall.

'It's the middle of February, fancy that…' he said dryly. 'Suppose it's about time you got out of the house… can't keep you cooped up here forever.'

'I don't know if you understand,' I said, retching. 'I think I've got a peptic ulcer. It has to be treated without delay.'

Feroze removed a doctor's notelet from a drawer in the writing bureau. Then, twisting the lid from his mandarin-coloured Parker Duofold, he scribbled a prescription.

'Go to the Swastika Chemist on Shakespeare Sarani,' he said, peering up from the paper. 'Give them this prescription and take the pills they give you… three times a day.'

As with eating, Feroze considered illness to be a waste of time. He disliked anyone associated with him to fall victim to the weaknesses of the human constitution.

'When you've got the medicine,' he went on, 'you are to go out and find your first example of insider information – the third element of your course.'

I clutched my belly like an expectant mother.

'Shouldn't I take a few days off?'

'For what?' he hissed viperously.

'Recovery,' I said. 'I once read a novel called *Broken Spirit*… the hero died an agonizing death from an ulcer much like mine.'

The Master swished his riding crop like a camel's tail.

'Sounds like a good read,' he gloated. 'I'll have to remember it.'

'What sort of "insider information" do you want me to find?'

'You'll know it when you find it,' replied Feroze. 'Now leave me... I have a rat to dissect!'

*

WITH ONE HAND on my stomach, and the other wiping the stream of sweat from my brow, I set out into Kolkata.

Through disorientation, I headed south by mistake, instead of northeast into the heart of town. Before I knew it, I was inching my way down the macadamized surface of Judge's Court Road. Famed as a haven of the sophisticated in days gone by, Judge's Court is one of Alipore's old imposing roads. Now a place of faded grandeur, it's home to a ragtag assortment of used furniture shops. Packed from floor to ceiling with roll-top desks, chandeliers, organs, and wall cabinets, bracket clocks and card tables, the shops are testament to changed taste. No longer do Kolkatans cherish the Indo-Baroque masterpieces of the past. Who wants a classical rosewood throne when they can recline in the comfort of a fluffy nylon easy chair?

As I wandered through the wide avenues of Alipore in search of a rickshaw, I considered the magician's medical prescription. How could I be taking medical advice from the person responsible for my condition?

'Bebtic ulcer very bainful,' mused the pharmacist at the Swastika Chemist.

'Yes,' I confirmed, 'it's desperately *baneful*.'

'Take six tablets every day for a week,' explained the professional.

'Shouldn't I be taking three tablets a day?'

The chemist shook his head.

'Oh, no, no, no,' he said, 'special offer... double dosage, same brice!'

I made a note of the Swastika's address. Mustn't forget about this place, I thought. This is a hypochondriac's fantasy.

'What about the pain?' I croaked. 'Will these red and white ones take away the pain?'

'Bain...?' said the pharmacist. 'Is the bain unbearable?'

'Yes, yes, yes!' I bellowed. 'That's just what it is... it's unbearable!'

The chemist screwed up his eyes like balls of paper. Then, sliding open an ankle-level drawer, he took out a brown glass bottle of lozenges.

'These relieve all possible bain,' he crowed, slapping them down squarely before me.

'How much do I owe you for them?'

'*Bain blockers*,' said the chemist grandly, tilting his head backwards, 'bain blockers, no charge... experimental.'

Sliding a wrinkled index finger to his lips, he winked.

Before choking down a bain blocker, something crossed my mind. A dangerous misunderstanding may have been about to claim a fresh victim. From the abyss of my unconscious mind a timid, lipless woman was signalling furiously. Had the chemist meant 'brain blocker', rather than 'pain blocker'? Was I about to induce a self-inflicted lobotomy? Prepared to try anything to dispel the gastric distress, I knocked a couple of the oversized chalky lozenges to the back of my throat and gulped. The experience was not unlike that of swallowing pebbles.

I counted to ten. Then to twenty. My brain still seemed to be generally intact. But, as I wandered down Shakespeare Sarani, I found myself floating like a ball of fluff in the wind. It was as if there were no gravity. The chemist's experimental painkillers obviously needed a little more work.

But as I glided towards the Maidan – Kolkata's immense central parkland – I reflected that, for the moment, the pills would be just fine.

Without faltering, I listed sloth-like and bewildered into the seething traffic of Chowringhee.

In a country where sedate driving is unknown, Kolkata's frenzied thoroughfare is the zenith of all motorway madness. Uncontrolled and maniacal, wild as a nine-headed Hydra, ferocious as ten thousand vampire bats, Kolkata's main street is more tempestuous than any act of God.

Bullock carts and Ambassador cabs, buses, their sides gashed like armour-plating peppered with anti-tank shells, herds of goats charging like migrating wildebeest, a vintage traction engine on a suicide run: fording the commotion is to play *Space Invaders* for one's life.

Dodge the heavy guns, and the stealthy cycle rickshaws creep up like assassins – laden high with sea trunks, and schoolchildren, *hilsa* fish and urinals, balloons and computer monitors. Miraculously, the press of wheels, spokes and tramping hooves parted, like a great sea, allowing me to cross.

In the Maidan, I drifted over to the Shaheed Minar, formerly the Ochterlony Monument – a throwback to the glory days of the British Raj.

Staggering somewhat, searching for insider information, I made my way from one performance to the next. At one, a girl of about twelve was demonstrating her ability to write with a pen held in her toes. For one rupee she would scrawl out a love poem or a secret astrological message. Opposite sat a young *swami* on crossed legs. His face was pasty, his hands tinged with orange specks. A single charred pot stood before him, positioned on a chequered handkerchief. The vessel contained crocodile fat, apparently a cure for arthritis, impotency and abdominal disorders. Beside it was a pile of 'miracle' shells from the Andaman Islands. An hour earlier, I might have solicited the luminary's advice and purchased a square of crocodile blubber. But now the pain of my peptic ulcer was nothing but a distant memory.

Further on, past a skinny boy and his tightrope-walking pye-dog, was another chap with wire-walking rats. Beyond him stood yet another lad. Like the others, he was in his early teens. But he was different. He had an engaging Charlie Chaplin smile, blinding teeth, and dimples as deep as sugarlumps. Although tattered, his clothes were well kept. Yet it wasn't his dress which caught my attention. It was his demeanour. This boy may have been operating in Kolkata's Maidan, but he was haughty beyond belief.

His pitch was being mobbed by enthusiastic punters, all eager to get his attention. Inquisitive at the source of the commotion, I floated over. Once I had pushed my way to the front, I watched the routine.

A member of the crowd would hand the lad a hundred-rupee note, itself a tidy sum of money in India. The bill would be folded in half, and then folded in half again. Then it would be slipped into a miniature manila envelope which was placed on a brick, before a green parakeet. The bird would grip the sachet in its bill, ripping the corner. Next, the boy would throw the marked envelope into a box containing other identical, yet unmarked envelopes. He would shake the box roughly. Only then would he invite the owner of the money to search for the envelope containing his banknote.

Invariably, the marked envelope had disappeared.

Despite swaying from the bain blocker, I felt certain I could catch the boy out. What's all my training been for, I asked myself, if I can't trip up an under-age hoaxer?

So when the boy challenged me, I accepted. My hundred-rupee bill was folded in half, then in half again, before being inserted into a crisp manila pouch. The parrot did its duty, and the torn envelope was thrust into the box. When the carton's lid was removed, the child – who was minting money – urged me to search for my note.

I waved the box aside. The crowd stared at me quizzically. The young magician frowned. Swaggering with all the pomposity I could muster, I ripped the stall's tablecloth away.

'This is where you hid my money!' I cried, sweeping the cloth back.

But the table was bare.

The crowd seethed with delight. Obviously expecting trouble from the foreigner, the entertainer slipped me his Charlie Chaplin smile, grabbed his parrot and props, and made off.

Back at the Alipore mansion, Feroze was pacing up and down the courtyard like a stallion before a race.

'Ah, back at last?' he puffed.

Without his captive, the magician had obviously been distraught with boredom.

'How was the rat?' I enquired, crossing the yard.

'Very interesting, actually,' replied Feroze. 'It had a tumour in its intestines. If it hadn't been frozen solid, it would have had an early death.' The Master groomed back his hair with his hands. 'That reminds me, did you get your pills?'

'Yes. Got some incredible painkillers, too. They're strong as a knockout punch.'

'Oh, can I see?'

Feroze examined the label-less bottle, then, removing the lid, he took a hesitant sniff. He raised one eyebrow, glanced at his pocket-watch, and then coughed.

'Do you mind if I take one away?' he asked.

'Help yourself. In pain, are you?'

The sorcerer chose not to answer. Instead, he enquired what example of insider information I had brought for him. When I retorted that I had come empty-handed – on account of medical reasons – he flew into a rage.

'Never...' he roared, 'never return here without completing the assignment I have set!'

Only as I apologized did I conceive the true extent of the Master's anger. By failing to bring him some nugget from my trip into town, I was in some way depriving him.

That night, in the dim light of my bedroom, I reflected on Feroze's unfounded animosity. Brooding, I tugged the inner sole from my shoe and inspected the rubber bands.

Revenge, when it came, would be sweet.

*

NEXT MORNING FEROZE met me as I descended the antique staircase.

It was still dark outside.

'Good morning,' I said, inquisitive as to why the magician should be hovering at the foot of the stairs.

'Tahir,' he replied in an unusually sensitive tone, 'do you remember those pills you brought back yesterday?'

'Yes, of course,' I replied, 'the bain blockers.'

'I've tested the one you gave me,' Feroze explained. 'It contained mercuric chloride. Take two or three more and you'll be dead.'

'Are you sure?'

'If you don't believe me,' Feroze responded coldly, 'keep taking them and see. Don't forget, this is India – when a quack tells you a potion is "experimental", take the hint and run off!'

For a few seconds I was touched by the magician's compassionate veneer. But, as I set out in search of insider information, I remembered the past. I had endured far too much to forgive and forget.

Where does one go in a tremendous city like Kolkata to find insider information?

I recalled India's golden rule: do the opposite of what would be normal anywhere else.

The subcontinent is a fine-tuned and well-practised place. To the outsider it may appear random, or directionless. But in India, what seems haphazard is the product of five thousand years of exertion. Go with the flow, I reminded myself – never strain against the nation's natural forces... and success must soon follow.

If ordered to scour a Western metropolis for trade secrets, I would have headed straight to the heart of the city. This being India, I turned my back on central Kolkata, and strolled towards the serene banks of Tolly's Nullah canal.

I sat beneath a banyan tree to eat a packed lunch prepared by Gokul. It was five past ten, but my constitution had grown used to the Master's timetable. A group of men were gathering cress with sickles at the water's edge. Others were fishing with wiry concertina keepnets, wading up to their chests like gazelle fording a river. Behind them, a family were flipping cow dung fuel bricks in the winter sun.

Four young boys were diving into the canal in turns, clouding the water, splashing carefree, shrieking like jackals beneath a full moon.

In Europe, the last person I would turn to for help would be someone with whom I did not share a common language.

When applying the golden rule of India, such a person becomes the obvious guide.

Sidling over to a bearded man of about my age, who was flipping dung bricks like dinosaur eggs, I struck up a conversation.

'Do you know where I'd find some insider information?' I asked.

The man looked at me with blank, swollen eyes.

'In-sid-er know-ledge,' I repeated, motioning obscure gestures like a psychotic mime.

Frowning as he strove to decipher my sign language, the brick-flipping man shook his head.

'Haa,' he murmured, as if he had understood my enquiry.

With a dung-clad finger he pointed at a distant building surrounded by a wall.

When I pointed to the same building, he nodded vigorously.

Excellent, I thought, I'm on to something here.

'Alipore Jail,' spluttered a boss-eyed *paan* seller, crouched outside the gate.

'Oh,' I said, sheepishly. 'That looks like a strange place to go searching for insider information, doesn't it?'

The *paan* seller clipped a pile of *sopaari*, areca nuts. 'Looking for Bhola Das?' he asked.

'Um, I'm looking for insider information,' I replied. 'Who's Bhola Das?'

The *paan* seller winked his good eye twice.

'Bhola Das... famous hangman of West Bengal!'

'Ah, yes... that's who I'm looking for. Yes, that's right. I'm looking for the hangman!'

Who could have better trade secrets than a hangman?

'Where do I go?'

The *paan* seller motioned to a low hatch within the main studded portal.

Pausing for a moment to get my story straight, I knocked twice on the door. There was no reply. I knocked again. Only then did a guard put his face to the door's grille.

'Bhola Das!' I shouted. 'I have come to see Bhola Das – the famous hangman of West Bengal.'

The guard slid the visor back across the grille. A bunch of keys rattled inside. The door within a door creaked inwards.

One guard ferried me to the next. To each I whispered the cryptic password... the name of the hangman.

After a long wait I found myself sitting before the warden.

'I have come to see Bhola Das,' I explained. 'I think you will find that he's expecting me.'

'Very good, sir,' said the warden, signing the necessary paperwork to authorize my visit.

He pressed a button beside his desk. Before I could turn my head, a watchman stepped from the shadows and led me through the fabled jail of Alipore.

Up and down stairs, around corridors and along straight passageways. The soles of my shoes rasped on the flagstones as we proceeded through the maze. The liveried guard halted before a robust steel door.

'Bhola Das?' he confirmed.

'Yes, it's the hangman I've come to see.'

'Very good, sir,' squirmed the watchman, as he knocked on the door. The door opened inwards.

Inside was a square, stone-walled chamber, illuminated by natural light. A solid wood table stood in one corner. On it was a noose, crafted from coarse hemp rope. Adjacent to the table a man was sitting on a three-legged stool. His hair was snowdrop-white, his cheeks were obscured by a rough grey beard, his steely eyes hidden behind scratched lenses, and his shirt and *lungi* were old, yet neat.

'Bhola Das?' I asked.

'Yes,' said the man. 'I am Bhola Das.'

'I would like to speak with you for a few minutes.'

The hangman glanced at a clock mounted high on the wall.

'Do you have an execution to administer?'

'No,' said Das dolefully, 'I have no work today.'

Whereas other states in India elect their executioners on their own merit, West Bengal employs hangmen from a single hereditary line.

'My father and his father and his father before him were all hangmen,' exclaimed Das, stretching his spindly arms behind him like locust wings. 'My father killed more than six hundred convicts. But that was in the time of the Britishers, and there were far many more to execute then. My father was sent to Glasgow during the Raj. He hanged Indians at the prison there. I suppose,' said Das solemnly, 'you could say that hanging is in my blood.'

'What's it like to hang a man?'

The hangman stared at the floor, then with eyes cold as sleet, he gazed at me, taking in the features of my face.

'To kill a man,' he said softly, 'is a dreadful thing. To bring a man's life to an end is almost too much to bear. I am a hereditary executioner. This is the work of my forefathers. I do not judge the profession which they have chosen for my line. But I ensure each man I kill dies with dignity and without pain. I believe I am the finest executioner in India. I do not claim that for an idle boast. Before killing a convict I cannot sleep for three days. I cannot eat either. I spend time alone, thinking about the life which I am about to end. Then, before I place the noose in position, I ask the criminal's forgiveness. I tell him I am only doing what the government and the court has asked me to do.

'When I hang a man,' declared Bhola Das, pressing his thick glasses to his nose, 'the victim remains intact. Blood doesn't ooze from his nostrils, from his ears or from his mouth. That's the mark of the professional.'

'Tell me,' I intoned in a hushed voice, as the footsteps of a guard tramped past outside, 'are there any secrets of the profession which have been passed on to you by your ancestors?'

Das nodded sagaciously, staring out at a pair of pigeons which were squatting on the window ledge.

'Yes,' he replied. 'There are family secrets…'

'Could you tell me what they are?'

The hangman squinted.

'The secrets of which I speak are,' he said, 'known only to me and to the man I execute.'

'Ah,' I winced, loosening my collar, 'I understand. But isn't there some meagre tip you could give, to prove the care you take in your craft?'

Bhola Das rubbed his palms together.

'First,' he whispered, looking from right to left, 'I lubricate the noose with a bar of soap. I make sure it gets into all the creases. This reduces friction. Then I rub it a second time, with a banana. Only after that can I be certain that the knot will slide easily. But,' continued the executioner in a low voice, 'the most important thing is to weave a brass nut into the noose. While slipping the noose over the inmate's head, I position a heavy nut at the side of the neck. As soon as the trap door opens, the nut swings round to the spinal cord and snaps it cleanly.

'Half an hour later,' the hangman went on, 'when I release the rope, there's sometimes an eerie scream from the convict's mouth – it's nothing more than air escaping from the prisoner's lungs.'

'Is hanging the only method of execution in West Bengal?'

'Unfortunately, it is. Four men were recently convicted of raping a nine-year-old girl,' continued Das. 'I was told to hang them. They ought to have been thrown into a cage of lions. The noose was too good for them!'

Bhola Das removed his glasses and rubbed his eyes. He was an honourable man, maintaining the work of his forefathers.

'Do your children want to carry on the tradition?'

'Yes,' said Bhola Das. 'My elder son wants to join the business. I have taught him how to twine a rope and craft a noose. He has helped me on some occasions. But,' imparted the hangman wearily, 'he wants the position to pay more and to have better job security. Without that,' he whispered, 'he says there's no future for the profession.'

Armed with the valuable insider information, I thanked the ageing executioner and summoned the guard to escort me from the prison. Bhola Das clasped his callused hands around mine and pressed his lips to my ear.

'If you ever require my services,' he murmured darkly, as I left, 'please don't hesitate to call upon me.'

That was an honest man, I reflected, as I trekked north up Baker Road towards the magician's compound. He had inner strength, and was compassionate under testing circumstances. As for Bhola Das's offer – it was hard to say whether I would ever need to avail myself of the private services of an executioner.

But the offer, I pondered, would be good to keep in reserve... for a rainy day.

*

IT WAS WITH elation that I entered the Master's mansion.

I was eager to share my newfound insider information. But before making my report, I slipped up to my room to wash and change. Gokul's assistant was polishing the brass carpet rods on the stairs. Climbing over him, I made my way up to the first-floor corridor. My bedroom was situated at its far end. Several other rooms led off the passageway. These were usually kept locked. Feroze was obsessed that they remain so. Noticing that the second door on the right was ajar, I was suspicious. Pushing it inward, I poked my head around the door.

The casual nature of my intrusion added to the surprise.

It was a young boy's bedroom. A home-made model aeroplane was suspended from the ceiling. Below it, a clutch of toy animals were poised on the bed. A leather satchel was propped up against a chair, its buckles unfastened. A child's sketches were pinned to one wall. The low desk was strewn with the elements of childhood. A catapult, a nest of marbles, cotton reels and a dismembered doll's head. It might have been like any other boy's bedroom. But it was not. The chamber was lit by a single bare red bulb. Its shutters had been closed like an iron visor, preventing daylight from penetrating in. A ghastly scarlet light filled the place.

Rattled by the sight, I stepped back to shut the door. But as I did so, I noticed a hunched figure sitting on a low stool with his eyes closed. It was Feroze. Surprisingly, he had not heard me. I tiptoed away.

When I had changed, I went out to the kitchen to find Gokul. Surely the Master's veteran servant would explain the room's mystery.

Gokul was busy roasting a ladle of spices over a gas flame.

'Hello, *Sahib*,' he said, without turning around.

'How did you know it was me?'

'Very noisy walker,' he snorted.

'Gokul… I've just seen something rather strange.'

'What strange?'

'There's a bedroom upstairs with a red light in it. The Master is sitting there with his eyes closed.'

The manservant raised the ladle from the heat. He turned to face me.

'Long time ago,' he said tensely, 'Master's son and wife was killed.'

'How? How did it happen?'

Gokul rubbed both eyes with his left hand, and sniffed.

'They taking cycle rickshaw in Kolkata,' he said. 'Rickshaw hit by petrol tanker… Master *Sahib* has kept son bedroom same way. Today,' mumbled the servant, 'anniversary of death.'

Leaving Gokul to his spices, I returned to the main house, my head hung low. The magician may have been my tormentor, but I was willing to agree to a temporary truce. Was his venomous attitude to his pupils connected to the death of his wife and child?

An hour later, Feroze found me in the study, where I was combing a copy of *Hobson-Jobson* for magical feats. He was less vitalized than usual. His eyes were circled by heavy rings, his face was drawn and pale, and his clothes quite dishevelled.

'How did you get on?' he asked, through gritted teeth.

'Well...' I began, snapping the book closed, euphorically.

'Did you find me any insider information?'

I reflected on Alipore Jail and upon the secrets of Bhola Das – hereditary hangman of West Bengal. Should I explain first about the soap, the banana, or the brass nut which snaps the spine? I glanced at Feroze. He wasn't his usual self. How could I discuss an executioner's tips with a man whose family had themselves met such a terrible end?

'I'm so sorry,' I said, 'but my stomach has been troubling me again. I'll make sure to bring back a double dose of insider information tomorrow.'

*

NEXT DAY, WELL before Gokul had shuffled up the passageway with a pot of milky tea, I had slunk out of the house. Today, I told myself, I am going to restore my reputation.

Early morning in Kolkata is a bewitching time. Like the back lot of a Hollywood film studio, it's either teeming with people, or silent as a ghost ship. Kolkata is either off or on. It's the only city on Earth with no halfway setting.

At six a.m. – like scene shifters and extras in a film – the first people saunter on to the set. They are well rested and prepared for another day of furious activity. Some scrape out the gutters, or scrub down the cobblestones, like studio janitors making ready for the arrival of the cast. Others set out dog-eared copies of *Time* and *National Geographic* on makeshift wooden stalls.

Nearby, beggars hobble into position, bracing themselves for the crowds. Street-side astrologers prop up their hand-painted boards depicting the constellations, perfume sellers dust down their carved glass bottles, toothpick vendors arrange their stock, pickpockets step stealthily into doorways. Fruit sellers divide sour green oranges into clusters of six. Traffic policemen tighten their white steel helmets and climb up on to their rostra. Then – and only then – as if an invisible director has ordered filming to begin, Kolkata is switched on.

Within moments, the streets are choked with vehicles. The air boils with exhaust fumes. And the pavements are packed with shoals of people, jammed shoulder to shoulder like lambs in a wagon.

Nothing in Kolkata is so important as the pavement. Far more than mere conduits for pedestrians, the walkways are dormitories, typing bureaux, markets, cafés, doctors' surgeries and umbrella repair shops, rolled into an endless profusion of activity. Kolkata's pavements are wider than in most other cities, constructed by the British for a grand imperial capital. Twenty yards of Kolkata pavement has more on offer than entire countries. Plastic combs and squashy toys, shower caps in camellia pink, hard-boiled eggs in trays, reconditioned engine-blocks, Bakelite telephones, mothballs in sackcloth pouches, beetroot and jackfruit, dental floss and wooden legs, Zimmer frames and pogo sticks, turbines and theodolites.

SHAH

*

AS I RECOILED from the force of the morning invasion, I noticed a man squatting outside the Writer's Building. He had no hands or feet. His stumps were well healed, their skin tight and smooth.

Dozens of unfortunates beg on Lal Bazaar Street. But this man was wearing a pair of alien antennae – popular with party-goers about twenty years before. As I bent over him, he twanged one of the springs with his stump. The bloodshot eyeball at the end jangled about, revolving wildly.

'Yes, *Sahib*…' he exclaimed eagerly, realizing that, as a customer from out of town, I was sure to buy the latest sensation. '*Panch rupia*, five rupees!'

'What would I use the apparatus for?'

'Very good quality,' he stressed, 'good price. I am crippling. No family. No money.'

I handed over the note and took the alien antennae. They might come in useful down the line, I thought. After all, this was Kolkata.

I tried on the tentacles for the first time. No one even looked round as I pushed through the crowds, the pair of demonic eyeballs jolting about above my head. Then I noticed a man waving at me from the far end of Lal Bazaar. Suspecting it to be another mendicant impatient to make an easy sale, I turned and hurried off. But a grinding of wheels indicated that the man was in pursuit. Without looking round, I slipped down a side alley, my alien eyeballs flapping about like teasels in the wind. The wheels followed.

'All right,' I snarled, facing the pursuer. 'What do you want?'

It was then I noticed that this was no cart-bound invalid, but a *rickshawalla*.

'*Jadoowalla!*' he shouted. 'Remembering? Mister Magician....?'

The man spoke gibberish.

He was sleek as a gondola, barefoot and extremely lean. His torn saffron-coloured vest revealed a scrawny back, pocked with dried sores, and with muscles as taut as a drum skin. When standing still, his body swayed back and forth. He was very drunk indeed.

'What do you want?'

The man pointed at me, then the rickshaw, and then acted out a little sketch.

He was beginning to seem familiar.

'Aren't you the *rickshawalla* who took me to Feroze's house on that first day – you were the runner in Purulia, right?'

The *rickshawalla* tilted his head from one side to the other. 'Haa, *Sahib*,' he said. 'Runner. I am runner. My name is Venky.'

The *rickshawalla* cracked his knuckle joints, as if demonstrating his enduring strength.

'Where you want to go?' he asked, squinting.

'Well,' I said, 'maybe you can help me.'

He shuffled forwards in concentration.

'I am looking for a special thing,' I explained. 'I am searching for *insider information*.'

Venky the *rickshawalla* raised his eyebrows as high as he could, and swayed his head from left to right. It smelt as if he had taken a bath in *chullu*.

'Do you understand? I want to be taken to someone with insider information.'

The man patted the rickshaw's seat with his leathery palm. I climbed up and we set off. He seemed to know where he was going.

Dodging the onslaught of taxis, juggernauts, and a great caravan of marching bandsmen who were out drumming up business, the *rickshawalla* scuttled towards the Bow Bazaar. The market is famous for selling fine jewellery, produced in cramped back workrooms behind each shop. The larger emporia have resident astrologers, advising on the appropriate design of jewellery.

Without warning, Venky dug his heels into the dirt and pointed to a cow. The animal, which had a wreath of flowers around its neck, was tied to a post. Beside it was a middle-aged woman, dressed in a simple white sari, tied in the Bengali way.

'How can an animal have insider information?'

The *rickshawalla* hesitated.

'Do not understand,' he said.

'Then why did you bring me to this cow?'

Venky stuck out his lower lip, revealing his gums. We had only just met, but somehow it was as if I had known him all my life.

'Well, since we're here, can you ask the woman what she uses her cow for?'

Promoted from *rickshawalla* to translator, Venky struck up a conversation with the woman. She held up a bunch of rough grass stems and he slurred a number of disjointed questions.

'She says,' began Venky in his best English, 'people pay a little money to feed the cow.'

'Why do people want to pay to feed the cow?'

'Feed cow lucky,' responded the *rickshawalla*.

'Does the woman own the cow?'

Again, Venky chattered away in animated conversation.

'Haa,' he said after some time, 'she not own cow. Milking man own cow. She is paying milking man for cow in day.'

'You mean that the woman hires the cow each day, once the milkman's finished with it, and she lets strangers pay her money to feed it?'

Venky thought for a moment. Then he smiled.

'Yes, *Sahib*... very good!'

The genius of the arrangement bore the unrivalled hallmark of Kolkata. Where else could you find such an ingenious system? The milkman milks the cow and then, instead of looking after it all day, gives it to a woman who pays him for the privilege of looking after the animal. Far from being left out of pocket, the woman charges people to feed the creature a few strands of grass. In turn, the cow's devotees attain a sense of inner calm from their charity. The woman sells the dung to fuel-brick makers as a profitable sideline. This was even better than the baby rental.

'Venky!' I declared, as Mehboob's Marching Band engulfed us like a sea of crude oil. 'You're a genius!'

Buoyed by the early success of Bow Bazaar, I set my sights on the street's other professionals.

If a humble cow could reveal such hidden wonders, then what could be waiting for me further along the street?

But even before I had a chance to put away my notebook, Venky pointed at a group of men cleaning out the gutters beside his rickshaw's wheel. '*Ghamelawalla!*' he cried.

'What are you saying? What's a *ghamelawalla*?'

The rickshaw puller was perplexed that I should not understand the term.

'*Ghamelawalla,*' he repeated, 'gold sweeper!'

'Venky,' I said, 'you're obviously wrong. These men are gutter cleaners. Look – they're sweeping up all the dirt and heaving it on to a metal cart.'

The *rickshawalla* wagged a finger.

'*Ghamelawalla* is looking for gold,' he said.

With Venky translating, I resigned myself to the fact that seeking out the truth might be a slow, uphill task. His English was limited. It was like deciphering a garbled tape recording made underwater. I put his wavering linguistic ability down to the flask of opaque liquid stored in the pouch around his neck.

Bow Bazaar is a street of astounding financial wealth. Bearing this in mind, it wasn't unreasonable that people should be dredging the gutters for gold. Renewing my faith in the man who had brought me the cow keeper's secret, I licked my pencil.

Gold dealers in the West value the dirt swept from workshop floors. An elderly Hasid jeweller in Manhattan once told me he had sold the antique floorboards from his factory. Their purchaser incinerated the planks to extract the gold dust which had worked its way into the crevices over the years. But as I came to realize, the clan of the *ghamelawallas*, Kolkata's unofficial army of gold scroungers, put even the great recyclers of New York to shame.

Taking their name from their *ghamelas*, heavy iron pans, the city's *ghamelawallas* begin work in the middle of the night. Long before the bazaar's jewellers are open for business, they turn up to sweep out the workshops. Like the tiny birds which peck the teeth inside crocodile mouths, *ghamelawallas* perform a vital, if not uncelebrated, service. Every grain of dust is meticulously collected. Once the business owner is paid a few rupees, the precious dirt is taken away to be treated.

Many *ghamelawallas* make their homes on the streets of Kolkata.

Nearly all are migrant workers, with wives and children who they see once a year. Most begin their careers as apprentice *ghamelawallas*, arriving to work alongside their fathers at the age of six or seven. They sleep on *charpoys*, rope beds, in alleyways, and wash at hand pumps. Wander the backstreets near the Bow Bazaar and you'll see them sitting on the pavements, toiling over the jewellers' dirt. Mixed amid the jumble of pavement life, the huddle of squatting figures could easily be dismissed without a second glance. But like so many in Kolkata, the *ghamelawallas* are masters of creating a living from almost nothing. The tattered sweepers, squatting at shin level, perform an intricate scientific procedure.

First, the scraps of paper and straw and larger pieces of rubbish are removed. These will be sold later to *ruddiwallas*, 'rag-pickers'. Then the actual dirt is washed in clean water. When it has been swilled about, a few drops of nitric acid are added. This dissolves all the metals except for the gold. The residue is then treated with a solution of barium, which amalgamates the gold particles.

After this, the remaining compound is burned in a crucible, on a *choolaah*, a little stove. As miniature hand-driven bellows blast air into the embers, a tiny nugget of gold is formed at the base of the crucible.

Some other Indian cities have *ghamelawallas* as well. But those in Kolkata dismiss their rivals as impostors. For nowhere on earth has recycling been taken to such exalted levels as in Kolkata. Whereas *ghamelawallas* working in, say, Mumbai, treat the salvaged dirt once, their fellow gold-seekers in Kolkata are far more ingenious. When the initial burning is over, the first group of *ghamelawallas* sells the dirt from which they have extracted gold to another group of *ghamelawallas*. More impoverished than the first, the second group repeats the process, removing even more minute traces of the precious metal. These *ghamelawallas* sell the dust on to yet another team of washers, who pan it on the banks of the Hooghly. When they are finished with the dust, they peddle it to builders, who turn it into bricks.

Subject after subject was discussed, and every time the intellectual cited books and precedents, false analogies and extraordinary presumptions without intuitive reality.

At length he produced a book which he had written, and Nasrudin stretched his hand forth to see it, because he was the only literate man present.

Holding it in front of his eyes, Nasrudin turned page after page, while the assembly looked on. After several minutes the itinerant cleric began to fidget. Then he could not contain himself any longer. 'You are holding my book upside down!' he screamed.

'I know,' said Nasrudin. 'Since it is one of the archetypes which seem to have produced you, it seems to be the only sensible thing to do, if one is to learn from it.'

Life and Death

Nasrudin climbed a tree to saw through a branch. A passer-by who saw what he was doing cried: 'Look out! You are on the wrong side of the branch. You will fall with it.'

'Am I a fool that I should believe you; or are you a seer that you can tell me the future?' demanded the mulla.

Soon afterwards, however, the branch gave way, and he fell to the ground. Nasrudin ran to catch up with the other man. 'Your prediction has been fulfilled! Tell me now, how shall I die?'

However much he tried, the other man could not now convince Nasrudin that he was not a seer. Ultimately he lost his temper and said: 'You might as well die now.'

As soon as he heard these words the mulla fell down and lay still. His neighbours came and found him and put him in a coffin. As they were walking towards the cemetery, there was a dispute as to the shortest route. Nasrudin lost his patience. Raising his head from the coffin he said: 'When I was alive, I used to turn left here – that is the quickest way.'

A Penny Less to Pay
Sitting near some stepping-stones across a river, the mulla saw that ten blind men wanted to cross the stream. He offered to help them over for a penny each.

They accepted and he started to take them across.

Nine were safely delivered to the farther bank. But, as he was making his way with the tenth, the unfortunate man tripped and was carried away by the flood.

Sensing something amiss the nine survivors began calling out: 'What happened, Nasrudin?'

'A penny less to pay,' said the mulla.

Why Ask Me?
Nasrudin was riding along one day when his donkey took fright at something in its path and started to bolt.

As he sped past them at an unaccustomed pace some countrymen called out:

'Where are you going, O Nasrudin, so fast?'

'Don't ask me,' shouted the mulla, 'ask my donkey!'

A SON OF A SON I

The Daughters

Nasrudin had two daughters. One was married to a farmer, the other to a brick-maker.

One day they both visited him.

The farmer's wife said: 'My husband has just finished sowing. If it rains, he will buy me a new dress.'

The other said: 'I hope that it does not. My husband has just made a huge number of bricks, ready for firing. If it does not rain, he will buy me a new dress.'

'One of you may be worth something,' said the mulla, 'but I could not say which.'

All Included

Nasrudin bought a handful of dates, and sat down to eat them. His wife noticed that he put each stone carefully in his pocket.

'Why don't you throw away the stones, like everyone else does?'

'Because when I bought the dates I asked the greengrocer if the price quoted for "dates" included "stones" as well. He said: "Yes, all included." So the stones are mine as well as the fruit. I can keep them, or throw them away.'

Why Shouldn't They Mourn?

Nasrudin used to breed chickens and sell them to the local butcher.

One day he was half-absorbed in the problems of his chicken-run when he noticed a man passing, dressed in mourning.

'Tell me,' said the mulla, rushing to the fence, 'why are you wearing those clothes?'

'Because my parents are dead: this is how I mourn them.'

The next day passers-by saw each one of Nasrudin's chickens with a black ribbon around its neck.

'mulla,' they cried, 'why are those chickens wearing black ribbons?'

'Their parents, as you may well imagine,' said the mulla, 'are dead. Why shouldn't they mourn?'

Not Worth Keeping

Seeing something glittering in the gutter, Mulla Nasrudin ran to pick it up. It was a metal mirror.

Looking at it closely, he saw his face reflected in it.

'No wonder it was thrown away – nothing as ugly as this could possibly appeal to anyone. The fault is in me, for I picked it up without reasoning that it must be something unpleasant.'

The Physician

A woman summoned the mulla in his capacity as a physician, because she did not feel well. When he arrived and tried to take her pulse, she was too shy, and covered her arm with her sleeve.

Nasrudin took a handkerchief from his pocket and laid it on the sleeve.

'What are you doing, Mulla?'

'Didn't you know? A cotton pulse is always taken with a silken hand.'

Appetite

'I have been unable to eat anything for three days.'

'Good heavens, Mulla – with your appetite? You must be very ill.'

'Not at all: nobody has asked me out to eat, that's all.'

The Secret

Nasrudin looked over a wall and saw a magnificent lawn, soft and green as finest velvet. He called to the gardener who was watering it:

'What is the secret of making a lawn like that?'

'No secret,' said the gardener. 'I don't mind telling you, if you climb down here.'

'Marvellous,' said the mulla, scrambling down beside him. 'I'll make one for myself, and turn my whole garden into a lawn like this.'

'The method', said the gardener, 'is merely to plant a lawn, remove the weeds, and keep it flat and smooth, cutting the grass frequently.'

'I can do all that! How long does it take to get it into this condition?'

'About eight hundred years.'

'I like the outlook from my window – without grass – anyway,' said Nasrudin.

Maximum Capacity

An ancient and valuable fragile Chinese vase had been found by the villagers. There was an argument in the teahouse as to its exact capacity.

During the wrangling, the mulla entered. The people appealed to him for a ruling.

'Simple,' said Nasrudin. 'Bring the vase here, together with some sand.'

He had the vase filled with layer after layer of fine sand, packing it down with a mallet. Ultimately it burst.

'There you are,' – he turned to the company triumphantly – 'the maximum capacity has been reached. All you have to do now is to remove one grain of sand, and you will have the precise amount needed to fill a container like this.'

Battle of the Sexes

In the teahouse, people were talking about the relative numbers of the sexes.

'Throughout the world,' said the baker, 'men and women are equally balanced in numbers.'

'On the contrary,' said Nasrudin, 'there are about ten per cent men.'

'How do you make that out?'

'Ninety per cent do what their wives tell them to do,' said Nasrudin.

At the Frontier

Nasrudin was carrying a basket of eggs across a frontier. The egg producers of the transborder country, anxious to preserve their rights, had petitioned the king. The king had decreed that no eggs were to be imported.

The customs officers on duty easily spotted Nasrudin, took him to their post, and started to interrogate him.

'The penalty for lying is death. What have you in that basket?'

'The smallest possible chickens.'

'That comes under livestock. We shall impound them,' said the officer, locking them up in a cupboard, 'while we make inquiries. But have no fear, we shall feed them for you. That would be our responsibility.'

'These are special chickens,' said Nasrudin.

'How?'

'Well, you have heard of animals pining, getting old before their time, when deprived of the attention of their master?'

'Yes.'

'These chickens are so sensitive, and of such a special breed that if they are left alone for a moment, they become young before their time.'

'How young?'

'They can even become eggs again.'

Try Anything Once

Nasrudin was lurking near a tavern. He was penniless, and besides, wine was forbidden to true believers.

The sultan's cup-bearer came out, carefully carrying a delicate flagon of wine.

They caught sight of one another at the same moment.

'Honourable Saki,' began the mulla, 'give me…'

'Give you what, Mulla?'

To ask for wine would be a direct admission that he drank it.

'Give me… a piece of advice.'

'Very well. Go and read a book.'

Half to himself, Nasrudin muttered: 'Oh, no, that won't do.'

'Why not?'

'Oh… er… I tried that, once.'

Seven With One Stroke

A soldier was back from the wars. The teahouse was agog.

'One day, on the Northern Frontiers, I slew no less than six infidels, all with red beards.'

There was a roar of applause.

'You can't cap that one, Mulla,' said a wag who had just tricked Nasrudin into swearing that he would tell the literal truth for the next twenty-four hours.

The mulla drew himself up to his full height.

'I do not boast much, and I have sworn to tell the truth. Very well: know, all of you, that I have myself slain seven unbelievers, with a single stroke.'

He stalked out, as everyone looked at him with new respect, back to his room, where seven unbelieving beetles lay in the shadow of his fly-swatter.

Raw Material

Everyone in the teahouse was criticizing Wali. He was generally admitted to be useless, and each person had something to say against him.

'That man,' opined the tailor, whose words were usually considered weighty, 'is a cabbage.'

Everyone murmured his assent – except Nasrudin.

'Not so, Aga,' he said. 'You must be fair. A cabbage can be boiled and eaten. What could Wali be turned into?'

Catch Your Rabbit

People were talking about strange, sometimes mythical beasts, and someone in the teahouse told Nasrudin that there were monsters to be found even near his own village.

As he was on his way home, the mulla saw a new animal. It had long ears, like a donkey, but it was brownish, furry and chewing. So preoccupied was it that Nasrudin was able to steal up to it and catch it by the ears. He had never seen anything like this before. It was, in fact, a rabbit.

He took it home and tied it in a sack, forbidding his wife to open it. Then he hurried back to the teahouse.

'I have found something,' he announced gravely, 'which has ears like a donkey, munches like a camel, and is now in a sack in my house. There has never been an animal like this seen before.'

Immediately the teahouse emptied, and everyone ran to the mulla's home to see this wonder.

Meanwhile, of course, his wife had opened the sack, unable to restrain her curiosity. The rabbit bounded out of the house and away. She could think of nothing better to do than put a stone in the sack instead, and tie it up again.

Soon the mulla arrived with his friends clamouring to see the monster.

He opened the sack, and the stone fell out. There was a dead silence. Nasrudin recovered himself first.

'Friends! If you take seven of these stones, they will be found to weigh three-quarters of a pound.'

Pity the Poor Natives

Nasrudin was on one of his many teaching journeys, travelling through a rich country, heading for the capital.

As his donkey plodded along, he was more and more impressed by the orderliness and prosperity of the farms on each side of the road.

He reached the city on the first day of the new moon. Here it was the custom for people to go into the streets to see the crescent. Nasrudin knew nothing of this until he realized that everyone was pouring into the open and looking up at the moon.

'They may have a nourishing country,' said the mulla to himself, 'but we, after all, have the moon almost all the time. She evidently appears here only when she is invisible to us.'

How Far Is Enough?

Nasrudin was at a loose end. His wife told him to go for a walk. He started up the road, and continued walking for two days.

Finally he met a man walking in the opposite direction.

'When you arrive at my house,' he said to him, 'go in and ask my wife if I have gone far enough, or if she says that I must walk farther.'

Economic Law?

During the Crusades, Nasrudin was captured and set to work on the ditch near Aleppo citadel. The work was backbreaking, and the mulla bemoaned his lot, but the exercise benefited him.

A neutral merchant passing by one day recognized him, and ransomed him for thirty silver dirhams. Taking him home he treated him kindly and bestowed his daughter upon him.

Now Nasrudin lived a life of fair comfort, but the woman turned out to be a shrew.

'You are the man, remember,' she said one day, 'that my father bought for thirty dirhams and gave to me.'

'Yes,' said Nasrudin, 'I am that man. He paid thirty for me; you got me for nothing – and I have even lost the muscles I gained digging ditches.'

Private Property

Trotting his donkey along a road one day, Nasrudin saw some beautiful flowers by the wayside. He dismounted to pick them, and when he returned with his posy found that someone had stolen his cloak from the back of the donkey.

'Very well,' said Nasrudin, 'I shall have your saddle instead. Fair is fair.'

He got on the donkey and placed the saddle on his own back.

Tie Up Below!

The mulla was aboard ship when a terrible storm blew up. All hands were ordered aloft to furl the sails and lash them to the masts.

Nasrudin ran to the captain, yelling:

'Fools! Anyone can see that the ship moves from below – and your men are trying to bind it up from above!'

Fire

Mulla Nasrudin was welcomed by an unctuous innkeeper who professed himself delighted to have such a distinguished guest. 'Anything you want, call for it,' he said.

During the night the mulla was thirsty. He called out for water, but nobody stirred.

His throat was parched, and he felt as though there was a fire in his mouth.

'Fire! Fire!' he cried.

The whole caravanserai awakened, and presently the host was at his side with a pitcher of water. 'Where is the fire?'

Nasrudin pointed to his mouth. 'Here,' he said.

Instinct

'There are some things,' said Nasrudin, 'that you positively know, inwardly, must be untrue.'

'Can I have an example?' asked someone who was always looking for evidence of the supernormal.

'Certainly. For instance, the other day when I was walking along, I overheard a rumour that I was dead.'

The Question Contains Its Answer

'Tell me the truth,' said Tamerlane to Nasrudin, as they sat in the steam-room of a Turkish bath.

'I always do, Majesty,' said the mulla.

'What am I worth?'

'Five gold pieces.'

The king looked annoyed. 'This belt which secures my bathing-trunks is worth just that.'

'You are without value,' said the mulla, 'and when you talk about "worth" I am forced to answer in terms of the question. If you are talking about money, I give you the exterior value – that of the belt. If you are talking about inner worth, it cannot be answered in words.'

Nosebags and Donkeys

'Where is Nasrudin?' said someone in the teahouse during a philosophical discussion. 'Let's ask him a difficult question.'

'But all he knows about is donkeys,' said another.

'There is philosophy in donkeys,' said the mulla, hearing the word as he entered.

'All right, Nasrudin,' said the baker, 'answer us this one: what came first, donkeys or nosebags?'

'Simple. Nosebags,' said the mulla without hesitation.

'But that is ridiculous!'

'Prove it!'

'Well... a donkey can recognize a nosebag, but a nosebag can't recognize a donkey.'

'I presume that you have the assurance of a nosebag,' said Nasrudin, 'that it cannot recognize a donkey?'

SHAH

The Mulla's Dream
One night the mulla woke his wife in a great hurry and said: 'Run, quickly, bring my glasses. I am having a wonderful dream, and more has been promised me by someone whom I have seen. I must have my glasses for this.'

The King Spoke to Me
Nasrudin returned to the village from the imperial capital, and the citizens gathered around him to hear what he had to say.

'I shall be brief,' said Nasrudin, 'and confine my remarks on this occasion simply to the statement that my greatest moment was when the king spoke to me.'

Overcome with wonder and staggered by the reflected glory, most of the people fell back, and went on their way to discuss this wonderful happening.

The least sophisticated peasant of all hung back, and asked:

'What did His Majesty say?'

'I was standing outside the palace when he came out, and he said to me, quite clearly, for anyone to hear: "Get out of my way!"'

The simpleton was satisfied. He had now, with his own ears, heard words which had actually been used by a king.

Nobody Really Knows
Suddenly realizing that he did not know who he was, Mulla Nasrudin rushed into the street, looking for someone who might recognize him.

The crowds were thick, but he was in a strange town, and he found no familiar face.

Suddenly he found himself in a carpenter's shop.

'What can I do for you?' asked the craftsman, stepping forward.

Nasrudin said nothing.

'Perhaps you would like something made from wood?'

'First things first,' said the mulla. 'Now, did you see me come into your shop?'

'Yes, I did.'

'Good. Now, have you ever seen me in your life before?'

'Never in my life.'

'Then how do you know it is me?'

Truth

'What is truth?' a disciple asked Nasrudin.

'Something which I have never, at any time, spoken – nor shall I.'

Last Year's Nests

'What are you doing in that tree, Mulla?'

'Looking for eggs.'

'But those are last year's nests!'

'Well, if you were a bird, and wanted a safe place to lay, would you build a new nest, with everyone watching?'

Head and Heels

'When you die, Mulla,' asked a friend, 'how would you like to be buried?'

'Head downwards. If, as people believe, we are right way up in this world, I want to try being upside-down in the next.'

Just in Case
Nasrudin was walking along the street enveloped in a dark-blue mourning-robe. Someone stopped him and asked: 'Why are you dressed like that, Mulla – has someone died?'

'Almost certainly,' said Mulla Nasrudin. 'It could have happened, you know, without my having been informed of it.'

Old Graves for New
'When I die,' said Nasrudin, 'have me buried in an old grave.'

'Why?' asked his relatives.

'Because when Munkir and Nakir, recording angels of good and bad actions, come, I will be able to wave them on, saying that this grave has been counted and entered for punishment already.'

From: *The Pleasantries of the Incredible Mulla Nasrudin*
Idries Shah

The Slaver is Ambushed

ABDUL GAVE ME a shock on our first halt from Mashed. I saw
him saying his prayers.

I concluded from this that he was unduly worried.

When he had concluded his prostrations he was in an
amiable mood, and rather foolishly, perhaps, I asked him
why he did not observe the Muslim rites more frequently.

Abdul was a scoundrel at heart, and had a reply for most
awkward queries, and he was not in the least abashed.

He turned upon me with a knowing grin and asked me if
it were not true that The Prophet had been a camel driver
and a raider in his time.

I had to agree that that was so.

He then proceeded to propound his creed.

The Prophet, he assured me, was well aware of the
hardships of the road, and he had indicated that all Muslims,
when engaged on long journeys, could be absolved from the
strict ritual of prayer.

Such is indeed mentioned in the Qur'an, but Abdul had
added his own interpretation. I had to assume that as his life
was an endless journey he considered himself under a full-
time dispensation.

With his usual insolence and arrogance, he asked me if I
had assumed the role of a *Pir*.

This was a direct snub, and one which he proceeded to rub well home.

With his coarse laugh he told me of a caravan man who had been persuaded to resume his devotions after a long interval of neglect. He began scrupulously to observe the ritual of five prayers a day.

Before many days had passed, his piety had become known, and robbers had denuded his caravan of two camels.

'Ah,' said the caravan man when the loss was reported to him, 'it is so long since I have made my presence known to Allah that he has forgotten me. I have recalled myself to his memory, and the loss of the two camels is a punishment for my long neglect. I must now pray for mercy.'

He continued to pray, and more camels disappeared. Other camels went sick for want of attention, and his flocks and his horses strayed.

In the end the caravan man took counsel with himself.

'Allah,' he cried, 'does not desire to be pestered with the prayers of one who is so unworthy. Prayer, after so long an interval, cannot seem but strange. It would be well were Allah to forget me again.'

And the caravan man ceased his prayers, tended his cattle, raided the robbers in their turn, and won back all that had been stolen from him, and much more.

That, in a nutshell, was Abdul's philosophy.

I do not know whether Abdul regarded that evening's news as proof of his beliefs, but from stragglers struggling along the road we learned that a large caravan ahead of us had been cut to pieces, and that some fifty persons had been killed and as many taken off as prisoners and hostages.

No matter what forces were out in the hills, Abdul was committed. He could not return to the more or less friendly shelter of Mashed without blackening his face, for to have got the better of the Mashedes was a point of honour with him. He had to trust to his own strength and fighting prowess in order to win through.

Had he not such a valuable load with him, I do not think that Abdul would have worried over much, but in some way he was linked with the Eminence of Turkomania, and was patently anxious to carry out his commission.

We were making for a place by the name of Gulshan, a high valley where for all time the people have suffered severely in the agitation which has racked the country. Nominally under the jurisdiction of Persia, they really acknowledged no authority, and regarded anyone dispatched to them from Teheran in the light of interlopers.

During the reigns of the late Shahs they looked upon the visit of Persian troops as the incursion of an enemy, and they had reasons. Times out of number the people had been pillaged and plundered by the very forces which had been sent to protect them from bandits. Their houses had been pulled down in order to provide wood for the troopers' fires, and their cattle had been killed and devoured without any semblance of compensation.

These people dreaded the appearance of Persian troops even more than they did the incursion of bandits. If anything, they preferred the latter, and wherever possible, fraternized with them.

In order to recoup themselves from the depredations of the periodical visits of Persian troops, the people of Gulshan not infrequently did a little raiding and camel-lifting on their own.

Gulshan and the surrounding country is such that it has no real trade if one excepts the manufacture of the *poshteen* – sheepskin coats to which I have already referred. The people merely trade or barter among themselves for their own domestic needs and their outside intercourse, as far as I could judge, was solely confined to the illegal inspection of caravans.

The *poshteen* manufactured by the people of this village in their more industrious moments is, however, worthy of mention because it differs so vitally from the rough and ready garment by the same name which is to be found upon the frontier of India and in the Afghanistan passes. The best of the coats are made from the skins of unweaned lambs, and some are so fine that they can be rolled into the size of an ordinary handkerchief. In the season there is a greater slaughter of lambs in these parts.

It is near Gulshan, too, that the famous Nadir Shah was assassinated.

Abdul did not appear to be unduly perturbed by the evil reputation of the people of the village, and when we encamped in the neighbourhood for the night, I discovered the reason. He had friends in the place. I might have surmised as much, for he had much in common with these turbulent townspeople.

We had not been encamped for long before Abdul disappeared. Next morning, he was missing from his tent – a remarkable occurrence in itself, but one which Umid, the wife of Abdul, accepted with solid phlegm.

Soon it went round that Abdul had been drinking with boon companions and had taken such potent doses of a spirit akin to brandy that he had taken to singing and dancing with the girls who had been provided for his entertainment.

The caravan was convulsed with the news, especially when it was seen that Umid was wearing a very grim expression which boded Abdul no good when he should eventually return.

It seemed, too, that Abdul, and his hosts, had become perfectly intoxicated and then, in a drunken frolic, had mounted horses, and, quite unmindful of the darkness, had gone off to spear pig.

Still later they returned, completely unsuccessful in their quest, and had fallen to the bottle again.

These libations were kept up for two days, during which Umid became more and more wintry.

We proceeded at length, and Abdul was as surly as a newly caged tiger. He growled at everyone within reach, and I took care not to be one of them.

We went on like this for two days while Abdul was massaging a tortured liver by jerking to and fro upon a camel, and he seemed to have thrown off all fear of bandits.

On this morning he appeared cheerful, and smiling, and the caravan reflected his mood. All was laughter, and idle chatter when the caravan came to a sudden halt.

I was about twenty camels from the head, but I could see in the near distance six dark figures which had suddenly materialized.

The men were armed, and they remained quite still. The silence was uncanny.

Abdul pushed along the line and examined the group. It was clear that he was unable to make up his mind. His excessive drinking had doubtless clouded his faculties to some extent.

He decided to give the men the sign of peace.

'*Salaam Aleikum*,' he cried, but there was no answering response. The six figures remained there, practically motionless, and without saying a word.

The situation was extraordinary, to say the least, and it was Umid who supplied a diversion. She came lumbering up on her camel, striking all within reach with a cane.

I watched her progress with some trepidation, for she was not weak in the wrist, though she was depending more upon her tongue for the purposes of castigation than her strong right hand.

'Oh,' she cried with fury, as she forced home each stroke, 'what is this? Look, you son of a sheep, look! Was your mother a worm that you have no eyes?'

Whack! would go the heavy cane, and another would feel the weight of her wrath.

'Had your mother no honour? Were you born in the gutter of the bazaar?'

And to another:

'Blind one with a pig's brain, look! Look!'

Umid was not the one for an emergency. Her sense of direction was completely dissolved in vituperation. She was the world's champion scold, and she had the whole line of caravan men ducking and squirming and looking apprehensively at her switch.

She rumbled up to her lord and master, and pulled excitedly at his arm.

'What have you among your men,' she screeched, 'hairless ones just escaped from the *purdah*?'

Abdul threw her a malignant glance, for her tongue had been rattling at full pressure for the past several days and its strident cadences made him wince.

'Camel men!'

The biting scorn in her tongue burned its acrid way through Abdul's phlegm, and he gave a gesture of anger.

'These begetters of imbeciles, they heed not –'

She swung her massive arms to indicate the rocks on her right. Abdul followed her gesture, but seemingly saw nothing. I, too, allowed my eye to roam over the rocks. There was no movement, but I discerned a dull gleam in a fissure between two boulders which was eloquently informative.

I slipped off my camel, and ran, under cover of the line, to Abdul. I caught his eye, and whispered urgently to him.

'The men ahead,' I said, 'are there to distract attention. There are others up in the rocks, and we are covered!'

As soon as Abdul realized the situation, he did not hesitate. Had he not been recovering from a very deep debauch he would never have allowed himself to be caught in such a trap, but once in it, he was determined to fight his way out.

He gave a cry of rage, and urged his camel forward, calling upon his fighting men to follow him.

A thin rattle of musketry came from the rocks, and one camel went down screaming.

The men ahead levelled their guns and fired also, but Abdul went unscathed, and we surged forward.

There was more firing on our right, and figures began to appear among the rocks. Some of our men returned the fire.

I succeeded in scrambling back upon my animal in the press and regretted the fact that I was unarmed. There was that unmistakable smell of warm blood around one, and it got into my nostrils. In such circumstances, the primitive urge is to fight.

Even as this thought was passing through my mind, the man ahead of me reeled in his seat, and sagged sideways on his camel. He had a curved sword in his hand, and this I snatched, more on impulse than with any idea of battling for Abdul.

Something in the subconscious told me, however, that it was better for Abdul to win out of this mess than for us to fall into the hands of the local banditry, and I allowed my frightened camel to charge its way forward.

I have a very indistinct memory of Abdul snapping away with his pistol, and of wildly flourishing swords. A man appeared in my path, well mounted on a horse. I saw him fire, and my face was peppered with the black powder which he used, but the missile itself went wide. I felt my newly acquired sword do its work, and again there was wild flurry of sweating bodies, gurgling camels, snap-shooting and hacking.

How long this went on I am unable to say. Such affairs are invariably blurred in detail for all except the onlookers, and from the manner in which my arm ached afterwards I am confident that I was no spectator.

All I recall is that the road ahead suddenly cleared, and that the camels, anxious to be away from the maddening smell of blood, broke into a panicky gallop. Such of the caravan which was still on its legs went forward, and the action was gradually broken off.

From: *Fifty Enthralling Stories
From the Mysterious East*
The Sirdar Ikbal Ali Shah

House of the Tiger King

WE ARRIVED BACK at the camp at twilight.

The temperature had continued to fall through the afternoon and the air was now filled with a sinister calm, the kind that can only lead to a massive, unrelenting downpour of rain. The porters were snuggled up together, some naked, others not. Richard was sitting alone by the river. He didn't say a word when we got back. He was shaking, rocking back and forth, as if he was very, very cold indeed.

The porters were reluctant to talk to me, and when they did it was only to say that Richard had been acting strangely all day. They said he had urinated into a cup and stared into the liquid for an hour or more, and that he had wept uncontrollably while they were praying after lunch.

'What's the matter with him?' asked Roberto. '*¿Qué pasa con mi verdadero amor?* What's the matter with my true love?'

I said that I didn't know, but that I was frightened.

'He has been trained to kill people,' I told them, 'so we must forget our differences and protect each other.'

I would have devised a plan to wrestle the shotgun away from Richard, but feared it would enrage him further. In any case, a man like that, I reflected, could kill us all with his bare hands. He was a killing machine.

Roberto got up in the night and made a secret meal for the old warrior. He took it to him in his lair in the forest. I don't know what he was expecting, or hoping, but he was chased away, yelping like a small dog that had been kicked hard by an unkind man.

At about two a.m. the temperature cooled a fraction of a degree, a rustle of wind streamed over our faces and it began to pour. The rain of Madre de Dios is similar to that of the Amazon, but there is a petrifying aspect to it, as if it seeks to wound rather than to nurture. It rips down in sheets, with anger, with hatred. We lay in our sleeping-bags hoping desperately, as always, that the water would stay out. But, as always, it found its path in, and was soon being sponged up by our bedding.

The rain continued to fall. It fell through the remainder of the night, all the next morning, through the next day and the following night. All the while, the river rose, inch by inch, until it was ten feet from our camp. We had the option of moving, pitching again in the forest, but the farmers didn't want to budge. They said that the rain would stop... and, sure enough, it did. It was how the world must have been in the wake of the biblical flood. Birds were seen twittering in the *chonta* palms, bright sunshine spilling between the fronds.

The river, which so recently had been little more than a creek, was now a surging body of water. Transformed from innocence to maturity, it was now our greatest foe. The current was so tremendous that we could not get across, let alone wade down it.

That morning the porters were slower than usual. At eight a.m. they were still cuddled up with each other beneath their long green tarpaulin.

'What's the matter with you?' I shouted.

'*Es sábado*, it's Saturday,' said Máximo. 'Seventh-Day Adventists don't do anything on Saturday.'

So they lay there all day. Their only breaks were to eat a meal of roasted fish heads and *yuca*, and to pray.

The next day, the river was still far too high for wading. There was only one solution: to blow life into the rubber boat. Máximo and Rogerio took out the Zodiac and unfurled it. Since I had purchased the boat, from a used-car salesman in London's East End, it had remained untested. Now was the chance to impress the locals, I thought. The porters gathered round. Their amazement lasted until the fragile foot-pump had begun to work. It was soon apparent that the craft was riddled with holes, twenty-three of them.

Marko, the Ukrainian banker, got to work with a repair kit. He glued and glued, until the boat was covered in patches. The problem was that in addition to the holes, the wooden floor was about to fall out, as the seams were in a terrible state. We decided to use it only for luggage, which would be placed on a platform above the waterline.

As the gluing was in progress, the farmers went out into the forest and hacked down a thicket of balsa trees. They felled about eighteen in all. Within an hour or two, they had stripped the bark of the smooth trunks and nailed them together, using pins made from *chonta* wood – the same wood that the Machiguenga used for their bows. Their skill and speed in making the rafts astonished me. Until that moment I had regarded them as good for nothing.

The equipment was packed onto the rafts and wrapped twice in polythene. Then they were launched, along with the antique Zodiac, and we set off back to Panataua.

The pinnacles might have been a disappointment but, as I saw it, there is nothing like testing equipment and men. As my grandfather would always say: 'Time spent on reconnaissance is seldom wasted.'

The Zodiac took in water the moment it was eased into the raging current. The balsa rafts fared much better: unlike the rubber boat, floating came naturally to them. Their other great advantage was their strength: they could be hauled effortlessly over the sharpest rocks.

It took only two days to retrace our route down the Inchipata. The farmers were thrilled at the prospect of returning to their homes. I longed to get to Panataua so I could talk Eduardo into setting out with us. If the porters from his village were the best around, I had no idea how we would ever transport our gear on a larger-scale journey.

For the moment the greatest concern was Richard. He lay on one of the rafts, outstretched and delirious, trembling with fever. At first I thought he was putting it on, that it was a bizarre act, perhaps to pull out of the main expedition. But as time wore on, I began to wonder if he was genuinely ill. The Richard Fowler we all knew and endured would have torn your head off for making fun of his past. But now he put up with the porters' taunts, and even allowed Roberto to stroke his thighs – until I ordered the young cook to move away. It seemed unfair to allow him to caress a man incapable of defending himself.

At Panataua, the porters lined up to be paid. They looked like a concert party about to put on a performance, rather than serious jungle porters. I counted out a wad of notes for each and forced myself to shake their hands.

'*Nunca encontrarás Paititi*, you will never find Paititi,' said Máximo, when his turn came.

'Why do you say that?'

'Because you do not have Jesus in your heart.'

I thanked him for his observation and handed him his money. Rogerio was next. He asked me if he and the other men could be given a Pot Noodle as a bonus. I said that none of them deserved a bonus but, as a gesture of goodwill, they would each be presented with one of the tasty dehydrated meals. They thanked me.

'You know, they are not to fill our stomachs,' said Máximo darkly, '*son para satisfacer a nuestras mujeres*, they are to satisfy our wives.'

It took me a moment to make the connection. He had referred to the supposed aphrodisiacal properties of the white plastic pots.

When the men had been given their Pot Noodles, we received word from Eduardo that we should come to his shack. I didn't know what to do with all the gear, so I coaxed the farmers to ferry it to his part of the village as their gesture of goodwill. Eduardo was standing under a *wayuru* tree, waiting for us. It was good to see him again. He was smiling, his mouth framed with white beard, a baseball cap pulled down tight on his head. 'I see that you survived the jokers,' he said.

'What do you mean?'

'The farm boys, *son débiles como los niños*, they're as weak as children.'

'Why didn't you warn me?'

The old man laughed ominously. 'If you really want to find Paititi,' he replied, 'you have to learn how to choose a team. Without the right people you will never succeed.'

Eduardo owned two modest wooden shacks. The one on the right was used for cooking and eating; there was an antechamber filled with general bric-à-brac and week-old chicks. The other building was larger. It consisted of a small sitting area open to the elements, a storeroom, and a room in which Eduardo, his wife, daughter and son slept. The shacks were surrounded by a mud garden. The arrangement was as primitive as one could imagine. Eduardo had come from the big city of Arequipa eighteen years before, but had not bothered to build a more permanent home. There was no running water, no lavatory or stove and, of course, no electricity. The family relied on candlelight, cooked on an open fire and washed at the stream like everyone else in the village.

The old man took one look at Richard, who was barely able to stand, and shook his head. 'You must all stay here with us,' he said. 'This man is in a bad condition, and he should not be moved.'

'He's used to a diet of hallucinogens,' I responded, 'but he can't get them. So he's getting weaker and weaker.'

The Maestro helped the old soldier to lie down on a bench in the shade. 'There is only one thing that can save him,' he said, '*el amor de Jesús*, the love of Jesus.'

With that, Eduardo ushered us in to eat. His wife, Gladys, was cooking a meal in the cramped kitchen. She was a short woman, hunched from years of stooping at the hearth, her head crowned with dull grey hair, her childlike eyes reflecting the flames.

We told Eduardo about the pinnacles, the porters, and what we had learned. I declared that the journey had been a waste of time.

'No, it certainly was not,' said Eduardo. 'It was the beginning of your preparation.'

We sat at the rough table and held hands in prayer. The old man's son, Enrique, said grace. He was about twelve, with the face of an angel, a complexion so delicate that we all gazed at it. The food was brought in by Luz, the teenage daughter we had met at the *chacra*. There were wide enamel bowls filled with creamy maize porridge, and boiled *yuca* on a bed of rice.

We ate in silence, and when the meal was over, Eduardo thanked Jesus on behalf of us all for providing the food. At first I felt I ought to confess my aversion to missionaries. Then I realized Eduardo might find it necessary to convert me. I asked the Swedes what to do. They talked animatedly in Swedish for a minute or two.

'Don't confess anything,' they said. 'It'll blow our cover.'

So we all agreed to endure the message of Adventism as best we could. After lunch Gladys spoon-fed Richard a bowl of chicken broth. His eyes had rolled up in an alarming way. I thought he might die. Eduardo was cordial, but wouldn't approach the sick soldier. He disliked even looking at him. 'He is filled with bitterness, with evil,' he declared, slapping his hands together. 'Only a diet of prayer can return his health. *Este hombre le ha dado la espalda a Dios*, this man has turned his back on God.'

'He's here to protect us,' I said, in a moment of enthusiasm.

Eduardo peered down at the outstretched figure, regarding him with absolute loathing. 'My friend,' he said, 'this man here could not protect anyone from anything. But let us pray for a miracle.'

We held hands and formed a circle around Richard: Eduardo, Gladys, Enrique, and Luz, Leon and David, Marko, Boris and myself. It was as if we were attempting to will life into the body of a dead man. Eduardo led the prayers, beseeching Jesus to give Richard another chance.

'He will be born again!' he cried. 'And will learn to walk and talk, and will be your child. He will love you, oh, Jesus, he will be your son.'

The film crew and I exchanged troubled glances. We were all concerned for our host. He was a religious maniac, but at the same time he was our best hope of finding the ruins.

That evening we sat on home-made benches on Eduardo's veranda. The candle wicks were long, their flames fanned by a gentle breeze from the west. Richard hadn't moved since we had arrived at the shack. He was still lying on the bench, his military clothing soaked with sweat. From time to time he would stir, ranting as if he was looking death in the eye.

Eduardo thrived in the darkness, when the candles were burning, projecting shadows across the walls like phantoms. He sat back, rubbed his beard and conjured his own world with words: '*Tienes que venir con el espíritu limpio*, you have to come with a clean spirit,' he said softly. 'It must be like a child who has not lost his innocence. To gain that purity you must cleanse your soul.'

'But how do we find Paititi?' I asked.

'I told you,' he said. 'The only way to find it is not to look for it at all. Only a man who has no greed, no avarice, can succeed. When you find Paititi you can take nothing from it. Touch anything at all and you will go blind.' Eduardo paused, picked up his tattered Bible, and pressed the soft leather cover to his lips in a kiss. 'If you do find Paititi,' he continued, 'you will have to repay the earth. How do you do that? Well, if you find a few ruins you will have to kill something small, a dog, perhaps. But if the ruins are great, you will have to kill something far larger.' Again Eduardo paused, but this time he looked at me through the ochre light. '*Si las ruinas son grandiosas*, if the ruins are great,' he repeated, '*tendrás que matar a un hombre*, you will have to kill a man.'

Eduardo walked the tightrope between lunacy and genius. Like everyone else, I was drawn in, willing to suspend judgement, for the Maestro mesmerized his audience, daring them to believe.

Before we knew it a week had passed, each day filled with a rigid routine of prayer, and sermons on how one might find Paititi. It felt as if we were growing roots, planting ourselves on the mud floor of Eduardo's home. Richard barely moved. He grew increasingly frail, and swore in a whisper at anyone who spoke to him. An attractive young nurse came from the village to examine him. In more usual circumstances, the veteran would have been all over her, but he was broken.

'What's the matter with him?' I asked her.

'*No es más que un resfrío*, it's nothing but a cold,' she said. 'Please try to make sure he washes. He smells very bad!'

Before she left, the nurse enquired about the strong medicine I had brought from my home country.

'The painkillers?'

'*No, señor*,' she said, holding a hand over her mouth as if she was about to utter an obscenity. '*Los afrodisíacos*, the aphrodisiacs.'

I squinted in confusion, then remembered the potent medication.

'Women all over the village are asking me for the medicine,' she said. 'They have heard it makes a man fiery, passionate.'

I handed her a Pot Noodle. 'It's a special new kind of drug from Europe,' I said. 'You take it orally.'

Every day Eduardo's harangues grew longer, and wilder, and every day I sensed that we were farther from reaching our goal, Paititi. The scruff of white beard that hid his mouth and quivered when he spoke gave our host an aura of sophistication. And when he spoke, those around him listened. You couldn't help yourself. You were drawn in, like a swarm of insects desperate to touch a flame on a tropical night. Eduardo would speak of veiled evil on a biblical scale, hinting of curses and *brujería* and ferocious, diabolical forces lurking between the trees, and in the mists of the waterfalls.

One night, he claimed to have seen a UFO. He said it wasn't a 'normal' extraterrestrial but was created by sorcerers upriver: the very same place to which we were planning to travel.

'*Era una bola de luz*, it was a ball of light,' he said, 'a sphere burning brilliantly like phosphorus. It glided through the sky, and down, down, down over the trees. Then, when it reached the river, it dived into the water.'

'Weren't you fearful?' I asked.

'No,' El Maestro replied stolidly, 'we had no fear, because we have Jesus.'

On the eighth day Eduardo had a visitor, a man we had not met before. He was wearing a simple uniform, part military, part civilian, and was called señor Franco. He was tall and had an uninteresting face; the kind of man your eyes would not pick out in a crowd. He walked with a dead straight back and chewed the corner of his mouth between sentences. The frosty reception put on by Eduardo and his family indicated their feelings for him. It turned out that he worked for the government and he had not come to speak to Eduardo, but to us.

'If you go to look for Paititi,' he said, in a clear, practised voice, 'we will have you arrested and incarcerated.'

'Paititi? What's Paititi?' I asked flippantly.

'You heard what I said,' he riposted. 'I am waiting for you. I am watching you.'

When he was gone, Eduardo warned us of the authorities. 'There is a layer of bad men plundering our country's wealth,' he said. 'It's big business, the business of a few.'

'Is señor Franco one of them?'

'No, no, he's low down in the chain of command,' Eduardo replied. 'He's employed by the government, but is really working for the oil company.'

A second week slipped by and, with each day, it was as if our roots anchored us a little more firmly to Eduardo's shack. He was now saying there was no point in leaving for the lost city before the next year. He had crops to plant, and money to repay. Again and again he declared that we were still not pure, our souls were not yet cleansed.

'Will we ever be ready to search for the ruins of the Incas?' I shouted in despair.

'*Quizás no*, perhaps not,' was his reply.

Meanwhile, Richard grew ever weaker. The villagers would troop in from time to time and look at him slouched in his camouflage hammock. Some would stretch out their arms and poke him, as if jabbing a strange animal to see if it was alive. They all had the same diagnosis: the Vietnam veteran had descended into hell and turned his back on Jesus. They were praying for his soul, they said coyly.

But then, one morning, Richard was standing up outside the house. We rushed over. He was smiling. We applauded. No one had seen him smiling in a very long time.

'I'm better,' he said angrily.

Eduardo praised Jesus for the miracle.

We must have been at the house too long, for we prayed to the Lord and were happy to do so.

'What's wrong with you?' Richard snapped at me. 'You gone all fuckin' religious or something?'

It was a great moment. The soldier was back to his old self. We were a team again. I went up and hugged him. 'It's good to have you back,' I said.

'Yeah, well, get me some chow, will ya?'

Gladys piled a plate high with roasted *yuca* and handed it to Richard as if her prodigal son had returned. Then, after the meal, we sat in the sunshine and Richard told tales of the wild times of his youth.

David was the one to stir the memories from him. 'What about Vietnam?' he said.

To us it was a single word, the name of a place, but to Richard it was a word whose intensity he had never found elsewhere. Like so many veterans, he relived it in his mind every day.

'Vietnam?' said Richard, drawing deep on his Marlboro. 'I'll tell you about Vietnam. Sure it was ugly, it was fucking obscene. But I had a ball down there. I'd be camped out in the jungle, inserted behind enemy lines and all that shit you see in the movies. If I got bored, and you did get bored, I could call in a fuckin' airstrike. There I was, a kid of nineteen, calling in a two-hundred-and-fifty-thousand-dollar airstrike. It blew your mind.'

'What about the killing?'

'Yeah, there was killing and death and plenty of it,' said Richard. 'They called our platoon the Widow Makers, and there was a reason for it. When you were new, what they'd do was to take you out on a trail with an experienced guy. All your life you're taught that killing is wrong, and all that Christian shit. But now you're out there, trained to do the shit. It's like cowboys and Indians when you were a kid. You're with these guys and they set you up. They put you in the bushes and you're sitting there watching, waiting. All of a sudden you see part of a guy and he's lookin' around and he's coming along… and now you're getting ready to kill him. He could have a wife but you don't think about that kind of shit. You got your weapon on automatic 'cos you're new to the game. You raise it up and lock on to the body. You let out a burst… Brrrrr! Then you take off, running like a madman up the trail.

'After a while, when you're more experienced, you get cool at it, and you can kill with one or two rounds. Then you got people saying to you, "Way to go, man! You rock! You finally got yourself a gook!" You get a case of beer and they're shaking your hand and you get this kinda sick fucking feeling. To do your job is one thing, but all of a sudden you've crossed the line with these guys and you're one of them. You've been initiated.'

Richard's illness had destabilized us all. I think it was because we feared he might kill us in the night.

SHAH

That evening, as I struggled to sleep, I thanked Jesus for bringing him back to us intact.

From: *House of the Tiger King*
Tahir Shah

Reflections

The Cheese

Once upon a time there was a cheese. A number of cheese-mites took up residence in it. As time passed, they bored more and more holes in the cheese, and, of course, they multiplied.

Then, one day, there were so many holes in the cheese that it collapsed into a powder, leaving the mites scrambling in the ruins of their home.

'What traitor is responsible for this?' screamed the mites.

They formed parties, each opposed to the other, whose objectives were to restore the former ideal situation.

Some mites, it is true, found another cheese. But as for the majority – they are fairly rapidly consuming the remaining cheese-powder.

Belief and the Impossible

There is a saying: 'I believe it because it is impossible.'

But if you make any study of people in a state of what they are pleased to call 'belief', you will find that you can usually best describe them by saying:

'I believe because I am impossible'; or even: 'My belief has made me impossible.'

Why He Was Chosen

The disciple of a dervish master whose name resounded from one end of Islam to the other, one day visited the Grand Sheikh of Korasan.

'I have been honoured by my acceptance as a pupil,' he said, 'singled out from among the hundreds who approach my master every day, and yet are sent away.'

'My dear brother,' said the Grand Sheikh, 'I will try to further your education by giving you a piece of essential information. You were chosen because of being in the greatest need of teaching, not because of qualities greater than those of the other applicants.'

New Names

People rename things and even other people; this makes them think that they are different from what they were before.

Let us take a neutral example.

Have you noticed how even at present the majority of buildings are made of mud, but people will not have it that they live in mud houses?

Every home is also an imitation of a cave, but we do not think much of cave-dwellers, so they are called houses.

The Dervishes From the Other World

Three dervishes returned from the Other World.

People, understanding that they had become altered, and wanting to follow their path, asked what had helped them.

'Pease pudding,' said the first.

300

'The Book of Wisdom,' said the second.

'Following a certain man alone,' said the third.

Some people thought that they were mad. Some thought that they were deliberately speaking in riddles. Some thought that this or that Way was the one to follow.

In reality, however, each had benefited from his own capacity and needs, in accordance with certain patterns which are only known to the men of greatest wisdom.

Clever and Profound

Statements which are merely clever and which have no development-potential, are often imagined to be profound, because they look or sound attractive. And profound remarks which have indeed got development-potential are as often deemed to be no more than clever.

The Reason

The cat said:

'What funny faces mice have! That's why I have to destroy them.'

Epoch-Making

People who feel it necessary to describe their activity as epoch-making are more often than not deluded. They try to make epochs because in this way their own importance will be created or increased in the minds of others.

What really counts is effect: not size nor noise, nor personalities, not even a sense of the colossal.

Permanence

Someone quoted the proverb: 'Nothing violent is permanent.'

What a nice hope. I am sure that everyone would agree with it.

It seems a pity that the originator of this saying did not admit his hearers further into his wisdom, by giving an example of something which is permanent.

The Toads in the Castle

Once, in a reverie, I saw a community of wholly admirable toads. They had taken over, and made their home in a castle, obviously, to me, originally built by men.

I spoke their language, in my dream, and asked them to explain to me, as a matter of information, the origins and uses of the various parts of their castle.

They were kindly and hospitable toads, and they gave me full details of their lives and thoughts, and the way in which the building was used.

Every single aspect of the castle and its surroundings, including the moat and the marshes and reed-beds in which it was set, had a thoroughly plausible use and a toad-origin in theory, indicative of toad-thought and toad-design – conclusive to the toad-mind.

I said: 'Brothers, forgive my seeming discourtesy. But this place was formed, designed, erected, by other beings. It was intended for quite different purposes than you have mentioned.'

Some did not hear at all. The whole idea was so strange that it did not even register with them. Some said, shortly: 'You are a liar, or a cheat.'

Others, trying to help me, said to one another: 'Poor fellow, he is raving mad.'

That of course quite disposed of me.

Man and the Tiger
A man being followed by a hungry tiger turned in desperation to face it, and cried:

'Why don't you leave me alone?'

The tiger answered:

'Why don't you stop being so appetizing?'

Thinking and Knowing
People think that they think things, and they also think that they know things.

They could usefully give some attention to the question of whether they know what they think and know what they think they know.

Teachers and Students
People often say: 'I must find a teacher who knows all.'

Some, at least, of such teachers have started by learning wisdom from the ignorant, as some learn conduct from the ill-mannered.

Many aspirants could do worse than start at that very point.

When you have been your own teacher for a time, you may be ready to find someone else who can teach you.

The Driver, Horse, and Cart
One day a driver thought: 'I'll let the horse and cart go where they like, maybe I am trying too hard to be the man in control.'

All went well for a time, since the horse took the cart on its accustomed route. But when the driver willed it to go another way, nothing happened.

'I need more will-power and less discipline,' said the man to himself.

One day the horse thought: 'Why should I obey?' And he started to pull the cart as and when and where he wanted to do so. The man sold him to someone who kept him on a very short leash indeed.

Yet another time the cart thought: 'I will assert my independence. At times my wheels will go, at others I will make them stick. Sometimes I will creak, sometimes not. And I will loosen and contract my nails as and when I feel like it.'

The cart, pronounced unreliable, was chopped up for firewood.

Who Cares?
It is not only a matter of not caring who knows – it is also a matter of knowing who cares.

A SON OF A SON I

Three Wishes

A man, after many years of study and effort, found out how to gain power over spirits. He conjured a jinn.

The jinn gave him three wishes.

He immediately wished for money.

Spending all his money on high living, he became an alcoholic.

His second wish went on making him well again.

Now he felt so undecided as to what to do, he used up the third wish to restore himself to his original state, and to forget his experiences.

Higher Perceptions

People imagine that higher perceptions might be attained by developing a certain inner sense.

But when a person has been working too much on the development of a certain inner sense, it is necessary to teach him by another method.

This method with the concept that the sense can be activated through the exclusion of factors which inhibit its operation.

Feed and exercise a lion in a cage: you may get a fine, robust lion. In order to fulfil his destiny, we may have to turn our attention from him to – the cage.

The Donkey and the Cactus

A donkey was chewing some cactus.

A dog came along and said: 'What are you eating?'

'The most delicious of food,' said the donkey.

The dog took a bite at it. 'You treacherous wretch,' he cried, 'you have deliberately misled me, and now my mouth is full of spines. The taste of this abominable vegetable is nothing like the juicy meat which I was thinking about.'

Positive and Negative

The way in which a statement is phrased is not what makes it positive or negative. It is positive or negative in accordance with its significance, not its appearance.

A 'no' which is constructive is far better than a 'yes' which is not.

Because 'no' is something which people don't like because of having heard it often in their childhood, they tend to behave as if it were something bad: that is to say, unpleasing to them. It is only a step (though a mistaken step) from here to be able to call it 'negative' and therefore not constructive.

In the Land of Fools

Once upon a time there were three wise men. They belonged to a place known as Fuzulistan: the Land of Fools. But this, of course, was only what its uncharitable neighbours called it. The inhabitants called it The Country of Civilization.

These three wise men decided that they would go on a journey, because, as everyone knows, travel broadens the mind; and even the most learned can profit by experience.

Quite soon after crossing the border they came across an unusual object. It was a minaret, towering into the sky.

'Ha, ha,' said the First Wise Man. 'Here is an item worthy of our observation. I will set you a test. How did this object come to be here, and what was the manner of its being produced?'

The Second Wise Man said: 'It is evidently a dead plant or tree. It grew from a seed, or even a certain kind of egg.'

The Third Wise Man disagreed: 'Not at all. This obviously was built. It must have been constructed lengthwise on the ground, and then hoisted to its present position.'

'You are both wrong,' said the First Wise Man, 'for it is evident that it was built by a race of giants. They were tall enough to lean down and place this thing here in its present position.'

It was concluded, after due consultation, that suitable care should be taken by the expedition to preserve itself from the giants, who might, after all, be dangerous.

Confession

'Confession is good for the soul' is an admirable sentiment.

It is valuable because it illustrates clearly something that its practitioners will ordinarily go to any lengths to conceal: that here they are not talking about a soul at all.

They mean: 'I have no conception of a soul, and therefore attribute the pleasure which confession induces in me not to its real source (the discharge of surplus emotional energy) but to something sublime.'

This is a fine example of the real information which we can collect from the hidden language of man.

Any number of comforting arguments could, of course, be found to deny or explain away this fact. There is no harm in listening to the arguments, so long as you are prepared to give an equal amount of attention to the observation of other people, to determine whether fact or argument is the more reliable.

The Spider

A child, dismembering a spider, found that he was left with a number of parts. There were legs, a body and fur.

Being a logical child, he concluded that the legs were from a camel, because camels have legs, the body from an elephant, and the fur from a mouse.

Now an adult would never reason like that, would he?

Defensiveness

When people are told things which they do not want to hear, they produce or borrow certain standard arguments to enable them to exclude the new information from their relatively closed minds.

You can usefully offset this tendency by remembering that most unfamiliar information is likely to be met by this response.

Remember, too, that the things which you already know are mostly facts which would seem to be impossible, unlikely or even symptoms of paranoia to a man or woman at a lower level of culture than yourself.

It is this kind of understanding, not emotional reaction, which will enable you and others to face the truth, and to learn more.

A SON OF A SON I

The Scholar and the Philosopher
A scholar went one day to see a practical philosopher, to determine the origins of his system.

As soon as the question was asked, the master handed the academic a delicious peach. When it had been eaten, the master asked whether he would like another. The scholar ate the second peach.

Then the philosopher said:

'Are you interested in where this peach was grown?'

'No,' said the scholar.

'That is your answer about my system,' said the master.

Suggestion and Attention
The effect of a suggestion tends to be in proportion to the prestige of the source of the suggestion.

Prestige is itself 'accumulated attention'. Accumulated and frozen attention.

Attention-fixing does not require the presence of the object. It may even occur, develop and become fixed through the absence of the object.

Dragon
'It is a dragon, destroyer of all,' cried the ants.

Then a cat pounced and caught – a lizard.

From: *Reflections*
Idries Shah

The Sheikh, the Sun, and the Sack

ON THIS PARTICULAR trip, he said, I was the guest of a sheikh. I would not mention his name. It will not be safe for you, for he shoots before speaking. He was a good enough host though; his whole camel-hair tent and his entire rations were placed at my disposal, for the Arab hospitality is proverbial.

He had only one joke, this sheikh. 'Ah, you Ajami,' he would say. For the rest of the world is Ajam, which is not Arab. He would show a tooth like a jackal's, and laughed at the idea that we Kurds could be of any use to the world.

We Afghans have a 'rep' in the East, I'll admit. There is a Persian proverb: 'In a row, look for an Afghan.' I suppose you would call us the Irish of the Orient.

I met the sheikh in the queerest way. I was riding camel-back from Maabilah, hoping to make Baalbec. I am not going to hand you out the old mossy tale about an eclipse of the sun, but it did just happen that one came along that very afternoon.

A shadow like the edge of a big bad penny began to creep across the disc of day. Of course, I saw at once what it was, and cursed. The beastly thing would last for over a couple of hours, and, as it threatened to grow pitch dark, I would perforce have to dismount. Hard cheese when I had figured to be at Baalbec by five o'clock.

Suddenly a bombardment like a second-class battle commenced to the south of me. On the other side of one of the big sandhills men were shooting like mad, and giving vent to the most bloodthirsty yells.

With the proverbial curiosity of my race I spurred my *heri* to the top of the mound and looked down. Some half-dozen Arabs were blazing away at the sky. On seeing me they stopped and, jumping on their camels, rode quickly to the summit of the rise.

'What are you firing at?' I asked. 'Aeroplane?'

'No, no,' irritably shouted a big man whom I took for the leader. 'Can't you see? Shaitan, he's swallowing the sun. We're firing at him to make him stop.'

'Waste of powder, my friend,' I laughed. 'There's no Shaitan there. It's only an eclipse and you know what that is surely?'

'If you're trying to hocus me with any of your modern stuff,' he shouted, 'you'd better think again, for I'm not having any.'

'If that's Shaitan,' I asked, pointing to the now very apparent shadow on the luminary, 'where are his teeth? And how comes it that his mouth is convex? You are duffers, you desert Arabs. Can't you see that's only the shadow of the moon? It'll disappear in an hour or two, as it always does. Surely you've seen an eclipse before without making all this hullabaloo about it?'

'Of course we've seen it before,' answered the sheikh, 'but in other cases it only disappeared because we fired at it.'

And 'suiting the action to the word', as the old story-spinners used to say, he raised his long rifle and banged away at the orb of day, followed by his faithful servitors.

'How many millions of miles off do you think it is?' I asked. 'Easy to see you never got The Story of the Heavens as a school prize.'

But I let them carry on without further argument, for, thinking of my own personal safety, I concluded it would be just as well that they should exhaust their ammunition.

This they very soon did, while the light faded into almost total darkness. When they had expended their last bullets the chief turned to me.

'Fire, can't you,' he commanded, but I shook my head.

'We're economical folk, we Kurdish Persians,' I said. 'I'm not wasting any Browning bullets on Old Man Sol.'

'So you're an Irani?' laughed the sheikh. 'Of course, that explains a lot. Where are you bound for?'

'Baalbec. I'm going to write about it.'

This statement was greeted with respectful silence. The desert Arab has an enormous veneration for anyone who can write.

'We are going in that very direction,' said the sheikh. 'You will not, however, reach Baalbec tonight for there are bandits in the pass. But I can offer you entertainment. Even if you are an Ajami you're a Muslim, ha, ha, ha! Come along.'

As I was the only man there with any ammunition I didn't mind 'coming along', but I resolved to keep my eyes skinned, for the gang looked rather a leery lot, and I didn't particularly want to wake up with the Sign of the Crescent across my throat. We rode for miles in almost absolute silence over the sands and gradually the light returned. At length we came to a fairly large encampment, which seemed to consist chiefly of tents, goats and smell.

We dismounted and the sheikh conducted me to his tent. 'Conducted' is good, for in reality we had to crawl in it. His *harem* was divided from the living apartment by a screen of filthy haircloth swarming with flies, but he ordered some quite passable coffee from a black slave, and handed me a *chibuq* filled with excellent Anatolian tobacco.

'Listen,' he said, 'when you depart on the morrow I want you to do me a favour.'

I indicated that I would be happy to oblige him if it wasn't anything too embarrassing.

'It's just to carry a sack of corn to a friend of mine at the mouth of the pass,' he assured me with a wink.

'Sack of corn, eh?' I laughed. 'Hasn't your friend any breadstuffs of his own? What's all the mystery about, anyhow?'

The sheikh laughed too. 'Oh, you Ajami,' he roared, 'you are such funny fellows.'

'Someone's told you that twenty years ago and you've evidently never got over it,' I said rudely, for all this jeering at my race was beginning to get on my nerves.

'It's all right, brother,' he giggled. 'Don't get angry. Now, see here. Karim, the son of my friend the Sheikh Abdul, got lost in the desert, and he offered a reward of two camels for the boy's recovery. I have found the boy. The camels came to

313

hand yesterday morning. Naturally I must now send the imp of Eblis back to his sire.'

'But why in a sack?' I asked.

'Well, if he's not tied up, he'll jump off your animal at once you see. Will you do it?'

'Well, since you've given me your hospitality I can't refuse, can I? All the same I don't much like the job. Looks as though you'd kidnapped the little beggar yourself.'

'It's really nothing,' he assured me, 'just carrying a sack on the hind-hump of your *heri* for an hour or two.'

We ate, and after more coffee and tobacco, went to bed, or what passes for 'bed' in an Arab tent.

I dozed off almost at once, and must have been asleep for several hours, when I was rudely awakened by the sound of a shot.

'What in the name of Allah?' I began, sitting up quickly enough.

'It's all right,' barked the sheikh. 'That infernal slave of mine, son of Eblis, tried to bag your spy-glasses, and I shot him, that's all. It's a pity, for he made such good coffee.'

'Good heavens,' I cried, 'you don't mean to say you shot the poor devil for that? Where is he?'

'Just outside,' laughed the sheikh. 'Oh, you Iranis, you are funny people.'

I dragged the unfortunate man in and found he was slightly wounded in the leg. I bound it up as well as I could in the circumstances.

There wasn't much more sleep that night, for the sheikh kept me awake with his laughter at the vagaries of the Kurds.

Why on earth should anyone worry about a slave or two? He passed from one fit of cachinnation to another. And then he began to snore, giggling every now and again in his sleep.

At last came daybreak and I made a job of the slave's leg and left him some dressings and antiseptic, which he promised in a bewildered sort of way to use. Then we breakfasted and the sheikh produced the boy whom I was to take to his father at the mouth of the pass in the Anti-Lebanon mountains.

When I saw the young shaver I had misgivings.

'It is seven miles to the mouth of the pass,' said the sheikh, 'and it is now bandit-proof, as I've ascertained. All the same, you'd better keep under the shadow of the hillside as much as possible. Got everything you want?'

'As man to man, Sheikh,' I asked, 'is there any catch in this?'

'I assure you that everything's straight and above board,' replied the sheikh, looking me fairly between the eyes. 'It is not in my heart to lie to you.'

'Well, I'll take your word for it, although I know what liars you desert Arabs are,' I said. 'But remember, if there's any hanky-panky about this I'll come back – and I won't come back alone.'

For answer the sheikh merely spread out his hands in a deprecating gesture. I kicked my camel in the ribs and started, the sack with boy complete bobbing at my rear.

We hadn't gone half a mile when that infernal young limb of Shaitan began to make such a hubbub that I was compelled to stop. He yelled like a stuck pig, but what he said I couldn't hear, for the sack veiled his words.

'Look here, my young friend,' I shouted, vigorously shaking the bundle in which he was tied, 'stop that song and dance inside there, or I'll chuck you off and leave you to be eaten by the vultures.'

This speech drew a louder howl than ever, although never a word could I make out of what the brat said – I knew why later. But resolving to take no notice, I rode on. I quickly covered the two or three leagues to the mouth of the pass which, as the sheikh had assured me, seemed to have not a single bandit left in its bounds, and came, rather too suddenly for me, on the 'village' of the local big-wig Abdul, whose son and heir I was conveying home.

And only then did it strike me – dolt that I had been! – how queer it was that I should have to deliver him in a sack!

Alas, it was too late to retrace my tracks, for just as the oddity of the thing struck me, a round dozen of Arabs suddenly appeared as if from the sand, and surrounded me.

'What do you want here *effen*?' asked one, who evidently took me for a Turk. 'You can't collect taxes nowadays, you know.'

'Nothing doing in that way, brother,' I said, as cheerily as I could. 'I've brought the sheikh's son home. Can I see his worship at once?'

It wasn't necessary to inquire further. At that moment the Sheikh Abdul came running out of his tent. I introduced myself with all the formality suitable to such an occasion, and told him of my errand. In another second he was pulling at the goatskin thongs which bound up the mouth of the sack, blaspheming lustily the while and muttering endearments.

'Karim, jewel of the desert,' he cried, 'hast thou then returned to thy father at last? And, wherefore, has this monster of cruelty brought thee back to me in a foul sack, smelling of the produce of the *Feranghis*? Rest assured that he shall suffer for the affront, my little star, my lambkin.'

Now this didn't sound any too reassuring, and I began to finger my Browning.

'Sheikh Abdul,' I said, 'I'm merely a messenger. I had nothing to do whatever with the affair, I…'

'Hold thy peace,' cried Abdul in a white fury. 'Do you see those black flags fluttering on the sandhills yonder?'

'Aye, Sheikh, I see them. What of them?'

'What of them! He asks "What of them?"' howled Abdul, tugging at the thongs in a frenzy. 'Here, Turk, thy knife.'

'With pleasure, Sheikh, but I'm no Turk. I'm a Kurd.'

'A wha-a-t?' bellowed the sheikh. 'A Kurd did you say?'

'What's the matter?' I asked lamely.

'He asks what's the matter!' screamed Abdul. 'Look dog, see the black flags?'

'Less of the dog stuff,' I growled, drawing my Browning. 'You're behaving like a fool, Sheikh. I don't get you at all.'

'The black flags,' murmured one of the 'suite', 'mean that the sheikh's beautiful daughter was abducted yesterday. Unhappily, the abductor chanced to be a Kurd.'

'And if one camel bites you, do you thrash another camel?' I asked sententiously.

But my old-time illustration was drowned in a series of maledictions, for by this time the sheikh had unbound the mouth of the sack and had drawn forth its occupant, who had been gagged. Howls rent the air.

'By all the fiends in Eblis,' yelled the sheikh, 'this is not Karim.'

'Not...your son?' I cried in a strangled voice.

'That spawn of a spavined dromedary my son!' spluttered Abdul. 'Seize that robber of children.'

'Look here, Sheikh,' I said, brandishing my pistol, 'I can make every allowance for your grief and disappointment as a father, but if you try on any funny business, you're apt to swallow some sand. Now, look here. If you'll return with me to the home of your kidnapping neighbour, we'll soon put things to rights.'

'I'm going there at once,' replied the sheikh with horrid calm, 'as soon as I've impaled you and this devil's offspring here.'

'Oh, if it's like that,' I said sternly, 'let's begin the impaling now. But there'll be some plugging first.'

Abdul looked somewhat alarmed. 'Be it as you say,' he croaked angrily, 'but if I do not recover my son, beware.'

We mounted with the yelling brat before me, and sped up the pass again.

In a little more than an hour our fast-trotting camels carried us over the rocky road. We were just in time, for the sheikh and his henchmen were in the act of striking camp.

'Accursed,' yelled Abdul, 'where is my son?'

'Produce that boy,' I shouted, handing him the counterfeit monkey, 'or, by Shaitan, it's your last morning, you dirty kidnapper.'

The sheikh looked dazed. 'What's the matter?' he said in amazement. 'I don't know what you're talking about. Put away that gun, Kurd. I don't like the look of it.'

Abdul hurled himself upon the sheikh and seized him by the throat. The pair rolled over and over in the sand.

'Get up,' I said, 'and listen to reason. Sheikh, where is Abdul's boy? Produce him at once, you wretched double-crosser – and the girl as well.'

'The girl!' moaned the sheikh, nursing his left eye, in which Abdul had inserted a probing thumb. 'I can give you the boy, but there's no girl here.'

'Liar,' I said quietly. 'You pinched Abdul's daughter yesterday and had it put about that I had done the job. So that's why you giggled in your sleep last night, eh? Now bring them both here before I start shooting.'

Sulkily the sheikh ambled to his tent, and after fumbling in the women's quarters, reappeared, driving before him a boy of some seven years and a girl about sixteen.

They at once ran to Abdul who embraced them rapturously. Then he turned to the sheikh.

'Jinn of the sand-hills,' he hissed, 'where are the camels I sent you?'

'The camels,' said the sheikh lamely, 'did you send camels? Well I suppose they'll be with the herd. I must be going. Business is slack about here.'

'Take this with you,' I said, kicking him in the proper place with my heavy riding-boot, 'and please understand that next time you meet a Kurd, you can't do him down as you tried to do me.'

As we rode off, a bullet or two whizzed past. I replied with my Browning, but the firing soon ceased.

The sheikh turned to me. 'Kurd,' he said, with a noble air, 'you are a hero. How I have misjudged you! But to make amends I shall bestow upon you my daughter's hand.'

'Sorry, Abdul,' I replied, 'but I am already married.'

'But do the Kurds not have more than one wife?' he asked in amazement.

'Not if we can help it,' I assured him. 'It's kind of you, very thoughtful indeed, but I must be getting on to Baalbec.'

'To Baalbec! But there's nothing doing there.'

'There's the ruins – nice quiet spot.'

'The ruins!' murmured the sheikh. 'Allah be good to him, for the poor Kurd is crazy after all!'

From: *Fifty Enthralling Stories*
From the Mysterious East
The Sirdar Ikbal Ali Shah

Flight of the Birdmen

JUST BEFORE HE died, Ramón's father had called his young son to where he was lying.

The old man had been in a trance for many days, getting weaker and weaker. Even though he was a respected shaman and a healer, his family knew he was about to die. He had finished his work in this illusory world.

Moments before he slipped away, he filled his lungs for the last time, and blew into Ramón's face.

'That breath...' said Ramón, squinting, 'that breath passed on to me *la sabiduría de la ayahuasca*, the knowledge of *ayahuasca*.'

'How long ago did your father die?'

Ramón thought for a moment.

'*Hace mucho tiempo*, a long time ago,' he said. 'I was no more than a child. I still had much to learn.'

'Without your father, who taught you?'

'The *ayahuasca* taught me,' he said, 'and it told me to speak to the trees and plants in the forest. They welcomed me, telling me how to use them. *Ayahuasca* is the pass which opens all secrets,' Ramón said. 'It's the most powerful medicine there is.'

When the third batch of water had more or less evaporated from the cauldron, Ramón filtered away the remaining liquid. It was the colour of caramel.

'We will leave it to cool,' he said, 'and when there is darkness, we can drink.'

I asked Ramón about the rumour that he could fly.

He widened his eyes and put a hand to the nape of his neck.

'*Ayahuasca* is very strong,' he said. 'I have already told you that. It can be used in many ways – as a purger of evil, as a medicine, a solver of problems... It can take you back in time, or into the future, show you miracles, transform you into a boa constrictor or a leopard.'

'What about flying... if you take *ayahuasca* can you actually fly?'

Ramón looked through me with his gaze, but said nothing.

I found myself thinking about *ayahuasca* and hallucinogens. I knew that my friends would give me pointed looks if they heard I was about to consume a mind-altering substance. In the West there's an extraordinary misunderstanding. Most people forget or merely ignore the link between plants and society. They may be condemning you while they're smoking a cigarette, or drinking a bottle of beer – both, of course, are made from plants which when smoked or fermented alter the state of the mind.

In our world we have grown away from the land and scorn natural preparations. Hallucinogens have a bad reputation, and rightly so. They are constantly misused by us in societies which are almost incapable of using anything correctly. Active ingredients are stripped out from plants and taken in massive doses for stimulation's sake. But the Shuar's use of *ayahuasca* is different. It is a medicinal plant used in the context of a specific culture. It is employed in unison with a rigid structure of ritual, which supports it as a framework. It is taken for answers, not to get high.

In the West people are preoccupied with the vision or sensation they may get by taking a drug. They don't give thought to the role of the concoction in healing, or its use as a tool. The shamans of the Amazon only take *ayahuasca* or any other hallucinogen when there's a reason to take it. When I hear of people in Europe experimenting with *ayahuasca*, it turns my blood cold. The plant-derived experience is only part of the equation, the other part being the ritual.

Our short-sighted approach is not entirely our fault. Compared with Asia or the New World, Europe has very few plant species. North America has a wide variety of remarkable species but, tragically, when the Europeans slaughtered their way across that continent, they destroyed the Native American knowledge which understood them, and replaced it with a crippled European system, touted by snake-oil salesmen. It must have put American medicine back centuries.

On a moonless night, a clearing in the jungle is very dark indeed. Save for the glint of the fireflies, or the odd flicker of a home-made wick burning in kerosene, there is blackness. Those who are not evangelists with late-night prayer sessions go to sleep soon after dusk. They rise long before it gets light.

Alberto sloped away to find a place to sleep. He had been feeling queasy since eating my beetle. The misunderstanding had cost me a great sum but, as I pondered it, I had got my just deserts. I should have released the insects when I'd had the chance.

Once Enrique had prayed quietly for our salvation, he followed the others to bed. Richard said to call him if I became distressed during the *ayahuasca* session. It struck me then that he had always appeared reluctant to talk of his own experiences on the hallucinogen while, at the same time, regarding the brew with the utmost gravity. I think he felt that *ayahuasca* was something which had to be tried to be understood. There was no point in him offering his own tales until I had been initiated. Without another word he wandered down to the tannin-brown water to swim. Only a man of Richard's resolution would have dared to swim there in the darkness.

Ramón and I were suddenly alone.

We were sitting at the far end of the *maloca*. It was a still night lit by a crescent moon. A pair of candles were burning before us, their flames perpendicular. In their light I saw the objects of ritual lying by the shaman's knee: a gourd of *ayahuasca*, a white enamel mug, a cloth bag, and a *chacapa*, the dried leaf rattle which I'd seen being used near Iquitos.

Ramón lit a pipe of *mapacho* and drew on it until his chest was filled to capacity. He blew the smoke at me. I tried to relax. The *maestro* opened up the cloth pouch and fished out a skull. It had long, threatening fangs at the front. I recognized it as a jaguar's skull. Sucking on his pipe a second time, Ramón blew down onto it. I watched as the swirls of grey smoke swept over the bone, before diffusing into the night.

Then, wiping his mouth with his hand, Ramón dipped the tin mess mug into the *ayahuasca*. He stirred the liquid with the cup, filling it almost to the top. I swallowed hard. The shaman put the mug to his lips and, taking small sips, drank the liquid. He leaned back, closing his eyes for a moment, breathing in through his nose. Stirring the cup in the brew a second time, he filled it again. I watched him in the dimness. With the brilliant macaw feather corona wrapped around his head, his face painted red with *achiote*, and the jaguar skull at his ankles, he made for a fearful sight.

He looked across at me, and then tipped a little of the dark liquid from the cup back into the gourd.

'This *ayahuasca* is special,' he said softly. 'I have made it with *toé*, *datura*. *Volarás muy lejos*, you will fly far.'

'But maestro,' I faltered, '*datura* will kill me. It is too strong.'

'I told you,' he replied, 'when you take *ayahuasca*, you die.'

He handed me the cup. I drank it in sips, as he had done. It tasted bitter, like the sap of a tree. Although not pleasant, it was bearable. As the last drops of *ayahuasca* made their way down into my stomach, the shaman blew out the candles. There was no light now, only the glow of his pipe when he inhaled.

Taking up the *chacapa*, he rattled it, at the same time breaking into a soft whirring chant. The tone was like an old gramophone player stuck on a single note. I knew it took time for the *ayahuasca* to take effect. At first I tried to keep up with the chemistry of the reaction. The harmaline would be inhibiting the monoamine-oxidase, I thought, allowing the hallucinogens to enter my blood. The illusions would begin shortly.

I took a series of deep breaths, relaxing my shoulders and arms, leaning backwards. Then I focused on the sound of the leaf-rattle and the smell of the *mapacho* smoke. My senses were heightened. I could hear the sound of Ramón's youngest child snoring at the far end of the *maloca*. The sound was almost deafening.

A few more minutes drifted by. I tried to think of the chemistry again. But I was no longer alert. The base of my spine felt warm, as if a hand was pressing on it. I could not focus my mind now, and I was losing a sense of space. A few more minutes passed, filled with the hum of the shaman's chant, the smoke, and the rustle of dried leaves. With every second I became more disorientated. My eyes had adjusted to the darkness. I gazed up at the eaves of the thatch, which seemed bowed inwards and cruelly distorted. So I peered out from the longhouse, up at the stars. They were bright, and they were constant. I thanked the stars for being there.

Then the *ayahuasca* took effect.

My stomach was signalling to my mind. I was about to be violently sick. I had been poisoned and had to get out of the longhouse.

Scrambling on my hands and knees, I crawled haplessly to the ladder. I was beginning to panic. My chest muscles were tense with fear. I could no longer trust my eyes. What they showed me was a distorted mess of colours and shapes. I closed them, feeling my way down the tree trunk ladder.

My bare feet were now treading in the mud. Rejoicing that I was on the ground I staggered, crawling, stumbling, into the undergrowth. Poison was in my blood. It was killing me. I was dying. The *ayahuasca* had tricked me. Fear took over. My chest sucked in air and I retched. I retched like I have never retched before. A flood of liquid spewed from my mouth. Panting hard, I reassured myself. The *ayahuasca* had been a mistake, I told myself. As soon as it was light I would hurry away from Ramón and the jungle. Within a few days I'd be back in a big city.

The reassurances did nothing to stop the reaction. I retched again, my stomach twisting itself in knots to purge the hideous brew. As I retched, my mind warned of more purging. This time from the rear end. In the nick of time I ripped down my shorts, just as my bowels opened.

Crouching there in the undergrowth of a Shuar village, unable to control my alimentary canal, I felt that this must be as bad as life can get. As I vomited, I crapped. And as I crapped, I vomited. All the while the undergrowth's nightlife was wondering what was going on. Frogs were jumping up, touching my buttocks with their heads. Moths and other winged insects were impaling themselves on the flow of faeces.

Yet, while in the undergrowth, I knew I was safe. There may have been frogs and moths, but I could lie low there and regroup. I coaxed myself to relax and, when the worst of the purging was over, I crawled back through the mud and up the ladder.

Ramón's chanting hadn't waned. The rustling of his *chacapa* and the low register of his voice dispersed. I took my place again, cross-legged on the hard bamboo floor. Soon after, a second bout of purging overcame me. Scurrying fitfully across the floor, down the ladder and through the mud, I found sanctuary back with the frogs. I glanced up at the stars, drunk and off-balance, questioning how they could allow such a predicament.

Back on the bamboo floor, as Ramón's smoke enveloped me, I sensed the *ayahuasca* moving on to the next phase. The hallucinations had begun. I leaned back, my eyes closed, my lungs breathing the dastardly *mapacho* smoke. It began with my arms sensing warmth, as the base of my spine had done. I questioned how anyone could take *ayahuasca* for pleasure. As I lay there, wondering, my body changed.

My shoulder sockets were growing warmer, as my arms evolved. They transformed from being feeble, feckless limbs. The bones altered first. I could see them. I watched astounded as they grew more delicate, shedding themselves of my sunburnt skin. After the bones, came the muscles – colossal ones, like those of a body builder. Only then, when my arms were fleshed with tremendous arteries and veins, did the final covering emerge – feathers.

White, fluffy feathers.

I might have panicked, but the shaman's chanting gave a framework to the experience. His song was mournful, like the dirge at a funeral. Appropriate, for I was dead. I could not distinguish the words, the individual sounds. But, despite this, they made perfect sense. The incantations were beyond a language. They were protecting me… comforting, teaching. I breathed in the sound, inhaling it until my diaphragm was taut.

The song was speaking to me in a language without a voice. It was ordering me to thrust my wings outwards, to soar up, high into the air. I called back that I did not know how to fly. The sound of the *chacapa* touched my wings and dragged them up on a cushion of air. I laughed maniacally. I was flying. My wings moved with unequalled ease. There was none of the frantic, feverish motion of a man emulating a bird in flight.

This flight was natural, an obvious sensation. Glancing down, I saw the desert far below. I saw *el colibrí*, the hummingbird. I was at Nazca. Circling round the symbols on that plain I understood the stupidity of the Western mind. *Ayahuasca* was the key which decoded the etchings, just as *datura* explained the witches' flight. Without one, the other had no meaning.

I flew on, guided by the *chacapa*'s sound, soothed by a spray of saliva from the shaman's lips. The colours were bright – purples and blues, yellows and pinks. I was on the far side of a magnificent wall, flying in a no-man's land of illusion. I felt the rush of air on my face, and learned to control my wings by tilting their edges up and down. Ramón was with me. He said this was no illusion, but was the real world. We had died and come to life. I was alive for the first time. I was meant to fly, to be a part of the air. I sensed the shaman's energy, the force of his knowledge. I could not see him, but I knew he was there. I was Icarus and he Daedalus. But our wings were not made of wax and feathers. They were living. We were birds, yet we were men; we were men, but birds.

*

WE FLEW FOR many hours.

I do not remember when the journey ended, or the moment I awoke. Sunlight streamed through the morning rain. I strained to open my eyes, retched, and rolled onto my back. The *maloca*'s palm floor was as hard as quartz.

At my sides, my arms ached, as if they had been flayed with a whip.

I roused the fingers of my left hand.

They were grasping something.

Still lying on my back, I raised the hand to my face.

In its grip was a long feather.

Three triangular notches were missing from the leading edge.

It had been dipped in blood.

From: *Trail of Feathers*
Tahir Shah

Hypocrisy

Q: WHY SHOULD a spiritual master be treated with respect and thought of with awe and humility?

A: Not for him, but for ourselves. It is the posture of mind which accompanies the feeling of respect which attunes us to reality and banishes self-satisfaction. Just as when people mourn the dead they are doing so because of themselves – the dead are unaffected by it – so, too, when people are too self-centred they cannot learn. They have to think of others as more important than themselves.

People sometimes become too man-worshipping, however, and think too much of their spiritual teacher. It is because of the need to balance the attitude to get it just right that this story of the sanctimonious dervish is told:

There was once a religious man, who liked to think of himself as a true dervish. He liked, too, to abide by all the rules of the divine and secular laws, and because he felt pride at this he became, like so many other people before and since, an unconscious hypocrite. This state, quite naturally, prevented him making any real progress on the spiritual path, and an angel decided to help him out of his difficulty.

One day, therefore, when the dervish was looking at a condemned man being led past his house, and feeling how right it was that the miscreant should suffer, the angel appeared before him.

The apparition said:

'For imagining sanctimoniousness to be real piety, you are condemned to wander the face of the earth, without hope of salvation, until buds shall appear and blossom on a dead branch!'

The dervish was at first indignant, and thought that the angel must be an impostor. Then, as events forced him from his home and onto the public streets, he realized that there might be some truth in the matter.

There was an old blasted oak tree at the top of a hill, which seemed completely dead, and the allegedly pious man used to go to look at this, pondering his fate and wondering about his potential.

One day he ran into a barber on the road. The barber said, 'If I do not keep in practice, I shall not be able to get a job when I get to my destination. May I shave you?'

The semi-dervish at first felt affronted that his reverend beard should be assailed; but suddenly the thought struck him that he was, after all, a fraud, and there was no point in keeping a beard if the man behind it had not attained perfection. So he agreed, and the barber shaved his beard off.

It was at that moment that the roots of the tree started to take in moisture and nutrition.

Then the dervish saw a very poor man walking along the road, without a rag to cover him. 'All I have myself,' he said to himself, 'is this patched dervish cloak…' Then he remembered that the sign of the patched cloak was to indicate his state, and yet his state was one of outward show while he wore it. So he took the cloak off and shared it with the poor wayfarer.

Then it was the sap began to rise into the trunk of the tree on the top of the hill.

Not long afterwards the dervish was sitting under the tree when two seekers-after-truth came along. Seeing this devout-looking figure before them, they asked him to teach them something. He said:

'What I can teach you is that whenever you see anyone who looks devout, who wears a beard, who is glad to teach you, who allows people to address him by religious titles; you are probably dealing with a fraud!'

At that moment buds appeared on the branches of the tree, and almost immediately afterwards, they burst into flower.

Missed the Point

A very distinguished religious figure was here today.

I asked him how he dealt with the fact that many of his ancient traditions were completely unacceptable to the people of today.

'That is easy enough,' he said, 'because I simply do not mention such things. There are plenty of beliefs, other than those you mention, which we can work upon.'

'But,' I went on, 'how can you manage when people insist upon discussing matters which contemporary knowledge finds anachronistic?'

'I simply say,' he told me, 'that these are minor points, and that they are worrying too much about them…'

All this reminds me of a tale. Read it and decide whether our prelate is not doing much the same as the cook in the story:

Irrelevant

There was once a cook who was surprised by his mistress while straining soup through one of her husband's socks.

'Whatever are you doing with the Master's socks?' she cried out in alarm.

'Nothing to worry about, Mistress,' said the cook 'as they are not his clean ones!'

Personally, I prefer the retort of Dr. Samuel Johnson, when asked by a lady why he had defined the word 'pastern' as 'a horse's knee'.

'Sheer ignorance, Madam,' he said.

Black and Blue

One of the most interesting – and little-known – facts about higher knowledge is that its pursuit is as much dependent upon exclusion as inclusion. It is as important to exclude certain elements as it is to include others. You may think that all you have to do is to find the right formulae of belief, ritual, exercise, but if you do not at the same time avoid doing or thinking or practising certain things, these unexcluded things can – often do – act as contaminants to your efforts. This is one of the functions of real teachers: to tell you what to avoid as well as what to do. Equally, of course, you can tell who is a real teacher and who is not, as often as not, by whether the teacher is merely giving you a bundle of instructions (prayers, meditations, fasting, concentration, and so on) and hence not excluding, or whether he is also telling you what should be avoided. The latter admonitions will deal with the time and places, the company and the response to reactions, which are part of the authentic knowledge of the real teacher.

In one story which is used as an analogy of this, a woman tells her husband to go to a reputed teacher, and to obey him in every particular. He is, in fact, to repeat everything that the teacher says. When the man arrives at the sage's house, the venerable one says: 'Who are you?'

'Who are you?' repeats the man.

'What do you mean?' continues the teacher, and the would-be student echoes, 'What do you mean?'

After a few exchanges of this kind, the sage orders the man to be beaten and thrown out. When he arrives home, the wife asks how he got on. 'Well enough,' says the husband, 'but I don't know how much more of this I can stand: they have beaten me black and blue, and this is only my first lesson!'

Slavish imitation, as the story tries to inform us, results in nothing, and may even be harmful. None of this is helped by the ordinary human mimetic habit, in which people very often copy the manners, acts and even dress of those whom they esteem.

The Barriers

A man is anxious to free himself from a prison, and yet he strengthens the bars. Will he escape? These bars are the habits of depending only upon the secondary self, the desire for emotional stimulus and greed.

Supposing someone were to want to rise above the surface of the water but persisted in holding on to stones at the bottom of the sea. What would happen to him and what would you call him? These are the attachments to outworn and irrelevant systems, ideas and slogans.

Suppose someone were to want to grow taller, but kept himself in a box which dwarfed his growth? This box is the reliance upon cults and organizations which dwarf people's capacities.

Supposing, again, that someone were to think that he wanted to travel, but yet placed great weights on his feet so that he could not walk or even move. What would you call such a person? Those weights are the desires for attention and for getting something before the time is right.

Supposing, yet again, that some people were to aver that they wanted to be better people, yet they constantly stole what belonged to others and told lies, working against being better in any way. What would you call such people? Those actions are paralleled by believing that one will get paid twice: once by feeling good after doing something good, and once in a future life.

Supposing, finally, that there were people who said that they wanted to see around them, yet who persisted in wearing blinkers, what would you call them? Those barriers are the habit of mixing attractive but useless formulae and totems with specific teachings.

Undigested

It is extremely important to absorb what one is taught, not just to taste it, or swallow it.

People generally are in such a hurry that they do not allow themselves to digest materials which, however, can be useful only if absorbed.

There is a parable about this, which helps to fix it in the memory; it is the story of the

Pieces of Gold

There was once a greedy miser who went to a king regularly and begged from him. Each time he went to the king, he came away with a piece of gold, which he had grabbed from the monarch's hand and stuffed into the recesses of his cloak.

As soon as he got home, he would drop the coin into a hole under the hearth.

One day the miser died, as we must all die.

When his money was found, it was noticed that on each coin was the name of the king, and all the treasure was returned to him.

Apricot Pies

There was once, in Afghanistan, an old woman who had been famous for thirty years for the deliciousness of her apricot pies. Everyone for miles around knew of the pies, and ate them whenever they could. Over the years, hundreds badgered her for the recipe.

She went on making the pies, in the soft-fruit season every year; she handed out pies right and left – but she would not tell anyone the recipe.

One day, fearing that the woman might die with her secret untold, a rich man – who was also something of a miser as well as a lover of apricot pies – offered a reward of a hundred gold pieces for the secret.

He could find nobody who could bake pies like the old woman, although there were plenty of people who clamoured for the reward, pretending that they could. Finally, however, he was surprised to find the woman herself at his door, offering to sell the recipe.

'I thought you would never tell anyone,' he stammered.

'Ah,' said the ancient one, 'I wanted to find a sign of sincerity first.'

'But how do you know that I am sincere?' asked the miser.

'You,' said the lady, 'are a man in love with gold. To be prepared to part with *any* of it, let alone a hundred gold pieces, for anything shows, in your own terms at least, that you are sincere. That is the nearest to real sincerity that we can arrive at in this region, it seems – so I shall give you the secret.'

The rich man was beside himself with delight. He took up a pen and a piece of paper and asked the woman to dictate. 'You won't need pen and paper,' she said, 'since there is nothing much to tell. I pick apricots, free, from charitable people's trees. Then I add water and a little honey – and that's all there is to it.'

'But that's how everyone else makes apricot pie!' shouted the man. 'I'm certainly not going to give you a hundred *ashrafis* for telling me that.'

'Take it or leave it,' said the woman.

'It's a lot of nonsense,' said the miser, 'but if the secret is not in the contents, it must be in the pie-crust. How do you make that?'

She smiled. 'I don't make it at all. I go to the village baker and ask him for some left-over pastry, cover the dish with it, and have him put it in his oven with the bread he bakes, and there you are.'

'But there must be something special about the pies,' said the man, 'and I want to find out what it is.'

'Very well,' she said, 'follow me and do as I do, and we'll see how you manage. We'll see whether you know what a recipe is.'

Together they went on a tour of the local apricot orchards. The old woman, as is the custom in those parts, was admitted free of charge, while the miser had to pay a copper coin before being allowed to pick as many apricots as he wished.

They took their dishes to the baker, and had him put some of his left-over pastry on the tops. Then they settled down to wait, until the pies were ready.

When the pies were cooked and had cooled, they tasted them. The old woman's one was delicious. But the pie made from the fruit collected by the miser was very ordinary indeed.

He shook his head in perplexity, and then started to berate the woman, calling her a fraud who had introduced some secret ingredient, then a fool who would not give the secret out, and finally a witch in contact with evil powers.

When he had exhausted himself, and was sitting on a bench outside the bakery, the old woman smiled again. 'After your huffing and puffing, after your superior airs and reliance upon money, after all that nonsense rooted in the disappointment of false expectations,' she said, 'I'll tell you where you went wrong.

'As you know, poor people are allowed to collect as much fruit as they wish from our orchards. In appreciation of this, I have never picked the ripe and perfect fruit for my pies, because the farmer is entitled to keep the best fruit to sell so that he can support his family.

'So I have always chosen the unripe and the over-ripe apricots, blended together, for my pies. That is the secret of their wonderful taste. You, on the other hand, are so greedy, for perfection and for gain, that you – like everyone else who has sought my secret – always picked the most attractive fruit.

'The result was ordinary apricot pies.'

With these words, she tucked the bag of gold pieces in her belt, and went on her way.

The greed, anxiety and compulsion to compare Sufi teachings with prior assumptions, conspicuous in the reactions of many students, causes parsimony of all kinds, produces barriers to understanding and blinds people to things which are perfectly obvious to those who approach the teachings in a simpler manner.

Loading and Unloading

When someone learns something from someone else, and starts to teach what he has learned, a situation exists which we should look at very carefully, because most people do not understand what is happening.

Forget for the moment that it is 'teaching' that we are talking about. The human being, at a far more basic level, 'gets' something from someone else. This thing may be a blow, information, money, the idea that he has had an experience.

As soon as this thing is 'got' or believed to be 'got', the next, automatic move of the human being is to try to pass it on. This is because the human is a communicator, or operates as such.

It is only at a later stage (even if this stage comes after only two seconds) that the individual decides that he has 'got' knowledge which he must communicate BECAUSE IT IS KNOWLEDGE. Because he is unaware of this characteristic, he will imagine that it is the fact that it is knowledge which prompted him to want to communicate it.

A certain, brief, verification of this is to be found in watching small children. They try to communicate. They try to get, and to give to others, any sort of object. And they seek a response.

Because of the socially determined ethic, of course, this getting and giving often reaps the richest rewards. A person getting a lot of money and giving most of it away will earn plaudits and honours.

Another important part of the getting-giving process is when ideas are offered to people. You often find that people who have ideas to communicate (whether these are of any value or not) will spurn or refuse to entertain other ideas. This is often because they are already 'getting' their ideas from somewhere, or have got them, and their giving-out process is at work.

We are all familiar with the situation of people wanting to hold forth on some subject and refusing to listen to anything else. This is exactly what happens when a person is being interrupted during his 'unloading' phase. This helps us to understand why people are sometimes bigoted. They are to all appearances intractable, but in fact what they are saying is: 'I am operating my unloading phase, do not interrupt it.' This comes out as 'Smith's ideas are of no importance'; or 'that is irrelevant to our theme', and so on.

Ignorance of the existence and operation of this phenomenon causes people almost to live in a dream: because they are wondering why Smith's ideas are of no importance, or why this or that is irrelevant. They should instead realize that they should not be interrupting an unloading process.

Diet of Grapes

Once upon a time, in the days of long ago, there was a wise and powerful prince, who lived within a walled estate. His palace was surrounded by orchards and gardens, and he was generally thought, because he did not explain his actions, to be uncaring of the people's interests, and neglectful of his duty to strive to improve himself. Those people who were considered wise were unable to understand him, and spoke against him. Those who knew little about him thought that he was bereft of qualities. Those who wished to curry favour praised him, but since such people are generally superficialists, this did not extend his repute far.

Now the territory in which this prince lived was, as is the way of life, attacked by barbarians, who successively reduced the neighbouring principalities until they were fast approaching his own. Time and again the prince sent messages to the other rulers, asking them to ally themselves with him against the invaders, but such was their arrogance, their ignorance of him, or their other tendencies, that they took no heed.

This behaviour on the part of his neighbours did not seem to distress the prince. All he said was, 'The burden of wisdom is almost too much to bear. I have, as a truthful man, been forced to tell them that I have to be their leader if the war is to be won in co-operation with them. Naturally they will not accept such a condition. Therefore the only option is to wait until the Second Stage.'

The barbarians continued to advance, until those who had been opposing them, in ever-increasing numbers, fell back upon the domain of our prince to make a last stand. They were the remnants of the knights and soldiers of every one of the vanquished princes.

Thus it was that one day when the prince was resting, his minister approached him and, after making the customary obeisance, said:

'O Point towards which the Compass turns: we have been unable to prevent the remnants of the defending armies from climbing the walls of the Domain, in their flight. They are now huddled in the vineyards, covered in mud and blood, in the last stages of exhaustion.'

The prince raised his head. 'And what else?' he asked.

'And,' continued the minister, 'they are too exhausted even to eat or to attend to their wounds. They are now lying fast asleep, like dead men, while the enemy masses without.'

'Very well,' said the prince, 'now you have made your report, you may withdraw. Return to me the day after tomorrow, to describe conditions then.'

The minister, though knowing that his master was possessed of wisdom, wondered why the prince did not take some action to defend the domain, but, like a good servant, made his salutation and withdrew.

Two days later he again approached the prince and said:

'Lord of Princeliness! I have come as instructed.'

'Give your report,' answered the prince.

'The exhausted warriors,' said the minister, 'have now slept for two days.'

'And what are they doing?' the prince asked.

'May your life be extended!' said the minister. 'They are now so famished that they are devouring grass, leaves and raw grapes.'

'Very good,' said the prince. 'Return in a further day and give me an account of conditions.'

The next day the minister announced: 'High Presence! The lords, warriors and ordinary people who fled to our domain are now eating the ripe grapes, having restored themselves somewhat.'

'Continue your report tomorrow, at midday,' said his master.

The day after, the minister said, 'May your Shadow never grow less! The refugees are now selecting the best grapes and eating them.'

'Excellent,' said the prince. 'Now call them to me, and I shall prepare them for the victory against the barbarians, for they are ready. Before this, they were in no condition to struggle, and had to get what nutrition they could from us. If we leave it any later, they will be so sated that they will start to argue among themselves, and will not listen to us. Prepare for victory!'

And that is the tale of the wise prince whose actions nobody understood. When the final battle came, and the barbarians were slaughtered, the victorious army fell out with one another. Returning to their own lands, their historians wrote conflicting accounts of what had passed. All accounts had this in common: they misunderstood the prince.

Attention

A teaching dervish was once asked why it was that the questioner found it so hard to keep awake, to remember the things which he had read or been told. In reply the dervish gave this lesson:

'There was once a dervish who used to lecture regularly before a group of people among whom were an old man accompanied by his grandson, a small boy.

'And, regularly as clockwork, the ancient one used to fall asleep as soon as the dervish had got into his stride.

'One day the dervish had an idea. After the meeting he took the boy aside and said, "I'll give you a silver piece if you jog your grandfather awake every time he falls asleep during my lectures." The boy accepted.

'For three meetings in succession, the old man was nudged every time his eyes closed, and the dervish was pleased.

'On the fourth week, however, the grandfather fell fast asleep, just as before.

'Taking the boy aside after that meeting, the dervish said, "I thought you were going to keep the old man awake for a silver piece?"

'"That's right," said the boy, "but when I told him, he offered me three silver pieces not to do it."

'And,' continued the dervish who was telling the tale, 'the single silver piece is your desire to pay attention. The three are your natural laziness, your habits and your unobserved opposition to the truth.'

From: *The Commanding Self*
Idries Shah

Fairies and Fairy-tales of Persia

THE OCCULT MARVELS of Persia are inalienably associated with the spirit race who, in order to make their nature more plain to European readers, it has been the custom to call fairies. It is, of course, a moot point what the word 'fairy' actually means, but a recent authority has put it upon record that English people employ the name in a manner wholly at variance with its derivation.

The word 'fairy', indeed, means a condition of enchantment, a magical effluence not unlike the Polynesian *mana*, and certainly cannot be applied to a supernatural being, the correct term for which in English is 'fay'. This word comes from old French *fae*, which again is to be referred to Latin *fata*, a fate, a supernatural protector. In such a sense, then, we can truly say that the Latin fates and the French and English fays are the same manifestation, that is they are spiritual entities who inhabit the world of faerie or magic and in this they bear a close resemblance to the various classes of Oriental spirits who, for the sake of a common denomination, we may designate fairies.

It is not essential that the fairy should be a power for good, and just as fays in Great Britain and France are frequently most malicious in disposition, so we find the supernatural agencies of Eastern countries frequently very vindictive in character. Among the Arabs, the Moghrebi is a sorcerer who has converse with demons, and from one of these men I received a good deal of information regarding the jinn, who are as truly fairies as those, let us say, of Brittany. He told me that the jinn were a pre-Adamite race who had lived hundreds of years before Adam and who, like the European Salamanders, were created out of fire. They were not immortal, and like the fairies must one day die, and they ate, drank and had children like mortal folk, lived in cities of their own and were ruled over by kings or sultans. They could assume any form they chose and were fond of haunting ruins, cross-roads, market-places and savage and desert vicinities. It is a comparatively simple matter, said my sorcerer, to bring them under the dominion of spells or talismans, and this made clear to me the numerous passages in Eastern tales where the jinns act as the complacent servants of anyone who may happen to possess a talisman which gives him sovereignty over them.

The word *jinn* comes from an Arabic term derived from a root signifying to 'veil' or 'conceal', Fruzabadi, author of the *Camus*, says: 'The word *jinn* signifies any spiritual being concealed from all our senses and, for that reason, the converse of a material being.' The Arabs speak of good and bad jinn, and since the establishment of Islam seem to have no more belief in them than the majority of the people in this country have in the existence of fairies, although it is only correct to say that Mussulman theologians maintain their existence as superhuman beings.

The Divs of ancient Persia resemble the European fairies even more than the jinn. They also are said to be pre-Adamite. The male *divs* seem to be of the nature of fiends or sprites, whereas the female, who are known as *peris*, are of gentler and more amiable disposition. Their chieftainess was Gian ben Gian whose dominion was disturbed by Eblis, the Satan of the Qur'an, who was the head of the rebellious angels and who formerly held dominion over the whole race of jinn.

The Daivers of the Hindus seem to be identical with the Persian *divs*. Their sphere is known as Daiver-Logum, and they number three hundred and thirty millions. Their king is Daivuntren or Indiren, whose court is capacious enough to contain the whole of his people. They are the sworn enemies of the giants, against whom they maintain feuds dating from antediluvian times. There are numerous species of Daivers, as for example the *kinnerar*, or players on musical instruments, the *kinprusher* or servants, who are represented with wings and angels' faces, the *paunner*, or jugglers, who amuse them, whilst others uphold the eight sides of the world. The exploits of these may be read of in the Zend Avesta.

The Burmese *nat* is a wood spirit for whom the villagers leave oblations of food and drink precisely as some people in France, England and Scotland were in the habit of doing only about a generation ago. He dwells in the thick jungle, and on occasion takes the forms of wild beasts just as the fairies did. It seems to me a striking illustration of the theory that the European fairies were probably the dead that the *nats* should be confounded with the departed. Also when the Burman wishes a wish he appeals to the *nats* in the hope that it may be fulfilled, in precisely the same manner as the European peasant or child appeals to the fairies to grant his desire. The *nat*, too, like the fays of France, Britain and Ireland is tricky and mischievous, not to say malicious. These spirits, too, are often conjured up by necromancers and this seems to me an important linking up of the idea of the fairies with that of Spiritualism.

After examing the question of Eastern spiritism with considerable detail, I have come to the conclusion that the great mass of it derives from Babylonia. Babylonia has a well-marked demonology, the figures of which seem to have been distributed through Oriental lands generally. Babylonia was indeed the mother of Eastern magic and witchcraft. Each of its gods was accompanied by groups of demons; the spirits of disease, for example, were the 'beloved sons of Bel', the fates were the seven daughters of Anu, the seven storm demons, including the dragon and serpent, belonged to the brood of Ea who was the great magician among the gods. His sway over the forces of nature was procured by the performance of magical rites. Almost any place, from a temple to a reed hut, was a suitable spot in which to conjure him. There was a class of priests in Babylonia known as the Asipu, who dealt almost entirely with magical things, and it was their business not only to drive out demons but to placate them and consult them if necessary. Demons haunted every department of life, and those which were connected with disease flourished exceedingly. To cure toothache, for instance, it was necessary to know 'the legend of the worm' which, vampire-like, absorbed the blood of victims and attached itself to the gums. When the worm heard the legend repeated it came under the power of the magician and was dismissed to the marshes while Ea was invoked to smite it.

But of all the extraordinary spirits which originated in Babylon, Baphomet appears to me to be the most curious. This spirit, indeed, has almost encircled the earth, for not only was he known in Palestine and the Mediterranean, but his worship was brought to England and Scotland and, at a much later date, to America. He is, of course, the goat-god of the ancient Babylonians, and at the same time of the Witches' Sabbath a most ancient deity who was probably at one time worshipped by people who lived the life of herdsmen and who drew their chief sustenance from goats' flesh and milk. Most occultists will remember that the Baphomet was the god of the Templars whom they were set to worship in their secret lodges. By some occultists it has been described as a Pantheistic figure of the Absolute. But the idol or head which the Templars are said to have worshipped they certainly procured in Palestine or Syria. Many Templars confessed to having seen this idol. Some said it was a frightful head with long beard and sparkling eyes, others that it was a man's skull. Some described it as having three faces, while according to others the idol had four feet.

The Baphomet belonging to the Templar order at Paris was said to be a silver head with two faces and a beard. Many Templars testify to having seen this idol and having been told to worship it by the officials of the lodges. But the majority of Templars said that they had heard this head spoken of but that they had never seen it personally. At the trial of the English Templars, however, it came out that there were four Baphomets in England, one in London in the Sacristy of the Temple, another at Bristelham, a third at Bruern, in Lincolnshire, and a fourth north of the Humber. The name Baphomet was supposed to be derived from that of Mahomet, but this seems improbable. He is found throughout India, where the goat is the sacred animal which carries saints and riches to heaven as well as the sacrificial beast of the lowest castes in the Carnatic.

This serves to show how, from a common centre, a belief in which there is any original force can become disseminated. Indeed the Baphomet reached America, where in modern times it was most assuredly found in certain lodges of the Reformed Palladium Rite, especially, it is understood, at Charlestown.

Demonism is rampant in Japan despite its veneer of civilization. In the mountains and forests are birdlike gnomes who frequently beset wayfaring men and women and steal away their wits. There are mountain men, huge, hairy creatures, not unlike the brownies of Scottish folklore who make sudden descents upon villages and have a knack of carrying their victims off on their backs for many miles before casting them from a great height to the earth beneath. Demon foxes, too, beset the unwary traveller. These are gifted with miraculous vision and hearing, and can read the thoughts of all men. These are also dowered with the capacity for shape-changing, and, loving to delude mankind, frequently take the form of beautiful women, whose embrace means madness or death. The cat is the Japanese vampire.

It is an outcast, as it did not weep upon the death of Buddha. But, oddly enough, sailors esteem it, as it is thought to have the power to ward off the evil spirits which infest the sea. But perhaps the most horrible department of Japanese enchantment, which may well be included in an article dealing with the belief in fairies and weird doings, is that which treats of the coming to life through the long, dark nights of bronze and stone images of dragons, horses and deer, which terrorize the people and are only laid to rest by summary decapitation. These are supposed to be inhabited by the souls of the living who may be dreaming or sunk in reverie.

All this seems to me to point to the circumstance that, so long as a race remains in a condition of savagery, its supernatural beings partake more of the nature of demons than fairies proper, and that it is only when it reaches the agricultural stage of development that it discovers those tendencies so unalterably associated in the West with the fairy folk. Indeed we can trace the development of fairies, as we know them, through the different stages of savage and semi-civilized life. Thus, in the less frequented parts of Burmah and China they are little better than demons, ever ready to wreak their spite upon the human race, and this, I believe, accounts for the malicious tendency of many Occidental fays.

In the folklore of the desert races, Arabs and other Semites, the demonic character is less apparent, and although the Slavs and Balkan peoples possess spirits of distinctly fiendish aspect and character, these are softer and less savage than the sprites of their Eastern neighbours. We come at last to the Teutonic spirits of house and field and their French counterparts, who strikingly resemble the inhabitants of these countries – so that we may say every country gets the fairies it deserves, and as Persia is a land of fairy-tales, a highly imaginative example in this regard may be cited in the following. It is called 'The Lost Arabian Nights' or 'The Mountain of Kaf':

Although our circumstances were those of extreme poverty, my mother had always assured me that I was the son of a prince. But she refused to gratify my curiosity any further, so that I remained in ignorance of my true origin. On my eighteenth birthday, however, she gave me a ring engraved with mystic characters, three pieces of gold and a scimitar with a hilt of silver and ivory, and embracing me affectionately addressed me as follows:

'My son, go to the court of the Sultan of the Land of Fountains which is five days' journey from here. Sit down in the garden behind his palace, and when the sultan himself makes his appearance, approach him and show him this ring and this sword.'

When she had blessed me, I set out upon my journey. By following the direction she gave me I came, in four days, to the capital of the Land of Fountains and sat down in the garden behind the palace.

Now in this palace is a summer-house of priceless white jade, carved in China, and carried thence on the backs of dromedaries. And as I was feasting my eyes on the beauty of it, which appeared to me as ice in moonlight, I espied through its lattice a loveliness still more exquisite, which burned as a flame in that shining place. A damsel of surprising beauty sat therein. She was like the shadow of a white lily in a dim water, and her eyes were smouldering shadows.

As I gazed in wonder, I was suddenly startled by the sound of a harsh voice, and, turning quickly, was confronted by a tall elderly man of majestic aspect, who was accompanied by two black slaves bearing drawn scimitars.

'How came you here, fellow?' he cried haughtily. 'Know you that this is the sultan's garden?'

'I seek the sultan,' I said simply – for, indeed, I had then no skill in courtesy.

'You seek the sultan!' he said with a laugh. 'You in your rags! Well, I am the sultan. What would you with me?'

'Your Highness,' I said humbly, 'I bring you this ring and this scimitar,' and I proffered him the circlet and the blade.

He took them and his face turned to the colour of ashes.

'Where did you find these?' he cried in an awful voice. 'Speak quickly, slave.'

'I had them from my mother,' I said with some spirit, although I confess I trembled. 'I am no slave, Your Highness, but the son of a prince.'

'Follow me,' he said shortly, and without another word walked quickly to the palace. We entered. I was amazed at the beauty of the place, for it was the first time that I had

seen such a paradise of gold and marble, being used to
nothing finer than our village mosque. The white ground
of the corridors and galleries was shot with rare stones. To
my simple eyes, indeed, they seemed the first steps in some
happy dream, and when, at length, we came to a chamber
hung with green silk and filled with silver cages of sweet
singing birds, I thought that no such wealth could have been
in all the earth.

'Your name?' asked the sultan, as he cast himself upon a
divan.

'It is Salim, Your Highness,' I replied, 'but I know not of
my father.'

He nodded, stroking his beard and looking at me
strangely. 'Yet you resemble your father: he was my younger
brother.'

'Then Your Highness is my uncle?' I cried in astonishment
and would have embraced him. But he repulsed me sternly,
and commanded me to stand back.

'It is true that I am your uncle,' he said in the most
ungracious manner possible. 'But you have been brought
up as a beggar. He may not mingle with princes who is not
himself as one of them.'

At this I felt the tears come into my eyes and the blood
into my face. Seeing my agitation, the sultan smiled, though
somewhat sourly, and bade me be seated.

'The true blood will show itself,' he said, 'and the
righteous man is just. I will provide you with an opportunity
of proving yourself fitted to take up your rightful position.
You saw the damsel in the summer-house of jade?'

I bowed low to conceal the colour which once more suffused my face at his question.

'She is my daughter, the Princess Zara,' he continued. 'She is under an enchantment. While she was yet a child she was engaged in casting pebbles into the lake which lies at the end of the garden. Suddenly the jinn of the lake arose in anger and cast back one of the pebbles, so that it struck her upon the lips. Ever since that day she has been dumb. I have searched the whole earth in order to find a cure for her affliction. Many sage and wise men have I sought advice from, but without avail, until I received letters from the learned Persian magus, Abra Melim, who has informed me that one antidote alone will cure my daughter's affliction. You have doubtless heard of the mountain Kaf, in Jinnistan, the country of the jinn?'

'Who has not, sire?'

'It looks four-square to the quarters of the earth. Its foundation is of emerald and possesses marvellous qualities, for with a shred of this magical jewel men can work wonders, can raise earthquakes and cure diseases. Only with such a fragment of this celestial gem can my daughter's speech be restored.'

'Is it your will, sire, that I should attempt the adventure?'

'It is,' replied the sultan gravely. 'It will allow me to discover whether or not you possess those qualities which will fit you for the position to which you lay claim.'

'I am perfectly willing to act according to Your Highness's wishes,' I said, 'but I am inexperienced and scarcely yet a man.'

'That is, perhaps, to your advantage,' remarked the sultan with a smile. 'The experienced man is more frequently daunted by such an adventure as I propose to you than he whose mind is innocent of the world's craft. Now come with me and we shall arrange for your departure at sunrise tomorrow.'

We visited the stables where more than two hundred of the choicest steeds were kept, and here I selected a white horse of graceful appearance, which the sultan assured me had yet a high turn of speed and great endurance. From the armoury I chose a scimitar of Damascus steel with a hollow back, into which, the sultan informed me, quicksilver had been poured to add weight to a blow. Then, as evening was drawing nigh, I asked the sultan many questions regarding the strange country to which I was bound. But of the marvellous things which he recounted to me I will not speak, for did I not behold them with my own eyes?

Before retiring to rest the sultan handed me a bag of gold sequins. Then, consigning me to the care of Allah, he bade me farewell, counselling me to begin my journey with the first streak of dawn.

No sooner had the sun risen above the edge of earth than I was in the saddle. I rode past the palace garden and the summer-house of white jade, where, alas, no light of loveliness now shone. But my vow to recover the boon of speech for the Princess Zara, my cousin, or perish, was strong in my heart, and whipping up my horse, I cantered on. The sultan had informed me that Jinnistan, the Land of the Jinn, or evil ones, was situated in the far East, so I set my horse's head in that direction.

The day was fair, the road excellent, and making good progress, I came at nightfall to a small caravanserai, which, so far as I could ascertain, had but one occupant – a shaven marabout, small, old and wizened, who replied to my questions in the briefest manner possible. Deeming him a holy man, I considered it more fitting to leave him to his devotions than to trouble him with inquiries. But what was my surprise on chancing to turn my head in his direction to see that he was engaged not in prayer, as I had thought, but in some magical ceremony. The cry of astonishment which I was unable to restrain at the sight caused him to look up angrily. I trembled, fearful that he should cast an enchantment upon me for my interruption. But the frown upon his face turned, to my amazement, to an indulgent smile and rising to his feet, he addressed me as follows:

'My son, I perceive that you are alarmed at what you have seen. But fear nothing. I practise no black art, but only that innocent and exalted sorcery which the wise call white magic. Indeed, the act in which I was engaged was prompted by a desire to aid you. You seem an amiable young man and I merely wished to discover whether your journey would be of advantage to you or otherwise.'

I stammered my thanks, which he cut short by a courteous gesture.

'I am aware of the nature of your venture, Salim,' he said. 'Know that I am the sage, Abra Melim, whom the Sultan of the Land of Fountains consulted regarding the malady of his daughter. You seek the Mountain of Kaf. Is it not so?'

Now I was in an excess of dread, for I feared that this strange being might be one of those jinn who are everywhere in the air, in the sea, and even in the bowels of the earth, and who, knowing of my quest, might seek to destroy me. Therefore I remained silent.

'Fear nothing, my son,' said Abra Melim kindly. 'I can read your thoughts, and I desire to assure you that your suspicions are misplaced. I am neither jinn nor afreet, as you seem to imagine. Indeed, I have command and authority over the spirits of the elements; if you will do me a small office, I will cheerfully assist you in your task, which is, I know, to obtain a piece of the great emerald which is the foundation of Kaf, the world-mountain, which cures all human defects and is the most potent of elixirs, as well as the repository of marvellous forces.'

'O sage whose name is known to the four quarters of the earth,' I replied, 'you will not be displeased with your servant if he asks the nature of the office you require of him.'

'By no means,' said Abra Melim. 'Listen: I formerly spent many years in Egypt mastering the hidden knowledge of that mysterious land. One day, while seated on the banks of the Nile, speaking with the priest of that country, my companion pointed to the mighty pyramids which cast their shadows on the place where we reclined. "My son," remarked the sage, "you behold these mountains in stone, the memorials of kings who died, while Greece was yet in the cradle and Rome was unthought of. All the lore that we can teach you is but as a drop of water to the ocean compared with the secrets contained in those monuments. In the heart of the Great Pyramid is a death-chamber, where rests the mummy of the High Priest who designed and built that stupendous pile. On his breast lies a wondrous book containing magical secrets of great potency – that book, indeed which was given to Adam after the Fall, and by the aid of which Solomon built the Temple at Jerusalem."

'From the moment I heard those words I could not rest. I resolved to find my way into the Great Pyramid and possess myself of the magic volume. Collecting a number of people of the land I addressed myself to the task of piercing the solid masonry, which concealed this ineffable treasure, until, after unheard-of labours, I came upon one of its hidden passages. For long I searched in the labyrinths of the vast pyramid ere I arrived at the sepulchral chamber. At length, groping in the profound darkness, and haunted by the rustling of the wrappings of the mummied pharaohs, I came upon the shrine where the corpse of the High Priest lay in grim state. I opened the sarcophagus, and, unwrapping the voluminous bandages, found the mystic tome lying among spices and amulets on the shrivelled breast. But as I attempted to seize it my hand suddenly grew numb, as if frozen at the wrist. I was unable to move. At the same time an awful voice pierced the silence of the chamber of the dead.

"'Forbear!" it cried. "This sacred volume which you covet may be borne hence by one only – one destined through the ages for the task. Depart, lest harm befall thee."

'Terrified, I hastened from the pyramid. For years I sought by magic arts to discover who might be that destined one who alone might bear away the Book of Secrets. At last it was vouchsafed to me that it was none other than yourself.'

'Myself!' I echoed in amazement.

'None other, as I say. For many years I have watched over you, waiting for the time when I might reveal this to you and ask for your aid. The day is now at hand. In short, it falls upon the morrow.'

'But, sage Abra Melim,' I cried, 'if what you say is true, what hope have you of regaining the treasure of which you have told me? We are far from the land of Egypt, and it would seem to me that the great opportunity is passed.'

'Not so, my son,' replied the sage with a smile. 'We shall be in Egypt by tomorrow morning.'

With these words he passed outside to where my white horse was tethered, and muttering some words I could not comprehend, struck him twice upon the withers. Immediately two large wings sprouted from the animal's shoulders, growing in size, and spread until they reached the ground. With an agility I could not have credited him with, the magician leaped into the saddle, and called me to take my place behind him. Then he whispered a word of power into the ear of my steed, and before I well understood what was happening, we were soaring high over the trees which surrounded the caravanserai.

I felt not the slightest giddiness, nor any fear that I would be cast to the earth below. We proceeded at a prodigious pace, at ten times the rate at which a horse gallops on the earth. Beneath us, cities, streams and deserts were spread out like the patterns upon a praying-mat. On and ever onwards we flew. At length the sun went down, and we continued our flight by the moonlight. All night we sped through the star-candled vault of the heavens. With the first light of dawn I could see the shimmering of a great river, which Abra Melim told me was the mouth of the Nile, a vast expanse of green, through which there meandered five streams spread out like fingers of a man's hand laid flat.

Scarcely an hour later we saw what seemed low hills of stone rise in the sands of the desert.

'These, my son,' said Abra Melim, 'are the pyramids. That one which towers above others is our destination. Prepare for the ordeal before you.'

Now the magician had mentioned nothing as yet regarding any ordeal through which I might have to pass, and as I heard his ominous words I trembled despite myself. To what doom of horror might I be devoted? Alas, it was too late to think upon such things or to draw back, and in another moment we had alighted at the base of the gigantic structure of granite, which frowned above us like the mass of a mountain.

Abra Melim uttered a spell which seemed to turn my horse into stone, so motionless it became. Then he signalled to me to follow him up the face of the great pyramid. Painfully I clambered up behind him, although I noticed that the ascent did not appear to trouble him in the least. Up and up we climbed, until at length, we saw a great doorway make a black mouth upon the shining granite. The magician entered as he might have entered his own house and in great fear I followed.

We halted for a moment while he produced and lighted a lamp with a flint and steel, and then, as if he knew the ways and windings of the place as familiarly as the depths of his own soul, we plunged into the gloomy labyrinth. On and on we walked through the hush of those dusty galleries of the dead, disturbing a thousand bats, and stumbling over the debris of centuries. At last Abra Melim stopped before a great pylon, on the sides of which he fumbled with his fingers. The stone which closed it rose to his touch upon the secret spring, and disclosed a shadowy interior from which came a strong odour of spices.

'Enter,' whispered Abra Melim, who himself appeared to be overawed. 'You will find the book on the breast of the royal mummy. Take it fearlessly, and return.'

'How shall I see without the lamp?' I asked, with chattering teeth.

'Enter, I say,' said the magician harshly. 'I will hold the lamp so that you might have light.'

I obeyed him and entered. I could perceive no tomb or even the semblance of one, nothing but a vast and empty chamber, and I was about to turn to acquaint Abra Melim with this, when a noise loud and terrible as thunder sounded upon my ears, and I heard the great stone door crash to the ground behind me. At the same time a peal of mocking laughter came from the other side.

'Fool,' cried the voice of the magician, 'perish in your folly. It was your desire to discover the mountain Kaf. Know, then, that you have indeed done so. For what you thought was a pyramid was none other than the mountain which stands four-square to the points of the compass, and in the recess of which you shall remain until the last day. The Nile you saw was a Nile of enchantment. As for me, I am the Jinnee Salac, guardian of the mountain in which you are now imprisoned. Farewell!'

Now when I heard these words I fell to the ground as one dead. My senses deserted me, so that I seemed to descend past walls of darkness into a great pit. When I came to myself I was still lying upon the ground in the chamber in which the cruel Jinnee, masquerading as a friendly magician, had imprisoned me. I recalled that he had described it as the interior of the magic mountain of Kaf, which it had been my hope to despoil of a portion of its emerald foundation. But there was small chance that I should do so now. I was doomed, I told myself, to perish in the hideous darkness which surrounded me. The thought was anguish and I wept.

But, as I was bemoaning my fate, I was startled to hear a small but quite audible voice proceeding from the scimitar I carried. At first I thought it must be a delusion of the senses occasioned by the horrible surroundings in which I found myself, but when it continued to address me, in tones of comfort and assurance, I listened attentively.

'O Prince,' it said, 'be not downcast, for I am able to assist you in the most powerful manner. You believe that it is merely quicksilver which is enclosed in your scimitar, for the purpose of adding weight to the swordsman's stroke. But I assure you that I am a spirit, imprisoned in the weapon you

wear for an ancient misdemeanour. If I aid you, and secure
your freedom, will you faithfully promise to break the blade
in which I am kept in durance, and let me go free once more?'

Desperate as I was, I immediately gave the required
assurance; and the afreet – for such I believed him to
be – continued: 'I accept your word. Know then that by
virtue of my presence in this scimitar, it has the power of
cleaving any substance, no matter how hard it be. Even
adamant will not withstand its edge. Strike boldly then at the
door of granite which separates you from the outer world,
and you will find yourself free.'

Hope arising in my heart, I immediately drew the sword
from its sheath, and, groping my way to the door, directed
a blow at it with all my strength. The good blade sheared
through the granite as though it had been made of parchment.
For a moment I stood amazed at the marvellous power of the
weapon in my hand, but, recollecting the danger in which I
was, I renewed the attack upon the stone, which presently
fell in fragments at my feet. Stepping from the chamber, I
found myself in the great gallery, where, for a moment, I
stood irresolute, not knowing which way to turn. But the
small voice from the scimitar spoke once more, advising me
to turn to the left.

Little by little I groped my way along the passage. The
feel of the walls told me what I had believed to be stone was
in reality, earth, and I knew that I was in the depths of the
mountain of Kaf. The voice from the scimitar continued to
guide me, advising me as to the turnings I must take, until

at length I beheld what seemed to be a star shining in the darkness of night.

Pressing on, I saw that it was night indeed in the other world; but when at last I came to the entrance of the mountain, and was about to descend, such a fierce wind arose that, despite my utmost efforts, I could not proceed a single foot. Again and again I threw myself against what seemed a very wall of wind, but without avail.

'Use me,' cried the voice from the sword. 'Cut at the wind, as you did at the granite.'

I did as I was bidden, and almost immediately the wind died down. Then, for I felt the surrounding presence of things evil, I made all haste to leave the mountain, down the side of which I scrambled in a panic of fear lest yet some other sleight of sorcery should seek to hinder my progress. Nor were my fears groundless, for, no sooner had I descended halfway, than I was seized as if by a score of hands, which sought to detain me. This time I required no advice how to act, but, whirling the scimitar above my head, slashed left and right. As I did so the most doleful shrieks and cries rent the air, as if proceeding from men mortally wounded. Presently they died away in hideous moaning, and I was not again molested. So making the best of my way to the foot of the mountain, I stood at last upon a substance so slippery to the feet, as to make me feel certain that it could be no other than the foundation of emerald, a shred of which the sultan had commanded me to secure.

Wielding my scimitar, I hacked mightily at the glossy platform upon which I stood. At the first blow there was a sound as of splintering. At the second, the jewel-mass crackled ominously. At the third, a fragment rebounded, and struck me upon the eyes. Instantly, the scene around me seemed as if plucked out of the shadows of night, and I could behold all objects within the range of my vision as clearly as if they had been suffused in the strongest sunlight. I now saw that I had indeed succeeded in detaching several pieces of emerald from the parent mass and, gathering them up, placed them in the folds of my turban. But what amazed me even more than the wondrous virtue of the sword I carried, was the circumstance that I was able to see the reflection of myself in the green mirror-like substance on which I stood, which told me that I had altered somewhat in appearance, and had, indeed, grown a small beard.

'Cease! O Prince! to marvel at what you see,' cried the small voice from the sword, 'for know that you have been immured in the heart of the mountain Kaf for more than a year – so quickly does time speed in the land of the jinn. Now keep your vow, and free me from the bondage in which I still remain.'

'But how, O Spirit, may that be accomplished,' I asked, 'seeing that even the most adamant of substances break at your touch?'

'Strike my hilt upon the emerald beneath you,' replied the voice. 'It is only in the blade that virtue resides.'

Seizing the scimitar by the curving blade, I struck the hilt sharply upon the green and shining floor. The handle at once fell away, and what seemed a ball of quicksilver ran out from beneath it. For a moment this writhed upon the glassy ground upon which it had fallen, then grew and grew, until, to my amazement, I was confronted by the semblance of a tall warrior clad in silver armour, which shone with the radiance of moonlight.

'I am the spirit of the scimitar,' he said, in a voice as loud and powerful as it had hitherto been weak, 'I thank you, gratefully, Prince, for my deliverance. You doubtless desire to return to the palace of the Sultan of the Land of Fountains. Well, you have but to hold a fragment of the emerald of Kaf in your hand, and desire to be there, to find yourself at your destination.'

With these words, and ere I could reply, he vanished. Acting as he had instructed me, I held a fragment of the emerald in my hand, and wished to be transported to the sultan's garden. Almost before the wish had passed through my mind, I found myself standing beside the summer-house of white jade.

It was still night to others, though not to me, but I boldly entered the palace, and made my way to the sultan's apartment. On being admitted, he at once recognized me, but informed me that I had been given up for lost. His joy on hearing that the desired antidote had been obtained was overwhelming, and he at once sent for the Princess Zara. When the jewel was placed upon her lips she regained the power of speech, and so grateful was her father for her release from the bondage of dumbness, that he immediately bestowed her hand on me. Our union is one of the most perfect happiness, and I have found in her

SHAH

a jewel more inestimable and more to be praised than the emerald of Kaf.

From: *Eastward to Persia*
The Sirdar Ikbal Ali Shah

A Conversation Paid for
in Postage Stamps

HICHAM HARRASS LIVES in a one-room shack he built himself
on the western-most edge of Casablanca.

The walls are made from third-hand breeze blocks and
the roof is laid with rusting tin. His home does not have an
address, but it does have a number.

It is number 2043.

All around it there's a jumble of other shacks, each with
their number daubed on the wall in dripping red paint. If
you turned up at the *bidonville*, the shantytown, you'd have
no hope in finding Hicham's place in the maze of alleyways.
But ask for him by name and every man, woman and smallest
child will jab a finger towards his door.

I met Hicham because of his passion for postage stamps.

Our house is half a mile from the Atlantic. Its gardens are
an oasis of date palms and mimosa trees, and are surrounded
on all sides by the breeze-block shantytown. When we first
moved into the house I must admit I was anxious. We had
no idea how our neighbours would greet us, whether they
could get used to a family of foreigners living in their midst.

One morning during our first week in Casablanca, there
was a tap at the door. I went to open it, and found an elderly

man standing in the frame. His skin was the colour of roasted almonds. He had a long, shiny face with a scrub of white beard at the end of his chin. He wore a frayed black and white wool *jelaba*, and old yellow *baboush* slippers on his feet.

Before I could ask how I could help him, the man extended a hand, smiled, said his name was Hicham, and that he collected postage stamps.

'Do you have any to spare?' he enquired politely. 'I could pay you money for them, a few dirhams.'

I thought for a moment.

'We haven't received any mail yet,' I replied. 'We've just arrived.'

Hicham's smile melted. I told him to come back in a week.

'Will you forget?' he asked.

I promised not to.

A week later Hicham was at the door again. I had collected five British stamps, all bearing the Queen's head. I handed them over, and a remarkable friendship began.

After that I collected all the stamps on my letters and gave them to Hicham. He was a proud man and insisted on paying me, although he had almost no money at all. I didn't want to offend him by refusing payment, and so we came up with a solution.

We agreed to meet at his home at the same time each week. I would pass over the postage stamps and, in return, he could tell me about his life.

Hicham Harrass was born in a village three days' walk from the southern city of Agadir. His father had been a farmer, with half an acre of dusty land. Along with five brothers and a sister, he grew up in a house made from flotsam, gleaned from the Atlantic waves.

When Hicham was seven years old, a *sehura*, a witch, came to the house and declared that he would drop dead within the next cycle of the moon. The only way to avoid such a fate, she said, was for Hicham's parents to give the boy away to a stranger. The family was very upset but, believing the witch's prediction would come true, they gave him to the next man who came into the village. Fortunately for Hicham, that man was a trader, a man called Ayman.

'He needed a boy to help him,' said Hicham, 'and so I travelled around Morocco with him and his cart, buying and selling scrap metal as we went. On the long journeys between small towns he taught me,' Hicham continued. 'He taught me about life, and how to live it.'

I asked what he meant.

The old man's wife bustled over with more mint tea.

'Ayman taught me to be selfless,' he said. 'That means giving more to the people you meet than what you take from them. And it means walking softly on the earth.'

As the years had passed, Ayman and the young Hicham criss-crossed the kingdom again and again. They travelled from Agadir to Essaouira, from Marrakech to Fès, from Tangier to Casablanca, always on the donkey cart piled high with scrap metal.

'We visited places that aren't on any maps,' said Hicham. 'It was adventure. Real adventure. You can't understand what it was like - it was like waking from a dream! Every mile that we travelled, Ayman would talk. Every mile was a lesson. He taught me about honour, and to tell the truth. It's because of Ayman that I cannot lie. Truth is the backbone of my life. It's my religion.'

'But Islam is your religion,' I said.

'It's the same thing,' said Hicham. 'Islam is Truth. It's the truth to believe in yourself, in those around you, and in God.'

Almost every week for a year, Hicham and I met and talked and talked, in conversation paid for in postage stamps. There are so many memorable conversations in my head, but few have ever been quite so revealing as those with Hicham. Over the months, I found myself grasping the basics of what must surely be real Islam.

One afternoon, Hicham invited me in, served me the ubiquitous glass of steaming mint tea, and said:

'You are young, your eyes are wide open, your mind is clear. But you must take care to understand.'

'To understand what?'

'To understand the right Path.'

Hicham called out of the door to his wife, who was chatting to a neighbour in the street. He apologized.

'I'm sorry,' he said, 'she forgets the duty of honouring a guest with food.'

I asked about the Path.

'To understand the right Path,' Hicham said, stroking his tuft of beard, 'you must understand what it is not. It's easy. It's a lesson in life. Islam is not complicated, or cruel, or unfair. Anyone who cannot describe it in the most simplistic way is telling falsehoods. He's telling lies. He's as bad as the fanatics.'

I asked about the fanatics – about Al-Qaeda, and other radical groups.

Hicham rubbed his eyes.

'They pretend that what they are doing is in the name of Allah, but it's in the name of Satan,' he said very softly. 'They are hijacking our religion. Open your eyes and see it for yourself! Islam teaches tolerance and modesty. It doesn't tell people to fly passenger jets into skyscrapers, or to strap plastic explosives to the waists and to slaughter innocent women and children. These people must be stopped.'

The next week, I handed over a fresh crop of postage stamps.

As always, the old man spent a few moments poring over them, commenting on each one. His favourites were from England but, 'Not those silly ones with the Queen,' he would say. 'I like the big, more unusual ones. They hint at the society, the tradition.'

I steered the conversation away from postage stamps, and onto the problems of the world. I asked Hicham how Islam could stop Al-Qaeda. He didn't say anything at first; he was too busy sorting through the stamps.

'I'll tell you,' he said at length. 'You have to starve them of publicity. That's what to do. Don't report their misdeeds. Ignore them. Pretend they don't exist.'

'Won't that just make them wilder for publicity?'

Hicham laughed. He laughed and he laughed until his old sagging cheeks were the colour of beetroot.

'Of course it would,' he said. 'But it doesn't matter how angry they get, so long as we rise up tall and spread the truth about Islam. We must tell people the facts, the real facts. That's what I'm saying.'

'What are the real facts?'

'Tell them that Islam doesn't order women to veil,' he said. 'The tradition was copied from the Christians of Byzantium. And tell them that Islam doesn't say you cannot drink wine – it just says you can't become intoxicated. And,' Hicham went on, his voice rising in volume, 'you can tell them that Islam says that all Muslims are equal. We are brothers. That means an imam or a religious scholar is equal to us. He can't tell us what to do!'

Three weeks ago I flew to London for a few days, leaving my wife and the children at our oasis in the shantytown. On the evening I returned to Casablanca, there was a knock at the door.

'That will be Hicham,' I said to my wife, 'he'll be wondering where I have been.'

I opened the door, expecting to see the old man's face. But it wasn't him. It was his wife, Khadija. She was crying.

'My husband died three days ago,' she said. 'He told me if anything ever happened to him, that I should give you this.'

The old woman was holding a box. She held it out towards me. I thanked her. A moment later she was gone. I went inside to my desk, turned on the lamp, and opened the box.

In it were Hicham's stamp albums. I sat down in the dim light. I was sad to have lost a wise friend, but at the same time I was happy – happy that we had found each other at all, and had enjoyed so many good conversations, each one paid for in postage stamps.

From: *Travels With Myself*
Tahir Shah

Understanding the Path

WE WELCOME THE scholars who want to understand the Path.

What of the others? They think that we do not welcome them, but it is in reality they who do not welcome us.

They cannot do so while they retain such strange conceptions of the Way.

I refer to two kinds: those who say: 'We deny the value of Sufism', and those who say: 'We accept Sufism, but this is not it.'

Of the two, those who reject the Sufis are better than those who pretend that the people whom they do not like cannot therefore be Sufis.

The former class are deluded by others into believing that Sufis are useless, and anyone may be deceived by others.

And the latter class are those who are deluded by themselves into imagining something which is not correct.

No scholar can decide who is or who is not a Sufi. People trying to do something of which they are incapable should always be a lesson to us.

Ajmal Hussein and the Scholars

Sufi Ajmal Hussein was constantly being criticized by scholars, who feared that his repute might outshine their own. They spared no efforts to cast doubts upon his knowledge, to accuse him of taking refuge from their criticisms in mysticism, and even to imply that he had been guilty of discreditable practices.

At length he said:

'If I answer my critics, they make it the opportunity to bring fresh accusation against me, which people believe because it amuses them to believe such things. If I do not answer them they crow and preen themselves, and people believe that they are real scholars. They imagine that we Sufis oppose scholarship. We do not. But our very existence is a threat to the pretended scholarship of tiny noisy ones. Scholarship long since disappeared. What we have to face now is sham scholarship.'

The scholars shrilled more loudly than ever. At last Ajmal said:

'Argument is not as effective as demonstration. I shall give you an insight into what these people are like.'

He invited 'question papers' from the scholars, to allow them to test his knowledge and ideas. Fifty different professors and academicians sent questionnaires to him. Ajmal answered them all differently. When the scholars met to discuss these papers, at a conference, there were so many versions of what he believed, that each one thought that he had exposed Ajmal, and refused to give up his thesis in favour of any other. The result was the celebrated 'brawling of the scholars'. For five days they attacked each other bitterly.

'This,' said Ajmal, 'is a demonstration. What matters to each one most is his own opinion and his own interpretation. They care nothing for truth. This is what they do with everyone's teachings. When he is alive, they torment him. When he dies they become experts on his works. The real motive of the activity, however, is to vie with one another and to oppose anyone outside their own ranks. Do you want to become one of them? Make a choice soon.'

Timur and Hafiz
The Sufi poet Hafiz of Shiraz wrote the famous poem:
> *If that Sharazi Turkish maid would take my heart*
> *Into her hand:*
> *I'd give Bokhara for the mole upon her cheek–*
> *Or Samarkand.*

The conqueror Tamerlane had Hafiz brought before him and said:

'How can you give away Bokhara and Samarkand for a woman? Besides, they are in my own domains, and I shall not permit anyone to pretend that they are not!'

Hafiz said to him:

'Your meanness may have given you power. My generosity has put me in your power. Your meanness is obviously more effective than my prodigality.'

Tamerlane laughed and let the Sufi go.

Full Up
A man came to Bahaudin Naqshband, and said:

'I have travelled from one teacher to another, and I have studied many Paths, all of which have given me great benefits and many advantages of all kinds.

'I now wish to be enrolled as one of your disciples, so that I may drink from the well of knowledge, and thus make myself more and more advanced in the *Tariqa*, the Mystic Way.'

Bahaudin, instead of answering the question directly, called for dinner to be served. When the dish of rice and meat stew was brought, he pressed plateful after plateful upon his guest. Then he gave him fruits and pastries, and then he called for more *pilau*, and more and more courses of food, vegetables, salads, confitures.

At first the man was flattered, and as Bahaudin showed pleasure at every mouthful he swallowed, he ate as much as he could. When his eating slowed down, the Sufi sheikh seemed very annoyed, and to avoid his displeasure, the unfortunate man ate virtually another meal.

When he could not swallow even another grain of rice, and rolled in great discomfort upon a cushion, Bahaudin addressed him in this manner:

'When you came to see me, you were as full of undigested teachings as you now are with meat, rice and fruit. You felt discomfort, and, because you are unaccustomed to spiritual discomfort of the real kind, you interpreted this as a hunger for more knowledge. Indigestion was your real condition.

'I can teach you if you will now follow my instructions and stay here with me digesting by means of activities which will not seem to you to be initiatory, but which will be equal to the eating of something which will enable your meal to be digested and transformed into nutrition, not weight.'

The man agreed. He told his story many decades later, when he became famous as the great teacher Sufi Khalil Ashrafzada.

Charkhi and His Uncle

It is related that a young disciple of Baba Charkhi was sitting in the hallway of his house when a man arrived and said: 'Who are you?'

The disciple answered: 'I am a follower of Baba Charkhi.'

The man said: 'How can Charkhi have followers? I am his uncle, and I would have known if he had. As to his being a "Baba", you have been misinformed, my child.'

Charkhi's uncle stayed in the house after that for many years, until he died. He refused to enter the 'assemblies of culture' held by the Baba, and he could never credit that Charkhi was a Sufi teacher. 'I have known him since he was a child,' he said, 'and I cannot see him teaching anything, because he was never able to learn anything.'

Even after Charkhi died, there were many people, some of them frequent visitors to his house, including merchants with whom he had business dealings, who did not believe that he was a saint.

Yunus Abu-Aswad Kamali, the theologian, spoke for some of these when he said: 'I knew Charkhi for thirty years, and he never discussed higher things with me. To my mind, such behaviour is impossible to a learned man. He never tried to describe his theories, and he did not attempt to make me a disciple. I only heard of his supposedly being a Sufi through the butcher.'

A SON OF A SON I

The Prisoner of Samarkand

Hakim Iskandar Zaramez and Abdulwahab el Hindi were passing the corner of a large house in Samarkand one day when they heard a wild cry.

'They are torturing some poor wretch,' said El Hindi, stopping and standing still as the cries increased.

'Would you have the suffering eased?' asked Zaramez.

'Naturally. As a *wali*, a saint, you can surely do it, if there be God's permission.'

'Very well,' said the hakim, 'and I shall demonstrate something.'

Zaramez moved five paces away from the corner of the house. The cries stopped.

'You withdraw, and the tumult ceases! Assuredly I have always heard that it is the nearness to an afflicted person which assuages pain,' said El Hindi.

The hakim smiled, but said no more, making the sign which among the Sufis signifies: 'A question may have no answer at a certain time because of the state of the querent.'

Many years later when El Hindi was in Morocco, he listened to a dervish relating his experiences to a group of students one night in the closed city of Maula Idriss.

Among other things, the dervish said:

'On such-and-such a day of the month of Ramadan el-Mubarak, so many years ago, I was seized as a vagrant because of my apparent poverty and meagre appearance. I was left in a stone-built cell at one corner of the outside wall of the Kazi's house, pending judgement. This was in the northern vicinity of Samarkand.

'I had been contented enough with my lot, and sitting in silent contemplation when I felt, quite unmistakably and from outside, not far away, the presence of a saint. I started to howl and shriek, and to throw myself about; because a power was upon me, and because I could not escape however much I wanted to approach him.

'Then I felt that he had moved away as if disturbed by my clamour. I tried to let him come near again by letting myself become as slack and silent as the night.'

The sheikh of the dervish circle said:

'Your experience could have instructed you that people are most profoundly affected by *baraka* (spiritual power) when for all apparent purposes it is beyond their reach. The *wali* was teaching you this, even though you were in prison and he may have seemed to outside observers to be doing something entirely different, or even nothing at all.'

El Hindi relates:

'This occasion was the beginning of my real understanding that it is not wonderful that people have "spiritual experiences". What might be wonderful is that so few people have them. What is certainly more wonderful is that instead of learning from them, they worship the experience and count it as something which it is not.'

The Book in Turki

A would-be disciple went to Bahaudin.

The master was surrounded by thirty of his students, in a garden, after dinner.

The newcomer said:

'I wish to serve you.'

Bahaudin answered:

'You can best serve me by reading my *Risalat* (Letters).'

'I have already done so,' said the newcomer.

'If you had done so in reality and not in appearance, you would not have approached me in this manner,' said Bahaudin.

He continued:

'Why do you think that you are able to learn?'

'I am ready to study with you.'

Bahaudin said:

'Let the most junior *Murid* (disciple) stand up.'

Anwari, who was sixteen years of age, rose to his feet.

'How long have you been with us?' asked El-Shah.

'Three weeks, O *Murshid*.'

'Have I taught you anything?'

'I do not know.'

'Do you think so?'

'I do not think so.'

Bahaudin said to him:

'In this newcomer's satchel you will find a book of poems. Take it in your hand and recite the entire contents without mistake and without even opening it.'

Anwari found the book. He did not open it, but said: 'I fear that it is in Turki.'

Bahaudin said:

'Recite it!'

Anwari did so, and as he finished the stranger became more and more affected by this wonder – a book being read without being opened by someone who did not know Turki.

Falling at the feet of Bahaudin, he begged to be admitted to the Circle.

Bahaudin said:

'It is this kind of phenomenon which attracts you – while it still does, you cannot really benefit from it. That is why, even if you have read my *Risalat*, you have not really read it.

'Come back,' he continued, 'when you have read it as this beardless boy has read it. It was only such study that gave him the power to recite from a book which he had not opened, and at the same time prevented him from grovelling in wonderment at the event.'

Beggars and Workers

It is related of Ibn el-Arabi that people said to him:

'Your circle is composed mainly of beggars, husbandmen and artisans. Can you not find people of intellect who will follow you, so that perhaps more authoritative notice might be taken of your teachings?'

He said:

'The Day of Calamity will be infinitely nearer when I have influential men and scholars singing my praises; for without any doubt they will be doing so for their own sake and not for the sake of our work!'

Unaltered

Nawab Muhammad Jan Fishan Khan was out walking in
Delhi one day when he came upon a number of people
seemingly engaged in an altercation.

He asked a bystander:

'What is happening here?'

The man said: 'Sublime Highness, one of your disciples
is objecting to the behaviour of the people in this quarter.'

Jan Fishan went into the crowd and said to his follower:

'Explain yourself.'

The man said: 'These people have been hostile.'

The people exclaimed: 'That is not true: we were, on the
contrary, doing him honour for your sake.'

'What did they say?' asked the Nawab.

'They said: "Hail, Great Scholar!" I was telling them that
it is the ignorance of scholars which is often responsible for
the confusion and desperation of man.'

Jan Fishan Khan said: 'It is the conceit of scholars which
is responsible, quite often, for the misery of man. And it is
your conceit in claiming to be other than a scholar which is
the cause of this tumult. Not to be a scholar, which involves
detachment from the petty, is an accomplishment. Scholars
are seldom wise, being only unaltered people stuffed with
thoughts and books.

'These people were trying to honour you. If some people
think that mud is gold, if it is their mud, respect it. You are
not their teacher.

'Do you not realize that, in behaving in such a sensitive and self-willed manner, you are acting just like a scholar, and therefore deserve the name, even if it is an epithet?

'Guard yourself, my child. Too many slips from the Path of Supreme Attainment – and you may become a scholar.'

Diagnosis

Bahaudin Naqshband once visited the town of Alucha, after a deputation of citizens, hearing that he was passing along the nearby highway, waited upon him and begged him to spend some time with them.

'Do you want to satisfy your curiosity about me, to entertain me and do me honour, or to invite me to impart my teachings to you?' he asked them.

The leader of the party, after a consultation with his fellows, replied:

'We have heard much of you, and you can have heard nothing of us. Since you apparently give us the rare privilege of receiving your teaching, we will gratefully accept this from the alternatives which you have offered.'

Bahaudin entered the town.

The whole populace assembled in the public square. Their own spiritual teachers ushered Bahaudin to a place of honour, and when he was seated, the chief of the philosophers of Alucha began to address him in these terms:

'Sublime Presence and Great Teacher! We have all heard of you, for who has not? But, since you are doubtless unfamiliar with the thoughts of such insignificant people as ourselves, we beg to be allowed to delineate our ideas to you, so that you may support, amend or refute them for us, to our certain profit…'

But Bahaudin stopped them, saying:

'I will certainly tell you what you can do, but you need not tell me anything about yourselves.'

He then proceeded to describe to the people their methods of thought and also their own shortcomings and the precise manner in which they looked upon different problems of life and of man.

After this, he said to the astonished citizens:

'Now, before I tell you how you may remedy this state of affairs, perhaps you will voice any feelings suppressed in your hearts, in order that I might explain myself for your edification, so that you could attend more completely to what I am about to say.'

The same spokesman, after conferring with the people, said:

'O ancient and guide! The unanimous cause of our wonderment and curiosity is how you could know so much about us and our problems and our speculations. Are we right in inferring that such knowledge can only exist where there is a superior form of direct perception, in an unusually blessed individual?'

In answer, Bahaudin called for a jug, some water in a pitcher, some salt and flour. He poured salt, flour and water into the jug. Then he said to the chief spokesman:

'Please be good enough to tell me what is in this jug.'

The man said:

'Reverence, there is a mixture of flour, water and salt.'

'How do you know the composition of the mixture?' asked Bahaudin.

'When the ingredients are known,' said the spokesman, 'there can be no doubt about the nature of the mixture.'

'That is the answer to your question, which surely requires no further explanation from me,' said Bahaudin Naqshband.

The Kashkul

It is related that a dervish once stopped a king in the street. The king said: 'How dare you, a man of no account, interrupt the progress of your sovereign?'

The dervish answered:

'Can you be a sovereign if you cannot even fill my *kashkul*, the begging-bowl?'

He held out his bowl, and the king ordered it to be filled with gold.

But, no sooner was the bowl seen to be full of coins than they disappeared, and the bowl seemed to be empty again.

Sack after sack of gold was brought, and still the amazing bowl devoured coins.

'Stop!' shouted the king. 'For this trickster is emptying my treasury!'

'To you I am emptying your treasury,' said the dervish, 'but to others I am merely illustrating a truth.'

'And the truth?' asked the king.

'The truth is that, the bowl is the desires of man, and the gold what man is given. There is no end to man's capacity to devour, without being in any way changed. See, the bowl has eaten nearly all your wealth, but it is still a carved sea-coconut, and has not partaken of the nature of gold in any respect.

'If you care,' continued the dervish, 'to step into this bowl, it will devour you, too. How can a king, then, hold himself as being of any account?'

The Cow

Once upon a time there was a cow. In all the world there was no animal which so regularly gave so much milk of such high quality.

People came from far and wide to see this wonder. The cow was extolled by all. Fathers told their children of its dedication to its appointed task. Ministers of religion adjured their flocks to emulate it in their own way. Government officials referred to it as a paragon which right behaviour, planning and thinking could duplicate in the human community. Everyone was, in short, able to benefit from the existence of this wonderful animal.

There was, however, one feature which most people, absorbed as they were by the obvious advantages of the cow, failed to observe. It had a little habit, you see. And this habit was that, as soon as a pail had been filled with its admittedly unparalleled milk – it kicked it over.

Individuality and Quality

Yaqub the son of the Judge, said that one day he questioned Bahaudin Naqshband in this manner:

'When I was in companionship with the Murshid of Tabriz, he regularly made a sign that he was not to be spoken to, when he was in a condition of special reflection. But you are accessible to us at all times. Am I correct in concluding that this difference is due to your undoubtedly greater capacity of detachment, the capacity being under your dominion, rather than fugitive?'

Bahaudin told him:

'No, you are always seeking comparisons between people and between states. You are always seeking evidences and differences, when you are not you are seeking similarities. You do not really need so much explanation in matters which are outside such measurement. Different modes of behaviour on the part of the wise are to be regarded as due to differences in individuality, not of quality.'

Paradise of Song

Ahangar was a mighty swordsmith who lived in one of Afghanistan's remote eastern valleys. In times of peace he made steel ploughs, shoed horses and, above all, he sang.

The songs of Ahangar, who is known by different names in various parts of Central Asia, were eagerly listened to by the people of the valleys. They came from the forests of giant walnut trees, from the snowcapped Hindu-Kush, from Qataghan and Badakhshan, from Khanabad and Kunar, from Herat and Paghman, to hear his songs.

Above all, the people came to hear the song of all songs, which was Ahangar's Song of the Valley of Paradise.

This song had a haunting quality, and a strange lilt, and most of all it had a story which was so strange that people felt they knew the remote Valley of Paradise of which the smith sang. Often they asked him to sing it when he was not in the mood to do so, and he would refuse. Sometimes people asked him whether the Valley was truly real, and Ahangar could only say:

'The Valley of the Song is as real as real can be.'

'But how do you know?' the people would ask. 'Have you ever been there?'

'Not in any ordinary way,' said Ahangar.

To Ahangar, and to nearly all the people who heard him, the Valley of the Song was, however, real – real as real can be.

Aisha, a local maiden whom he loved, doubted whether there was such a place. So, too, did Hasan, a braggart and fearsome swordsman who swore to marry Aisha, and who lost no opportunity of laughing at the smith.

One day, when the villagers were sitting around silently after Ahangar had been telling his tale to them, Hasan spoke:

'If you believe that this valley is so real, and that it is, as you say, in those mountains of Sangan yonder, where the blue haze rises, why do you not try to find it?'

'It would not be right, I know that,' said Ahangar.

'You know what it is convenient to know, and do not know what you do not want to know!' shouted Hasan. 'Now, my friend, I propose a test. You love Aisha, but she does not trust you. She has no faith in this absurd Valley of yours. You could never marry her, because when there is no confidence between man and wife, they are not happy and all manner of evils result.'

'Do you expect me to go to the valley, then?' asked Ahangar.

'Yes,' said Hasan and all the audience together.

'If I go and return safely, will Aisha consent to marry me?' asked Ahangar.

'Yes,' murmured Aisha.

So Ahangar, collecting some dried mulberries and a scrap of bread, set off for the distant mountains.

He climbed and climbed, until he came to a wall which encircled the entire range. When he had ascended its sheer sides, there was another wall, even more precipitous than the first. After that there was a third, then a fourth, and finally a fifth wall.

Descending on the other side, Ahangar found that he was in a valley, strikingly similar to his own.

People came out to welcome him, and as he saw them, Ahangar realized that something very strange was happening.

Months later, Ahangar the Smith, walking like an old man, limped into his native village, and made for his humble hut. As word of his return spread throughout the countryside, people gathered in front of his home to hear what his adventures had been.

Hasan the swordsman spoke for them all, and called Ahangar to his window.

There was a gasp as everyone saw how old he had become.

'Well, Master Ahangar, and did you reach the Valley of Paradise?'

'I did.'

'And what was it like?'

Ahangar, fumbling for his words, looked at the assembled people with a weariness and hopelessness that he had never felt before. He said:

'I climbed and I climbed, and I climbed. When it seemed as though there could be no human habitation in such a desolate place, and after many trials and disappointments, I came upon a valley. This valley was exactly like the one in which we live. And then I saw the people. Those people are not only like us people: *they are the same people*. For every Hasan, every Aisha, every Ahangar, every anybody whom we have here, there is another one, exactly the same in that valley.

'These are likenesses and reflections to us, when we see such things. But it is we who are the likeness and reflection of them – we who are here, we are their twins…'

Everyone thought that Ahangar had gone mad through his privations, and Aisha married Hasan the swordsman. Ahangar rapidly grew old and died. And all the people, every one who had heard this story from the lips of Ahangar, first lost heart in their lives, then grew old and died, for they felt that something was going to happen over which they had no control and from which they had no hope, and so they lost interest in life itself.

It is only once in a thousand years that this secret is seen by man. When he sees it, he is changed. When he tells its bare facts to others, they wither and die out.

People think that such an event is a catastrophe, and so they must not know about it, for they cannot understand (such is the nature of their ordinary life) that they have more selves than one, more hopes than one, more chances than one – up there, in the Paradise of the Song of Ahangar the mighty smith.

The Treasure of the Custodians

A prince of the illustrious House of Abbas, kinsfolk of The Prophet's uncle, was living a humble life in Mosul of Iraq. His family had fallen upon evil times, and had reverted to the common lot of man to labour. After three generations the family was somewhat restored, and the prince had the status of a small shopkeeper.

As is the custom with the noble among the Arabs, this man, whose name was Daud el Abbassi, merely called himself Daud, son of Altaf. He spent his days in the marketplace, selling beans and herbs, trying to repair the family's fortunes.

This process continued for some years until Daud fell in love with the daughter of a rich merchant: Zobeida Ibnat Tawil. She was more than willing to marry him, but there was a custom in her family that any prospective son-in-law would have to match a rare gem specially selected by the father, in order to prove his resourcefulness and also his material worth.

After the preliminary negotiations, when Daud was shown the glittering ruby which Tawil had chosen for the test to win his daughter, the young shopkeeper's heart became heavy. Not only was this gem of the finest water, but its size and colour were such that the mines of Badakhshan could surely never have yielded anything of that kind more than once in a thousand years…

Time passed, and Daud thought of every means he could to find the money which he would need even to try to match the jewel. He at length discovered from a jeweller that he had but one chance. If he sent out criers to offer anyone producing its equal not only his house and all his possessions, but also three-quarters of every penny which he would earn for the rest of his natural life, there might be a chance to find a similar ruby.

Accordingly, Daud caused this announcement to be made.

Day after day the word went forth that a ruby of astonishing value, brilliance and colour was being sought, and people from far and near hastened to the house of the merchant to see whether they could provide anything so magnificent. But, after a lapse of almost three years, Daud found that there was no ruby in Arabistan or Ajam, in Khorasan or Hind, in Africa or the West, in Java or Ceylon, which came anything near the excellence of the one which his prospective father-in-law had found.

Zobeida and Daud were at the point of despair. It seemed as though they were never to marry, for the girl's father refused adamantly to accept anything less than a perfect match for his ruby.

One evening, when Daud was sitting in his small garden trying to think, for the thousandth time, of some means to win Zobeida, he realized that a tall and emaciated figure was standing beside him. In his hand he had a staff, on his head was a dervish cap; slung at his waist was a metal begging bowl.

'Peace upon you, O my king!' said Daud in the customary salutation, rising to his feet.

'Daud, the Abbassi, scion of the House of Koreish!' said the apparition. 'I am one of the guardians of the treasures of the Apostle, and I have come to help you in your extremity. You seek a matchless ruby. I shall give it to you, from the treasures of your patrimony, left safe in the hands of the penniless custodians!'

Daud looked at him and said: 'All the treasure which was in the possession of our House was spent, sold, plundered centuries ago. We have nothing left but our name, and we do not even use that for fear of dishonouring it. How can there be any treasure left out of my patrimony?'

'There can still be treasure, precisely because it was not all left in the hands of the House,' said the dervish, 'for people always first rob those who are known to have something to steal. When, however, that is gone, thieves do not then know where to look. This is the first measure of security of the Custodians.'

Daud reflected that many dervishes are reputed to be eccentrics and so he only said:

'Who would leave priceless treasures such as a gem like Tawil's in the hands of a ragged beggar? And what tattered beggar, having been given even one such thing, would forebear from throwing it away, or selling it and spending the proceeds in an insane bout of recklessness?'

The dervish answered:

'My son, this is exactly what people are expected to think. Because beggars are ragged, people imagine that they desire clothes. Because a man has a jewel, people imagine that he will throw it away if he is not a thrifty merchant. Your thoughts are the things which help to make our treasure secure.'

'Then take me to the treasure,' said Daud, 'so that I may end my intolerable doubts and fears.'

The dervish blindfolded Daud and made him ride, dressed as a blind man, for several days and nights on a mean donkey. They dismounted and walked through a mountain cleft, and when the cloth was removed from his eyes, Daud saw that he was standing in a treasure-house where incalculable quantities and unbelievable varieties of precious stones glittered from shelves in serried walls of stone.

'Can this be the treasure of my forefathers? Because I have never so much as heard of anything like it, even from the time of Harun al-Rachid,' said Daud.

'You may be sure that it is,' said the dervish, 'and more than that: this is only the cavern which contains the jewels from which you may choose. There is much more.'

'And it is mine?'

'It is yours.'

'Then I will take it all,' said Daud, who was almost overcome by greed at the sight.

'You will take just what you have come here to take,' said the dervish, 'for you are as little fitted for the proper administration of this wealth as were your forebears. If this were not so, the Custodians would have handed back the entire treasure centuries ago.'

Daud chose the only ruby which exactly matched Tawil's, and the dervish bore him back to his house in the same way as he had brought him. Daud and Zobeida were married.

And in this way, it is related, the treasures of the House are handed out to their proper inheritors whenever they have real need for them. Today the Custodians are not always patched dervishes in appearance. Sometimes they are to all outward appearances the most ordinary of men. But they will not yield the treasures except when there is a real need.

The Attachment Called Grace
A studious and dedicated seeker after truth arrived at the *tekkia* of Bahaudin Naqshband.

In accordance with custom, he attended the lectures and asked no questions.

When Bahaudin at last said to him: 'Ask something of me,' this man said:

'Shah, before I came to you I studied such-and-such a philosophy under so-and-so. Attracted by your repute I journeyed to your *tekkia*.

'Hearing your addresses I have been impressed by what you are saying, and wish to continue my studies with you.

'But, since I have such gratitude and attachment to my former studies and teacher, I would like you either to explain their connection with your work, or else to make me forget them, so that I may continue without a divided mind.'

Bahaudin said:

'I can do neither of these things. What I can do, however, is to inform you that one of the surest signs of human vanity is to be attached to a person, and to a creed, and to imagine that such attachment comes from a higher source. If a man becomes obsessed by sweetmeats, he would call them divine, if anyone would allow it.

'With this information you can learn wisdom. Without it, you can only learn attachment and call it grace.'

'The man who needs *malumat* (information)

Always supposes that he needs *maarifat* (wisdom)

If he is really even a man of information, he will see that he next needs wisdom.

If he is a man of wisdom, he only then is free from the need for information.'

Correction

Abdullah ben Yahya was showing a manuscript, which he had written, to a visitor.

This man said: 'But this word has been incorrectly spelt.'

He at once deleted the word and wrote it in the manner of which his guest approved.

When the man had left, Abdullah was asked: 'Why did you do that, considering that the "correction" was in fact inaccurate, and you wrote the wrong word where the original one had been right?'

He answered: 'That was a social occasion. The man thought he was helping me, and thought that the expression of his ignorance was an indication of knowledge. I applied the behaviour of culture and politeness, not the behaviour of truth, because when people want politeness and social interchange, they cannot stand truth. Had I stood in relation to this man as teacher to student, matters would have been different. Only stupid people and pedants imagine that their duty is to instruct everyone, when the motive of the people is generally not to seek instruction, but to attract attention.'

The Saint and the Sinner

There was once a dervish devotee who believed that it was his task to reproach those who did evil things and to enjoin upon them spiritual thoughts, so that they might find the right path. What this dervish did not know, however, was that a teacher is not only one who tells others to do things by acting through fixed principles. Unless the teacher knows exactly what the inner situation is, with each student, the teacher may suffer the reverse of what he desires.

However, this devotee one day found a man who gambled excessively, and did not know how to cure the habit. The dervish took up his position outside the man's house. Every time he left for the gambling-house, the dervish placed a stone to mark each sin upon a pile which he was accumulating as a visible reminder of evil.

Each time the other man went out he felt guilty. Each time he came back he saw another stone on the pile. Each time he put a stone on the pile the devotee felt anger at the gambler and personal pleasure (which he called 'Godliness') in having recorded his sin.

This process continued for twenty years. Each time the gambler saw the devotee, he said to himself:

'Would that I understood goodness! How that saintly man works for my redemption! Would that I could repent, let alone become like him, for he is sure of a place among the elect when the time of requital arrives!'

It so happened that, through a natural catastrophe, both men died at the same time. An angel came to take the soul of the gambler, and said to him, gently:

'You are to come with me to Paradise.'

'But,' said the gambler, 'how can that be? I am a sinner, and must go to hell. Surely you are looking for the devotee, who sat opposite my house, who has tried to reform me for two decades?'

'The devotee?' said the angel. 'No, he is being taken to the lower regions, since he has to be roasted on a spit.'

'What justice is this?' shouted the gambler, forgetting his situation. 'You must have got the instructions reversed!'

'Not so,' said the angel, 'as I shall explain to you. It is thuswise: the devotee has been indulging himself for twenty years with feelings of superiority and merit. Now it is his turn to redress the balance. He really put those stones on that pile for himself, not for you.'

'And what about my reward, what have *I* earned?' asked the gambler.

'You are to be rewarded because, every time you passed the dervish, you thought first of goodness and secondly of the dervish. It is goodness, not man, which is rewarding you for your fidelity.'

The Sheikhs of the Skullcaps

Bahaudin Naqshband was approached by the sheikhs of four Sufi groups in India, Egypt, Turkey (Roum), and Persia. They asked him, in eloquently worded letters, to send them teachings which they could impart to their followers.

Bahaudin first said: 'What I have is not new. You have it and do not use it correctly: therefore you will simply say when you receive my messages, "These are not new".'

The sheikhs replied: 'With respect, we believe that our disciples will not think thus.'

Bahaudin did not reply to these letters, but read them in his assemblies, saying: 'We at a distance will be able to see what happens. Those who are in the midst of it will not, however, make the effort to see what is happening to them.'

Then the sheikhs wrote to Bahaudin and asked him to give some token of his interest. Bahaudin sent one small skullcap, the *araqia*, for each student, telling their sheikhs to distribute them as from him, without saying what the reason might be.

He said to his assembly: 'I have done such-and-such a thing. We who are far will see what those who are near to events will not see.'

Now he wrote, after a time, to each of the sheikhs, asking them whether they had abided by his wishes, and what the result had been.

The sheikhs wrote: 'We have abided by your wishes.' But as to the results, the sheikh of Egypt wrote: 'My community eagerly accepted your gift as a sign of special sanctity and blessing, and as soon as the caps were distributed each person regarded them as of the greatest inner significance, and as carrying your mandate.'

And the sheikh of the Turks wrote, on the other hand: 'The community regard your cap with great suspicion. They imagine that it betokens your desire to assume their leadership. Some are afraid that you may even influence them from afar through this object.'

There was a different result from the sheikh in India, who wrote: 'Our disciples are in great confusion, and daily ask me to interpret to them the meaning of the distribution of *araqias*. Until I tell them something about this, they do not know how to act.'

The letter from the aheikh of Persia said: 'The result of your distribution of the caps has been that the Seekers, content with what you have sent them, await your further pleasure, so that they may place at the disposal of their teaching and of themselves the efforts which should be made.'

Bahaudin explained to an audience of hearers in Bokhara:

'The dominant superficial characteristic of the people in the circles of India, Egypt, Turkey and Persia was in each case manifested by the reactions of their members. Their behaviour when faced with a trivial object such as a skullcap would have been exactly the same if they had been faced with me in person, or with teachings sent by me. Neither the people nor their sheikhs have learned that they must look among themselves for their choking peculiarities. They should not use these trivial peculiarities as methods to assess others.

'Among the disciples of the Persian sheikh there is a possibility of understanding, because they have not the arrogance to imagine that they "understand" that my caps will bless *them*, will threaten *them*, will confuse *them*. The characteristics here are, in the three cases: Egyptian hope, Turkish fear and Indian uncertainty.'

Some of the epistles of Bahaudin Naqshband had meanwhile been copied as a pious act and distributed by well-meaning but unenlightened dervishes in Cairo, Hind and the Persian and Turki areas. They eventually fell into the hands of the circles surrounding these very 'Sheikhs of the Skullcaps'.

Bahaudin, therefore, asked one wandering Kalendar to visit each of these communities in turn, and to report to him how they felt about his epistles. This man said on his return:

'They all said: "This is nothing new. We are doing all these things already. Not only that, but we are basing our daily lives on them, and by our existing tradition, we keep ourselves occupied day in and day out with remembrance of these things."'

El-Shah Bahaudin Naqshband thereupon called all his disciples together. He said to them:

'You who are at a distance from certain events connected with these four sheikhly groupings will be able to see how little has been accomplished by the working of the Knowledge among them. Those who are present there have learned so little that they can no longer profit from their own experiences. Where, therefore, is the advantage of the "daily remembrances and struggle"?

'Make it a task to collect all the available information about this event, inform yourselves of the whole story, including the exchange of letters and what I have said, as well as the report of this Kalendar here. Bear witness that we have offered the means whereby others could learn. Cause this material to be written down and studied, and let those who have been present witness it so that, God willing, even reading about it might prevent such things happening frequently in future, and might even enable it to come to the eyes and the ears of those who were so powerfully affected by the "action" of inactive skullcaps.'

From: *Wisdom of the Idiots*
Idries Shah

Opium Den Drama

A ROAR OF 'Hurra!' from a thousand Indian throats had not died down as the favourite passed the winning post, when someone gently touched me.

'Hallo, Colonel,' I greeted my chief, 'I hardly expected to see you here.'

'Aay, yes,' he drawled, chewing his cigar, 'I don't much care for this second-rate racing at Meerut, but,' he dropped his voice, 'I had to come, knowing that you would be here. I wanted to get in touch with you quickly.'

Then he explained that whereas from his headquarters at the Indian capital of Delhi, Meerut was only fifty minutes' motor-drive, he had found it more advisable to come personally and start me on the job right away, his secret reports that morning indicating Meerut to be the real starting point.

As the race meeting melted away from our gaze, and he sped his car through the cantonment beyond the polo ground, taking the long, straight road to the canal, he pulled up at the bridge.

Passing the bridge, he ran his car right into a low-lying sugar-cane field, and then stopped.

'Here we can have a half-hour's talk,' he said, mopping his brow, for in spite of early spring, the weather was none too cool.

There he showed me a map and chart of the native quarters of Meerut, handed me my bag of tricks, that is, a suitcase containing my Indian clothes, and told me a whole lot of other things.

'Get going at once, boy – get going.' He gave me a friendly shake. 'Would you slip into your loin-cloth business in the back of the car?' he asked, pulling down the blinds of the windows.

We sped fast towards Meerut again.

'And, here – see this; I was almost forgetting to give it to you,' I heard him shout above the roar of the car, as he handed me a small gold ornament.

It was certainly charming. Two small fishes, mouth and tailwise, were engraved on a gold mount, no bigger than a shilling in size.

'It's very pretty – a lovely brooch!'

'Look at it carefully, it's their emblem –'

'Their what?' I shouted.

'The emblem of those rogues that you are to capture,' came back his resounding voice. 'The Sign of the Fishes – you know the heathen sign of the Zodiac.'

The dying sun was painting the mango-tree-tops with pale gold, as the chief dropped me near the cantonment railway station, assuring me that the entire resources of the secret police would be at my disposal; he drove off to cover the remaining forty miles to Delhi.

And, as I waited for the sun to sink, even that last half-hour before the dusk I found difficult to kill; so I watched the men and women of my nationality play golf quite happily near the railway line.

Dressed as a peasant wayfarer, I sat on the *nallah* bridge, toying with my rustic flute, as I heard a young woman golfer at the fourth hole say: 'Father! look at that man playing the flute. Is he a snake charmer?'

'Damn them,' came back the gruff reply, 'play on, child, play on. I hate cobras.'

Replacing my flute and slinging my cotton bag upon my back, I walked away towards the temple of Mother Kali, laughing inwardly. If those golfers had known!

With the setting sun, droves of buffalo and donkeys, followed by sacred bulls, were moving towards the narrow lanes of the native city. Enveloped in the dust of their own making, they mooed and brayed and jostled each other, endeavouring to push themselves into the mouth of the alleyways.

Their herdsmen shouted to me to mind the bulls, the sacred bulls, as they applied their long sticks mercilessly upon their kine.

Past the sweetmeat shops, and the grain merchants' booths, I picked my way through the zigzag lanes; in the *dowriz* – porches – crude oil lamps were giving a sinister light to the interior of the houses. Here and there an over-devout Hindu woman was plastering the floor of her kitchen with cow-dung, thus giving it the necessary sanctity before her husband's home-coming; a few urchins were being amused by a grandfather who lighted their fireworks.

At last I saw the lofty pinnacle of the Temple of the Black Mother. Like the eye of a demon, a solitary lamp shone brightly under the giant brass bell, hung as it was by means of heavy silver chains to the entrance of the temple.

The interior was already becoming crowded. I saw each worshipper come. He removed his shoes, tolled the gong gently, and with a quick gait was approaching the idol of Kali – the Black Mother, the Hindu goddess of death – laying his offerings at the feet of the Black One.

Then he touched the ground in front of the idol with his forehead, reciting magic formula. He was now dipping his hand in a bowl of gore and smearing his caste-thread with it. Next, he paid his fee to the priest before he retired to a dimly lit corner of the temple, giving place to his next co-religionist, and to await the grand ceremony.

Not being over-devout, I spared myself the first two or three gestures of worship, but paid my rupee to the priest, and, slinking past him, took my seat on a cold-looking marble slab; behind a pillar where prying eyes might not discover me; ostensibly muttering prayers, but watchful of things to come.

When inside the temple and outside in its courtyard the number of worshippers must have reached several hundreds, the chief priest advanced to the altar of the Kali, and tinkled a tiny brass bell.

In the dead silence that ensued, he chanted loudly and long; others yelling out responses as the man passed.

Presently the chanting became general; and I saw the row of the worshippers part, three kids being escorted by three priests to the foot of Kali's Shrine.

Before the giant figure of the Black One, the necks of these three kids were secured in vices. Chanting was led by the high priest, men fell upon their faces, the drums were thudding, three naked blades rose and fell upon the necks of the kids and their unfortunate heads rolled down to the pool at the foot of the goddess, whilst their bodies, held still firm by the vices, trembled in death.

The sacrifice to the Black Mother was performed. A sacrifice in which blood must be shed.

In the strained atmosphere of that gruesome spectacle, when little bells were jingling, and prostrated forms had straightened themselves before the goddess, the high priest still shrieked out his prayers; I saw a priest dip his fingers in the kids' gore, and smear it upon the blood-stained palms, eyes and tongue of the idol; a second application was upon her necklace shaped in the form of human skulls, and a girdle of snakes.

Seeing this, my head reeled. A people who think that their goddess of destruction would be appeased with nothing less than blood, small wonder that they think so little of poisoning and murder. In effect, it hardened my resolve to do my best against such men, who would stick at nothing.

Somewhat stunned, mentally, from what I had seen, I did not realize that even as I sat mutely watching that overpowering scene, the number of worshippers was already getting less and less; and that, too, rather quickly for it to be the normal procedure. There was something more afoot, and I had guessed aright.

When the two innermost recesses of the temple near the goddess were practically empty, I noticed that three men, hitherto wrapped in their cotton coverings, who were administering the 'blood-tokens' from the pool, were now going round the temple and mumbling something to each.

'The Sign of the Fishes,' said one to me, as they came round in my direction.

The brooch that the colonel had given me; the thought came to me at once.

Now, slowly I saw a man's face thrust itself from under the plinth on which sat the goddess. His lips moved dimly, and the visage disappeared. A second and a third time, the man came up – though at different levels of the plinth, and, doing as before, vanished.

By now the temple was practically deserted, save those, who – like me – watched the face appear and disappear. With this difference, that they perhaps knew what it was all about, and I did not – till later.

Blowing out the larger flaming torches, a priest was now lighting tiny lamps, in which a wick of twisted cotton rag burnt smokingly; and all this had reduced the light in the interior very appreciably.

A man was coming stealthily towards me: 'If you are a new recruit to the Sign of the Fishes, brother –'

Cutting him short by showing my Sign to him was easy enough, but where was I going to, as I followed half a dozen tough-looking ruffians down a roughly hewn step, just behind the gigantic image of Kali, into the cavernous depths of a dark passage?

Presently a door opened at the farthest end of the passage: 'Examine them!' shouted a hollow voice.

Sensing it to be a dangerous corner, I straightened myself against the wall in the gloom, meaning to let others go in first, thus enabling me to notice the method of examination.

Not seeing me, others passed me hurriedly through the darkness; and when, after a knock, the door was again opened, I saw how each person was being examined. They only wanted to see the Sign.

Boldly, I advanced, showed my Sign, and was admitted into a remarkable hall – a hall of mirrors. Even the roof was decorated with looking-glasses; and there again was an image of Kali, and a head priest was bending low before it.

When about seventy-odd had been admitted, the priest turned his hard and tricky face towards us. He was reciting prayers. At each stanza he tinkled a bell.

All had taken the vow of death. They were prepared to die for the cause, they shouted with the frenzy of religious ecstasy. The priest blessed them, by giving them the leaves of Tulsi to chew.

And, as I chewed mine and my tongue burned, I was completely at a loss to know the nature of the cause. So persistent was the feeling that I could have asked the man standing next to me.

When we all trooped out, and as everybody seemed to know what was required of him, I was puzzling my brain over the mystery. I could do worse than linger in the shrine, I thought.

I would even hide behind Kali's image, and wait for developments, for something was bound to happen, I assured myself.

That something did happen, for when the rest of the members of the Sign of the Fish had gone, I saw three men emerge from an alcove. They were talking earnestly. One of them was the high priest.

I lay quietly as a cobra and listened, but their tones were suspiciously low. Only once, the eyes of the priest, that looked soft and kind, leaped into a flame.

'Come, now – we go,' I heard him whisper.

I had to climb up the temple pepal tree, and swing myself out to the outer wall, before I could follow them hurrying towards a courtyard.

My chief was as good as his word, for as soon as I was hastening towards the courtyard, a man saluted.

'We have been watching the temple, since you went in Sahib,' he said huskily. 'What, Hukum, order?'

Instantly a huge car swung out of the courtyard where the priest with his two companions had disappeared, and those three men were in the car. The priest was at the wheel. They cut out on to the Delhi road.

After telephoning to Delhi to watch for the car, it was not long before I was chasing the priest on his hitherto unknown mission. The whole police service was alive.

By the time I arrived at Delhi, the hour was not much past midnight, and the report of the doings of the three men was handed over to me at the Jumna bridge.

The three had driven straight to the Kutra of the Hindu jewel merchant bazaar, hauled a noted gem expert out of his bed, and, posing as maharaja's officers, had forced him at the point of a revolver to assess the value of a string of pearls, if they were like the artificial ones that they showed him. The price judged was about ten thousand pounds, and ten thousand pounds in India is a fortune.

'A maharaja.' Something raced through my mind.

'Which maharaja is staying at the Viceregal Lodge?' I asked, my nerves tingling with excitement, for I thought that I was beginning to see daylight in that case.

It was, as I anticipated, His Highness, the Maharaja of Panipura – famous for his pearls.

But why all that secret society business? Am I following a third-rate theft and robbery case? I thought depressingly.

The moon of late night was now paling, as I strode upon the verandah of a police station in the outskirts of Delhi, when the sergeant came rushing to give me the news that they had now found the car abandoned at Bhojla Pahari near the Viceregal Lodge.

'Akh! a wild goose chase,' I growled. 'The scoundrel must have had a scent and escaped.'

But I had not finished my sentence, when another police station announced the finding of a dead body near the River Jumna.

When I arrived at the spot where the body lay, what did I see? The priest; his head completely severed but for about an inch of skin.

More baffling was the fact that the murderers had wrapped the dead person in a sheet, ready to be cremated.

But where were the culprits, and who was going to cremate the corpse?

Time was precious, and I made a quick decision.

The dead body was immediately removed, by the police, and, wrapping myself in the death-shroud, I took the place of the murdered priest, and waited.

It was an eerie feeling, lying there 'to be cremated', and listening to the sighing waters of the holy Jumna glide past me.

I had not long to wait when I heard footsteps, and although I'm no coward, I must own my heart pounded.

It could not be my police guards, for I had given them strict instructions not to make the slightest noise.

Nearer and nearer came the footfalls. That they were those of men carrying heavy loads was apparent to me, as they occasionally rested and, panting and blowing, one spoke hardly above a whisper:

'A nice egg, two *lakhs* rupees' worth. Ah!'

'Yes, we could do with a *lakh* each,' replied the other as he plunked something which sounded like a large tin canister.

'Oh, a rope!' moaned the first.

'*Chup* – silence, chicken-hearted,' scolded the other. 'He will soon be ashes, and ashes swallowed by Mother Jumna's waves tell no tales.'

'Besides,' hoarsely continued the man, 'besides, look at the outrage upon our cult, the national cult, as the high priest inciting us all to fire the Viceroy's house in the name of national terrorism; and on the sly only meaning to get a hulla-balloo started by that fire, so that he, with his selected men, could rob the maharaja of his jewels, and escape…'

'And escape to – ' continued the other, excitedly.

'Come on, come on, Narungi,' exhorted the other, 'let's get going. Time is short. You build the pyre, and we will pour the *ghee*; don't spare the fat… and it will soon be a blaze.'

While the two were busy in the Jumna sands, I thought that I had heard enough: but again, had I? I would wait, I thought. My men were within call, and I was armed.

They had built the fire on which I was to be placed and, as they came back towards me, I caught snatches of their conversation.

'Would you act in his stead?' One was asking the other.

'Nay, brother, we will just say that he has gone to Calcutta to get those arms through.'

The 'arms'. Ha, ha. I had another secret.

'But Krishna would say –'

The other slapped the younger man on the face.

'You are always anticipating evil news.' Murder spoke in his voice.

'I knew Krishna had been a shipping agent, and he would say that the priest could not go so early to Calcutta, because the *Motui Marro* would not be docking for three weeks yet.'

At that instance, throwing aside my death-shroud, I faced the two murderers.

'Stand where you are,' I shouted, 'or I will shoot you like the dogs you are!'

I think that it was fright at seeing a corpse rising to shoot which paralyzed them to a fainting point, as my men soon handcuffed them; and by the early morning train, I was travelling Calcutta-wards to 'prepare to receive' the ship of the gun-runners.

Their information was true to the minute, as *Mouti Marro* duly docked at one of the Hooghly ports, declaring some eighty passengers, and cargo of timber-logs.

It was so manoeuvred that the landing of those logs could be delayed, till the next boat brought their owner Chandi from Shanghai, for in the hollowed-out trunk of each log, revolver parts and ammunition were found.

The eighty passengers were kept in a concentration camp, for although they formed a nucleus of arm-wielders throughout India, it was necesrary to catch their ring-leader, Chandi, the mastermind of the gun-running.

On the third day, he was allowed to land from his lugger boat, and made a bee-line to the less respectable quarters of Calcutta – to be precise, to an opium den, kept by an ancient Chinese laundryman.

It would have been quite easy to have arrested him at the port, but we wanted also to lay our hands on others of his agents from North India, so as to squash the whole gun-running business, which was taking an alarming aspect by then up to Bombay.

It was for this reason that I knocked at the door of Suchi Chow, one night darker than other nights, when our report had it that a large number of suspicious-looking passengers had arrived from North India. They must have a grand council, we thought, that night; and that fact could not have been hidden from the Chinese, as he did not reply to my repeated knocks.

As I rapped for the third time, a dark form detached itself from the heavier shadows of a little alleyway going down to the river's edge, and spoke to me in a series of sharp, short grunts.

I looked down upon him, and was dazzled by his torch-light.

Presently, lurching up, he brushed past me, and instantly I noticed he had a gun in his hand.

He would have fired, but someone moved between me and the gunman, quietly, silently. It was the Chinese.

With no suspicion in his manner, he was now conducting me to a low-roofed cellar, the first whiffs from which were enough to stupefy one.

Chattering like an aged monkey, he asked my business; and when I bared my arm, and showed him the two painted fishes, he became cringing and obliging, and beckoned me to take a seat on a broken-down chair.

"E plenty late, topside,' he muttered in a piping voice, then, changing his mind, he led me to a nearby bunk. The whole place reeked of opium smoke.

A long pipe was handed to me; another man dead to the world was automatically sucking his pipe as he lay on a rough mat beside me, whilst a third was smiling to himself for probably having attained his paradise.

I pretended to smoke, but dared not take even a short puff. Then I saw the Chinese approach me, a lighted taper in his hand.

I gave him three rupees, the price of the pipe; and lay back pretending to be smoking, watching fascinatedly the smoke curling up and up from the tiny bowl at the end of that long pipe.

A man groaned, another thudded down from his bunk; and the Chinaman ran to pick up his precious pipes, smiling the while, getting ready for other customers.

Then there was silence. A ghostly silence. No one moved; only an occasional inarticulate grunt broke the swish-swish sound of the Hooghly's lapping water coming up through the rafters. The sleepers lay as the dead.

Suddenly the sinister silence was rent by a yell and the raving of a giant sailor. His brain aflame, he swore; he hit his head against the wooden column, then he fell like a log of wood as one in a swoon.

An evil peace descended upon the scene again; and I surveyed the living-dead men around me. I thought that I saw one of them move – and move in a manner that made me feel he was conscious – even alert.

I now saw the Chinaman open a door, so dexterously hidden behind a curtain; and the man whom I had spotted as conscious quickly disappeared through that door.

It was all quiet again, but again another man moved, and in the manner of the first disappeared behind the curtain;

several other men did likewise, till I was left with only a few whose turn must come soon – very soon, then my turn.

When only five of us remained in the den, the Chinaman lit a hurricane lantern, and began to scan the faces of the remaining 'corpses'. Upon my face I am sure, he could not find much life, when I saw him make a sort of pass; and a door opened right in front of where I lay, through which a gust of clean river air gave me a welcome breath.

From that door no less than twenty-seven men entered and passed to the door behind the curtain. All were armed.

They were followed by others, bringing in wooden packing-pases.

'Gently, they might explode. You, Sala, may thy sister be given in marriage to a donkey –' swore Chandi to one who had dropped a suitcase.

Lying there I counted one hundred and seventy cases, and it was now no mystery to me that they contained arms and ammunition, and that we had now the grand council of arms-smugglers within the precincts of this vile opium den.

If these men came by way of the river, our river patrol had blundered in some way; but we had them in the hollow of our hands now. What if these other four men lying beside me were also Chandi's men?

For a second the door leading to the river was left unguarded. That second I leaped towards it. Only one man was minding the two empty flat-bottomed rowing-boats there. I descended upon him, and the unexpectedness with which I pounced upon him disturbed the balance and I found myself struggling with him in the black water.

His knife had gleamed a second too late, a bullet hit him fairly and squarely on the jaw; and now my men hiding behind the rafters were ready.

A fusillade of shots greeted my police officers from the hideouts of the den; for those men were now fighting for their lives.

I had to give orders to fire; and, as the guns spat, hell itself seemed to have been let loose, shouting, yelling men, more like demons, with the names of Kali upon their lips, swarmed out of their rat-holes to fight to a finish.

As we rushed them inside the den, I saw Chandi's teeth gleaming whitely in his scraggy black beard as he shouted to his men to fight. 'For the hour has come, *maro, maro* – kill! kill!' he commanded, standing on an empty water-butt.

But the courage of his gun-runners gave way. They were now running hither and thither; only the solitary figure of Chandi surrounded by a smoky torch, stood yelling hoarsely, adding to the bewilderment of the cursing shapes who were throwing themselves in the waters of the Hooghly. Finally, when we made another dash to break down the door to the inner chamber, I saw Chandi hold his revolver to his head and collapse, as if a blade had cut him off from the knees.

Although deadening fatigue was bowing me down to exhaustion, my clothes were soaking, my face and hands blackened, I sat till dawn, making my report to Headquarters regarding the capturing of the whole gang of gun-runners, as well as a quantity of ammunition that could have provided weapons enough for several regiments.

SHAH

'I write this report, sitting in the opium den,' I penned. 'There is no sickening smell in it now, and,' I added naively, 'when cleaned up, this would make an ideal spot for a riverside afternoon tea-house.'

From: *I Spy for the Empire*
The Sirdar Ikbal Ali Shah

Godman

THE MAYBACH CRUISED through the crested gates of
Pimperne Hall, and crawled along the three-mile driveway
at walking pace, allowing His Celestial Highness to take in
the landscape.

On the back seat, Bitu grunted.

'You ready?'

Harry flicked his head down in a nod.

Taking the last bend, the limousine halted a short distance
from Pimperne Hall. Between the car and the house was
an eight-thousand-strong crowd of devotees. All wearing
identical emerald-green robes, they knelt in unison, hands
over their faces in honour of Sri Omo-ji.

'Jesus Christ,' Bitu groaned under his breath. 'Marney's
outdone himself.'

'Not bad,' the godman added with understatement.
'Looks like everyone got here.'

The Maybach's door was opened by the chauffeur liveried
in green, and the godman stepped onto a green carpet.

As he glided forwards to the house, hands pressed together
in Namaste, an army of children hurried up, scattering green
rose petals at his feet.

Kneeling at the front of the house, Marney hoped the
guru would single him out for praise.

But he did not.

Instead, Sri Omo-ji walked past, his emerald-green Versace slippers padding silently into the house.

*

THE FIRST TWO months of life at Pimperne Hall were marked with a frenzy of activity, the *poonyas* working shifts round the clock.

Zap the fixer spread rumours in the surrounding area that a charity music festival, called 'Greenstock', was taking place. It explained why so many thousands of people dressed in varying shades of green were descending on the quiet corner of Dorset.

While still under the radar of the British establishment, the devotees embarked on a raft of ambitious plans. The first job undertaken was to upgrade Pimperne Hall, especially the areas reserved for His Celestial Highness. The private apartments were fitted out with luxury furnishings, and with the latest security gear.

As at the ashram in Varanasi, a secret lift descended to a bunker – one that none of the rank-and-file *poonyas* knew existed. Fully autonomous from the main house, it housed the usual range of facilities – including a communication hub, an armoury, a gym, a cinema, as well as walk-in bank vaults, storerooms, and escape systems.

Outside the house, the devotees set about constructing a hexagonal auditorium the size of a soccer pitch, called the 'Great Hall of Verdant Sanctity'. Once it was completed, they built a hospital, two schools, and a multitude of office buildings. So as not to contravene the area's strict planning laws, many of the new buildings were recessed into the ground. As an afterthought, Pimperne Hall's farm buildings were modernized, the fields ploughed and sown with crops.

With donations pouring in from all over the world, there was no shortage of funds for even the most extravagant plans. Rosco, who was in charge of investments, made tens of millions more through his connections in Silicon Valley.

Meanwhile, a nature trail was laid out in the forest along the banks of the River Stour. For the first time in the property's history, the habitat was protected from huntsmen.

A bookstore, cinema, beauty salon, and bowling alley were constructed too, as well as a boutique packed with clothing – all of it in vibrant emerald green.

Another shop on the compound, The Sri Omo-ji Emporium, stocked hundreds of products relating to the godman. Everything on offer bore the guru's face – from tear-off calendars, dishcloths embroidered with proverbs, board games, and of course the bestseller, *The Path of Omo*.

Most important of all, an enormous rock was delivered on a flat-loader, the kind designed to transport military tanks. Embossed with the curious hexagonal symbol, it was even more impressive than the original Great Stone, abandoned at the ashram in Varanasi.

*

MR. AND MRS. Singh were slumped on the sofa in the front room at 10 Henry Street, as they were every evening between the hours of six and ten.

The ritual was always the same:

Four hours of game shows, reality TV, and the odd Hindi classic thrown in, with supper served on their laps. Ranjit Singh would make sure the kitchen was always stocked with plenty of off-cuts. Some of the meat may have been well past its sell-by date, but his wife piled on the spices so much that they never noticed. A lifetime in butchery had blessed them both with cast-iron stomachs.

At six o'clock, Mr. Singh burped long and hard, then reached for the remote control.

'What about an oldie?' he grunted. 'I'm in the mood for *36 Chowringhee Lane*.'

'You and your Shashi Kapoor, Ranjit!'

'Quiet, you like him as much as me.'

Burping again, Mr. Singh turned on the TV and began making the long journey to Amazon Prime. Technically challenged to the point of absurdity, the Singhs spent almost as much time each night finding the right show as they did watching it. The process involved flicking their way through hundreds of channels one by one.

While Ranjit Singh hunted, his wife put on her bifocals.

'Keeps taking me to that damned Sky News,' he growled. 'Nothing I hate more than Sky!'

'Shall I do it? I've got my glasses on.'

'Hush! I will find it! You're no good with this thing!'

In the world of Mr. Singh, the TV remote was a weapon never to be relinquished from the grasp of a man. His thumb aching, he rested for a moment.

Inexplicably, Sky News flashed up again.

'I'll just catch the headlines,' he said firmly.

'Thought you hated Sky.'

'I do! But a man must see the news to know what's going on.'

Turning to face the other camera or the next item, the anchor read her script:

'And now for something that strains the boundaries of plausibility... An Indian guru who's set up an ashram in a sleepy Dorset village is enraging locals with a world of free love and miracles, all of it washed in emerald green. We managed to get a secret camera inside. Hugh Thomas has the story.'

A well-presented Englishman explained how he was donning sacred robes and a secret body-cam to lift the lid on the Path of Omo. After a quick piece-to-camera he was shown emerging in the grounds of Pimperne Hall, his voice stressed to breaking point.

'I'm now in the ashram of His Celestial Highness Sri Omo-ji,' he whispered, 'whose Eighteenth Incarnation is taking place not in the wilds of far-away India from where he's come, but at a leafy West Country retreat. The cult's devotees are all heading into the Great Hall of Verdant Sanctity, where the guru is about address them.'

A series of indistinct shots followed, while the secret camera struggled to focus. Then, amid a tremendous swishing noise, the undercover reporter managed to pan over a sea of people in emerald green. There were thousands upon thousands of them. Many missing ears and a few missing their thumbs.

Their curiosity piqued, the Singhs watched.

'Bloody nonsense!' Mr. Singh barked.

'Look at them all,' his wife muttered.

'It's a shame on India. No wonder everyone gives us so much trouble.'

Slowly, the camera focused on a lone heavily bearded figure seated on the stage.

Mrs. Singh nudged the bifocals up her nose.

'Wait a minute, Ranjit…' she said.

'Wait a minute, *what*?'

'That guru… look at him.'

'What about him?'

Mrs. Singh gasped.

'He looks like Hardeep!'

Her husband grunted.

'Well it's not. That crook sitting there has fame and fortune – two things lazy good-for-nothing Hardeep will never have!'

'But I'm sure it's him!'

His face flushed, Mr. Singh grabbed the remote control and turned the TV off.

'I've told you a hundred times, never to mention his name in this house!' he cried.

*

AT THE FAR end of the gardens stood an ancient oak, its colossal trunk etched with the initials of lovers stretching back a century and more, the boughs alive with birdsong.

As the shadows lengthened each day, afternoon ebbing towards dusk, Karnika would sit alone beneath the oak and pray for the soul of Sri Omo-ji.

From the other end of the gardens Marney would watch her sitting there in the lotus position, a vision of feminine beauty. Shy by nature, he couldn't quite bring himself to go over and sit with her.

But then one morning Karnika made eye contact with the timid Canadian in the breakfast queue, and she smiled. Not the absent smile of one acquaintance to another, but a smile of enduring affection.

That evening, Marney waited for Karnika to take up her position. As soon as he spied her there, he made a beeline to where she was sitting beneath the oak.

Her eyes firmly closed, back ramrod straight, she smiled as the Canadian approached.

'Been hoping you'd join me here,' she said with a grin.

Marney was overcome with lust.

'How d'you know who it is?' he asked gingerly.

'X-ray vision,' Karnika replied with a laugh. 'Come sit down beside me. Come close.'

Marney did as he was told, and there began a love affair the likes of which he'd never known. Love for a woman who understood him, and loved him in return.

Over the following days, the pair became inseparably close. They shared every detail of one another's lives.

Confiding secrets and exchanging whims, they laughed and wept together. Most profound of all was that their love for Sri Omo-ji was mirrored in the other, as though viewed in the sacred lens of a kaleidoscope.

One evening as they sat close together beneath the oak, Karnika stroked a hand over Marney's knee.

'I loved you from the first moment I saw you,' she said tenderly.

'And I loved you even before that,' the Canadian replied.

Leaning in, they touched lips in a kiss.

Hush prevailed, until the last strains of light gave in to darkness. Never in his life had Marney been so close to anyone that he was comfortable in their silence. He was about to pledge his eternal love, but Karnika spoke first.

'You know I share my love for you,' she said.

'And I mine for you.'

'To think he's so selfless that he's asked us all not to love him… not to worship him.'

Marney's eyes welled with tears.

'It's the only request of his I can't agree to.'

Karnika sighed.

'I feel as though my soul is knitted up to his.'

'I'd die for him.'

'So would I… and even then the sacrifice would be too little.'

Leaning in, they kissed again.

As they did so, Karnika shivered.

'You OK darling?'

'Yeah. Just got spooked, I suppose.'

'D'you see something out there?'

'No, no, it was something I thought of.'

Marney wrapped his arms around her, and held her tight.

'Don't be frightened, I'm here.'

'I had a terrible dream last night,' Karnika whispered. 'I dreamed that Sri Omo-ji went to sleep and didn't wake up.'

'Don't say such things!'

'But what if it happened?'

Almost choking at the thought, Marney smoothed a hand down Karnika's hair.

'Our lives are in his hands,' he answered, 'and we are here to serve him, to protect him.'

Again, Karnika shivered.

'Perhaps,' she uttered in a voice so quiet as to be almost silent, 'perhaps it would be better for Sri Omo-ji not to live.'

Unsure he'd heard the comment correctly, Marney pulled back, his bloodstream becoming fortified with adrenalin.

'What d'you say?!' he voiced with alarm.

'It's just that things are so perfect, so serene. I'm worried they'll go off the rails.'

Reeling, Marney was at a loss for words.

'He MUST live,' he responded resolutely. 'And nothing – and I mean *nothing* – is gonna go off the rails!'

Karnika shuddered a third time, more forcefully than before.

'I hope and pray things stay as they are for an eternity,' she said.

*

OVER THE FIRST hundred days Sri Omo-ji made the occasional appearance in the great hall, but remained largely hidden from view.

While the inner circle spread word that he was praying for the souls of the Unloved Children, a rumour circulated that he was unwell – still weakened by the long hibernation.

The truth was rather different.

Having escaped from Pimperne Hall through the tunnels, Harry and Bitu had taken a taxi to Salisbury, then the train up to London and on to Blackpool. Dressed in regular clothes, they successfully cultivated a high-end hipster look.

At Salisbury railway station, Bitu took out a wad of crisp fifty-pound notes and asked for two first-class return tickets.

Harry nudged him hard.

'Let's go second class.'

'Whatever for?'

'For a taste of how things used to be.'

Late in the afternoon the train rolled into Blackpool North Station.

'First stop where it all began,' Harry said.

'Where's that?'

'Where The Great Maharaja Malipasse dropped dead.'

Strolling the half-mile stretch down Talbot Road, they reached the North Pier at sunset. Minds clouded with memories, Harry and Bitu ambled down the pier, pausing at the spot where on that soaking day they'd walked out on their old lives.

'Back then we were nobodies,' Bitu said reflectively.

'No we weren't,' Harry shot back. 'We were who we are now, but no one else knew it.'

'Wish I'd have known it would end as well as it has.'

'If you'd have known it the journey would've been impossible,' Harry said. 'We had to jump through the hoops to be exactly where we are.'

That evening at a hole-in-the-wall diner across from the football stadium they devoured a feast of black pudding, mushy peas, and fish and chips, washed down with Boddingtons bitter. The walls were layered in a film of beige grease, accumulated through decades of serving up what Marlene, the owner, called 'Heart Attack on a Plate'. An officious old battle-axe, she took the orders at the counter. Bent double much of the time by a smoker's cough, she was as much an institution as the diner itself.

'Beats our friggin' chef and the posh dinner plates,' Harry said, a hand clasped to his stomach.

'Maybe we could get a place like this done at Pimperne,' Bitu suggested. 'I'm sure Marlene would be willing to branch out.'

'Can't believe she hasn't recognized us,' Harry grumbled. 'I've been coming in here since I was a kid.'

'C'mon,' Bitu answered, 'let's get to bed.'

Vetoing Travelodge as being too up-market, Harry had insisted they stay at a low-end B&B on Henry Street. Deficient in every way, it was two doors down from the Singh family home. They took the most modest rooms with a shared bathroom.

At breakfast next morning both asked for the 'full English'.

Blustering back to the kitchen, a trail of cigarette smoke following her, the landlady got the frying pan out.

'Mrs. Jeffries doesn't recognize me either!' Harry snapped. 'Jesus Christ! I've known her forever. Her bloody son Marty used to duff me up every break time.'

Bitu opened the morning's copy of *The Sun* which was perched at the edge of the table.

'It's not the same since they got rid of Page Three,' he muttered. 'There's nothing else worth looking at in here.'

Mrs. Jeffries lurched through the door, a plate of fried fare in either hand.

'Hope you two like ya eggs well done, boys,' she said. 'I do them how my son Martin likes them. Course he can do them a whole lot better than me. He's a chef in Manchester. Got his own restaurant, he has.'

Harry was about to shoot out a suitable reply, when his gaze fell on the red-top's front page. A massive headline blared:

INVASION OF THE GREEN GURU!

Leaping up, Harry told Bitu to pay the bill, while he messaged Zap to lay on emergency transport back to Dorset.

As he stood on Henry Street, his mother and father came out of their house and walked straight past him.

They were arguing in Punjabi about the best way to cook spinach.

*

A MAN WHO loathed confrontation, Marney found reasons to avoid his beloved Karnika rather than try and make sense of her inexplicable comment.

Uneasy in one another's company, they each made excuses as to why they couldn't spend time together.

The divide deepened.

Within a week their love affair was dead.

Karnika stopped meditating beneath the oak, and spent her time sitting on the bench beside the Great Stone. But rather than meditating, she was seen mumbling to herself. With every day that passed, her hair and clothing appeared a little more unkempt, as though she were suffering from some kind of malady.

Keeping a distance, Marney monitored Karnika, worrying and wondering if he ought to speak out to other members of the inner circle. Each time he had made up his mind to break his silence, something caused him to hold back.

Unable to keep the secret of Karnika's deranged state any longer, he was about to send a message to the members of the inner circle, expressing an urgent need to speak to them, when the Maharaja of Patiala called an extraordinary assembly. All members of the inner circle and the blue faces were requested to make their way immediately to the hexagonal meeting room. Filing in with the others, Marney scanned the room for Karnika.

She wasn't there.

The rushed return from Blackpool had involved a chartered Sikorsky S92 helicopter scooping Harry and Bitu up from Stanley Park, and depositing them in a field outside Pimperne.

Slipping down into the labyrinth of tunnels, they found the fixer waiting for them with a golf cart. Before they knew it, they were in the godman's private apartments.

Ten minutes later, they were in costume and in character at an emergency meeting.

The Maharaja of Patiala addressed the trusted devotees on the godman's behalf, while His Celestial Highness sat in silence.

'It was just a matter of time before the press heard about us,' he said, holding up the crumpled copy of the morning's *Sun*.

'Journalists have been snooping around for the last week or two,' Marney reported.

'Bet they were tipped off by the guy at the Anvil Inn,' Rosco said darkly. 'He's had it in for us since Day One.'

The maharaja cracked his knuckles.

'We've got to lock down,' he said. 'That means barbed wire and laser alarms until we get a ten-foot wall built around the entire property. We need to ramp up security on the gates, and put thermal cameras in the grounds. From now on, everyone coming in or out gets screened.'

Stepping forwards, Marney put up a hand.

'I think we ought to check everyone already within the perimeter,' he said loudly. 'And I mean *everyone!*'

The maharaja shot the Canadian an unspoken instruction to sit down. As soon as Marney was seated, Rosco leapt to his feet.

'Your Highness, the problem is the locals in Pimperne and Stourpaine,' he blurted. 'They don't trust anyone wearing green, and are calling us a "cult".'

Motionless, Sri Omo-ji cleared his throat softly, indicating for the maharaja to approach him. When Bitu's ear was in line with his mouth, the godman's lips parted and he whispered something.

Striding back to the trusted inner circle, the maharaja cracked his knuckles again.

'His Celestial Highness says we are to buy the villages,' he said.

'Which one?' asked Rosco.

'Pimperne and Stourpaine... and all the surrounding farmland as well.'

From: *Godman*
Tahir Shah

The Legend of the Cattleman

THERE WAS ONCE a cattleman, who travelled far from his homeland in order to earn his living and also to share his special skill and knowledge with the cattle-raisers of other lands.

When he arrived in the country where he had decided to settle, he gave himself out as a cattle expert. At first people crowded around him, anxious to learn his knowledge.

They said:

'We welcome you, for we are specialists in cows and oxen, and we need such as you, although this is not a good country for raising such animals, as they become sick and die very frequently, in spite of all our science.'

He asked them:

'And how do you feed and treat your animals?'

They described their methods to him, and he at once saw that because of deep but false imaginings about the nature and treatment of cattle, they were actually preventing their own herds from multiplying and even from flourishing.

To them, their own feelings were more necessary than the proper raising of cattle, though they imagined that they were serving their herds.

When he tried to point this out to them, they displayed such horror and dismay that he was compelled to say, 'I am

440

only jesting; of course you are right in the way in which you treat your animals.'

Because he had said that, the people allowed him to work with their animals. They appointed him in the end to be their main administrator of cattle.

This meant that this man had employment in the country of his choice. But when it came to the matter of being able to carry out his principal ability – that of tending and treating cattle – his condition was one of great anxiety and trouble for him.

Because he was compelled by local requirements to treat the cattle with famous but useless remedies when they were sick, he had to spend one-third of his nights, when he could have rested, in making the rounds of the herds and administering the right curatives to them.

Because he had to feed the cattle with insufficient nutrients, since these were the ones which the local people considered right, he had to spend another third of his free time in secretly feeding to the cattle what they really needed.

Only one-third of the necessary allotment of rest ever remained to him.

His life was shortened by this way of living, but he attained high repute among the cattle-people, who regarded him as a paragon of the virtues in cattle-wisdom which was enshrined in their own previous history and aspirations.

The cattle herds improved and flourished. When he died and the puzzled cattle-people tried to redouble what they imagined to be correct formulas for dealing with their herds, the animals died even more often than they had done before they had ever known the newcomer.

It was only because he left a son sworn to secrecy, who eventually took his father's place, that the people's welfare, and that of their cows and oxen, was, in spite of themselves, maintained.

The Handicap

A Persian carpet-weaver challenged a Turkish weaving master to a contest.

Each was to make the best carpet that he could, so that a panel of judges might finally decide who was the greatest weaver in the world.

But the Turk was a philosopher whose teaching for many years had been summed up in this phrase:

'Never refuse, but never contend.'

So he accepted the challenge, saying only:

'I must make one proviso, because of the known disparity between your work and mine.'

'Yes, indeed,' said the Persian, 'I am prepared to agree to a handicap.'

'Very well,' said the Turkish master, 'the condition shall be that I give you a start of twelve thousand years.'

How Things Work

There was a venerable dervish, who, being able to ignore certain anxieties due to the degree of his development, was much respected by the local people.

One day they made a collection and presented him with a sheep, which he took to his retreat, and looked after carefully.

A thief, however, heard that the old man had a sheep, and decided to steal it. He started along the road towards the dervish's abode.

On the way, he met a devil, and asked him where he was going. 'As a matter of fact,' said the devil, 'I'm on my way to the cave of such-and-such a dervish. He is interfering with the customary operation of human weaknesses, and I have decided to kill him.'

'We have no real diversity of aims,' said the thief, 'for I am going to the same dervish's place. My mission is to steal his sheep.'

So they walked on in silence and amity for some time.

Presently the devil began to think, 'If I let the thief steal the sheep first, he may alert the dervish, whom I need to surprise when he is asleep.'

The thief, for his part, was thinking at the very same time, 'If I let this devil get to the dervish first, he may cause such a commotion that the people of the neighbourhood could be aroused. They might prevent me getting the sheep, and my night would be wasted.'

When they arrived outside the dervish's cavern, the devil said, 'Let me go in first, then I can kill the man and you can walk in and carry away the sheep.'

'No,' said the thief, 'let me go in first and get the sheep. I can tell you if he is awake or not.'

They started to argue, and then to exchange blows, and finally to scream at each other so loudly that the dervish came to the cave-mouth to see what was going on.

At the sight of him the devil, overcome with hatred for the thief, shouted out, 'Look out, dervish! This is a thief, and he's going to steal your sheep.'

The thief, furious with the devil and affronted by his impudence, screamed, 'This is a devil, and he's going to kill you!'

As the dervish stood there, everyone in the neighbourhood, wakened by the din, came pouring from their houses and surrounded the fighting pair. They were given such a buffeting that they fled, and neither a thief nor a devil has been seen in that locality for centuries.

Three Villages

There was a wise man who divided his time between three villages.

In the first village, he gave instruction to groups of people, one party at a time. He told them and showed them things, and gave them observances to perform.

He used to spend a great deal of time away from this village. The result was that the villagers split into even smaller groups. Some of them believed that he would come back, others felt neglected. Some of them invented their own teachings, and some of them made use of his name to influence fellow-villagers. Many of them weakened in resolution because of his absences.

There was a second village. The wise man used to spend most of his time there, and people came to visit him, and attended his contemplation-hall regularly. These people sang his praises and always seemed to do what he asked, and believed that they were in harmony with him and with each other.

One day the wise man went to a third village. Taking some pupils from there, he showed them each village in turn.

'The first village is in the condition in which we saw it because you have not given enough attention to its people – you must nurse them,' said the newcomers, thinking that they had understood his point. 'Look how well behaved the people are where you spend so much more of your time,' they continued.

The wise man answered them, 'On the contrary. You have to leave people alone from time to time, so that you and they can see what they are really worth. The pot is stirred in order to mix, but also in order to produce the scum and the dregs. If you spend all your time with people, they become accustomed to you, and they have no self-reliance in your absence, as in the first village; whereas, as in the second, their self-reliance is invisible, because it is never tested.'

'Then,' asked the observers, 'which is the better method?'

'Neither. Each is an incomplete part of a total method. In order to produce learning, you must have those who are frequently seen to mix with those who are seen sometimes. And a few of those who – like you – are prone to misinterpret, may be included as well.'

The Sutra of Neglectfulness

It is the duty of Khidr, the Hidden Guide, to travel about the earth in various guises, in different ages, provoking a state of mind in man, such that he shall have a chance to gather his scattered self.

There were once three men whom Khidr had to test.

The first one was suffering from a terrible disease, and Khidr went to him. He said, 'What do you want?'

The man said, 'I want relief from this distress.'

'And what else?'

'I would like money, so that I may flourish in the world.' Khidr gave him both wishes.

Then he heard the supplications of a second man. He went to him and said, 'What do you want?' The second man said:

'I want only that my friend and adviser, who is being tortured, should be released, for he is near to death because of his enemies.'

'And what else do you want?'

'I want that I should have property, so that I may have the respect of men.' Khidr gave him both of his wishes.

Then Khidr went to the third man, who wanted something very badly. 'What do you want?' he asked him.

'I want protection for my children, for they are in fear and terror.'

'And what else do you want?'

'I want importance, so that men shall respect me and make my life easy.' Khidr granted these wishes.

Some time later, however, he visited the three men again to see what they had made of their lives, and how they were living them. To the first he appeared in disguise, and said:

'I am a poor traveller, and I need some help, some money, to reach my destination. The way is long, and I have no recourse other than you.'

'Am I a banker?' asked the first man, for he had made himself forget the days when he was needy himself. 'I can give you nothing – unless you can help me, because in the past few years, although I have money, I have become lame in one foot.'

'Do you not remember me?' asked Khidr.

'No,' said the man, 'I do not remember you. Be off!'

Then Khidr went to the second man, who was in a flourishing condition. 'I am a poor traveller,' he said to him, 'and I need your help, for many are dependent upon me, and I must reach my destination, so that I can help them by my work when I get there.'

'But you are not a member of my community,' said the second man. 'And I can help only those who adhere to my laws. Why should I help you?' So Khidr went on his way.

He arrived at the door of the third man, and said, 'You may have forgotten me. One day I helped you, when you wanted protection for your children, and also to become respected by men, so that you could flourish.'

The man looked at him for a long time. 'I have no memory of such a transaction,' he said, for he had forgotten it, 'but I will help you, for I do not think that I should always give something away only in payment of a debt or in expectation of gain for myself.'

A superficial and sanctimonious theoretician of the Sufi lore who was present turned on Khidr and abused him roundly. 'This friend of mine is clearly a saint,' he said, 'and his words should make you ashamed of yourself, trying to manipulate his feelings!'

Remedy

A certain dervish spent many years in perfecting a remedy for the illness of a man who happened to be rich. So excited was he by the success of the preparation that he set off to carry it to the patient without consulting his Sufi mentor, to see whether circumstances had changed. On the way, however, he met another man in a caravanserai, and told him the formula and the wonderful effects of his discovery.

As soon as he was asleep for the night, this villain stole the medicine, substituted sugared pomegranate juice, and hastened ahead to cure the sick man, hoping for a reward.

The villain gave some of the medicine to the rich man, but it immediately made him worse. And the thief crept away, convinced that the dervish was mad and that his remedy was useless. And so even his knowledge of the recipe was of no value to him. He even felt relieved that he had not been found out, and that the patient's servants had not beaten him as a charlatan.

When the dervish arrived at the patient's bedside and gave him pomegranate juice – it cured him with one mouthful.

In the Land of Fools

Once upon a time there was a man who strayed from his own country into the world known as the Land of Fools.

He soon saw a number of people flying in terror from a field where they had been trying to reap wheat. 'There is a monster in that field,' they told him. He looked, and saw that it was a watermelon.

He offered to kill the 'monster' for them. When he had cut the melon from its stalk, he took a slice and began to eat it. The people became even more terrified of him than they had been of the melon. They drove him away with pitchforks, crying, 'He will kill us, next, unless we get rid of him.'

It so happened that at another time another man also wandered into the Land of Fools, and the same thing started to happen to him. But, instead of offering to help them with the 'monster', he agreed with them that it must be dangerous, and by tiptoeing away from it with them he gained their confidence. He spent a long time with them, in their houses, until he could teach them, little by little, the basic facts which would enable them not only to lose their fears of melons, but even to cultivate the fruit themselves.

Cooking the Cabbage

Two thieves met one day in the Land of Fools.

As with all people of the same profession, they started to boast of their exploits.

One of the thieves said:

'I once stole a cabbage as big as a house!'

449

The other said:

'I once stole a saucepan as big as a palace.'

The first thief said:

'What would anyone want a thing like that for?'

Said the second thief:

'It was needed to cook your cabbage in!'

The Branch

Once upon a time, in the Land of Fools, a stranger to the country found that the branch of a tree had broken and was about to destroy a dam full of water.

He seized the branch and held on to it. Soon afterwards a party of people of the Land of Fools came walking by.

They said:

'What are you doing with that branch?'

He answered:

'How lucky you have arrived! Help me to lift this branch, for otherwise the dam will be broken, and we shall all die.'

They laughed and laughed. Finally the wisest among them said:

'Dear friends! This is a delicious moment: savour it. Not only does this man, talking about a branch, imagine that we are stupid enough to think that it has some relevance to a dam – but he imagines that by relating it to an ancient fear of ours he will make us obey him!'

And so, in paroxysms of laughter, the people of the Land of Fools went on their way.

The end of the story is exactly what you think it is.

The Fruit

It was reported to the Very Wisest Men of the Land of Fools that the trees were bearing, and so they went out to collect fruit.

The trees, sure enough, were laden, their branches pulled down almost to the ground.

When the Very Wisest Men reached the trees, they fell to discussing which crop they would harvest first. Since they could not come to any agreement on this, they tried another subject. Now they discovered that there was no accord about whether to pluck the fruit with their left or right hands. Then there was another problem of equal difficulty; and another, until they realized that they must withdraw to a more suitable place to thrash things out.

Finally, after full participation of all the learned institutions, all was settled. The Very Wisest Men again found themselves under the trees. But by then it was winter. The fruit had fallen and lay rotting on the ground.

'What a pity that these trees are so treacherous,' exclaimed the Very Wisest Men. 'Those branches had no right to swing up again like that. But never mind: you can at least see that the fruit was rotten anyway.'

The Magic Word

The three wisest men of the Land of Fools, by some lucky chance, met Khidr, walking the earth trying to impart wisdom.

'Would you like to know the Word whereby everything can be accomplished?' he asked them.

'Yes, indeed,' said the Three Wise Men.

Khidr said:

'Are you ready to hear it?'

'Yes, indeed,' said they.

So Khidr told them the Word.

The First Wise Man said:

'But this is a word which anyone could pronounce – this cannot be of any use.' So he promptly forgot it.

The Second Wise Man said:

'This word is too inelegant for me,' and he found that he could not remember it.

The Third Wise Man said:

'It can be written down – so it cannot be of any use. It does not sound like what I expected – so it is not the right kind of Magic Word.'

Then they all noticed that a deputation of ordinary citizens of the Land of Fools was waiting to hear some of their wisdom, so they hurried off to fulfil their obligations.

How to Prove It

Two people of the Land of Fools were talking.

The first said:

'I'm no idiot, I can multiply numbers!'

The second said:

'I don't believe it!'

'I bet you this silver coin that I can,' said the first.

'Go ahead then, let's hear you,' said the second.

'Here you are,' said the first man. 'Two and two are ninety-nine!'

'Fair enough, here's your money!'

Yearning

A man said to the sage Humayuni:

'In my earlier years, I used to yearn for a teacher and for instruction. But I never found any which fully satisfied me, and now I no longer feel such a need.'

Humayuni said:

'If you had sought a teacher and a teaching, being content with what you found, you would have been a Seeker. In fact, while you were only seeking the fulfilment of a yearning, you were unteachable at the time. The thirsty man may be incapable of recognizing water if over-thirstiness has maddened him.

'The way to find water is not always to increase your thirst. It depends upon the degree and nature of the thirst at the right moment.'

Man and Sufi

It is related that someone once said to Mulla Jami:

'You do not behave like a great poet and Sufi: how do we know that you are genuine?'

He replied:

'You, on the other hand, behave almost exactly like a human being – that is how we know that you are not yet one!'

The Book

A young man was about to be married, and his prospective father-in-law was an unbearably pious and literal-minded cleric.

The youth went to his Sufi mentor and asked how the old man might be directed towards the Path of Understanding.

'He will be directed,' said the sage.

'But in what manner?'

'The question has been formulated, the answer will develop, the question is not permissible,' said the Sufi.

'Then how should I act towards my father-in-law, if that is a legitimate question?' asked the bridegroom.

'Put up with him.'

When the wedding day came and the couple moved into their new home, the cleric followed them, bearing on his back a huge leather-bound box. On its cover was inscribed: 'The Holy Recital'.

The newlyweds put the case on a shelf and left it there.

Some months later things went wrong for the young man. He lost his job, his small capital was soon exhausted, and he thought about approaching his moneyed father-in-law for help to set himself up in a small business and to meet his growing debts.

'Approach your father-in-law by all means,' counselled the Sufi sage.

The young man wrote a letter outlining his situation to his wife's father, and the old man arrived in short order, bringing with him the local judge and a couple of other scholars.

When all were assembled in the sitting room, the old man quavered:

'You have been brought to this pass through your own flagrant disregard for the *Sharia*, the Sacred Law.' So saying, he pointed to the Qur'an-case, and called for it to be brought down and opened.

'But why should you say that we do not have regard for the Law?' asked the young man.

'You do not read the scriptures,' said the cleric. Sure enough, when the box was opened, it was found to be filled with gold pieces.

Then the young man said, 'But has it not been said that "Knowledge is better than reading"?' And he explained that he knew the Qur'an by heart.

The judge said, 'You brought me here in order to pronounce whether this young couple were pious or not. I certainly cannot say that you can find fault with this son-in-law of yours.'

'No indeed,' said the ancient, 'and I do sincerely repent, for this youth, modestly refraining from having made any play of his erudition before this time, has shown me that he is a better scholar than I am, both in conduct and in knowledge. I acknowledge myself to be outdone, and henceforth I shall strive to learn the Qur'an by heart.'

The two scholars exclaimed, 'How excellent is his humility, and how admirable his resolve to perfect his erudition!'

'But,' said the judge, 'it has also been said that "Public humility ceases to be so when it is the subject of dramatic show."'

'Yet what is better than following the example of one who does not simply read the Qur'an, but has gone to the trouble to learn it by heart?' asked the ancient.

'Because public drama is destructive to real achievement, I shall tell you privately,' said the judge.

And what he told the academic made him exclaim:

'This has saved me from becoming one learned from books: I will henceforth follow the path of the Sufis, the people of practice and being.'

And he became a Sufi, whose life illuminated, and still suffuses, the thoughts and deeds of the People of the Way.

What the judge had told him was:

'You and your fellow intellectuals read the Qur'an. The young man knows it by heart. But your daughter, his wife: she thinks and lives in accordance with it, although she can neither read nor write, nor dispute, nor recite.'

Dervishhood
Abul Hasan insisted:

'Thinking about the affairs of this world is nothing to do with the matter of the dervish path.

'Thinking about the next world is nothing to do with the matter of the dervish path.

'They stand in relation to one another as yesterday does to tomorrow.

'Today – something similar but having its own individuality – that is the dervish path.'

The Reflection Chamber at Doshambe
The manner of tiling of the walls of the reflection chamber of Doshambe was thus:

Hamid Parsa asked his disciples, some of them tile-craftsmen, to arrange for the chamber (*Dar el Fikr*) to be tiled.

They made a start on the work, and then it was delayed by a variety of obstacles.

Hamid Parsa made inquiries from time to time, and in the end the master craftsman said:

'O Pathfinder (*Rahnuma*) we have not enough men and we have not succeeded in tiling the walls and we think it would be better to say this now, since such a long time has elapsed, and you may probably wish to make other arrangements so that the chamber shall be completed for whatever use you desire it.'

Hamid Parsa answered:

'Very well. Leave this work, and I will arrange for its completion.'

The craftsmen were assigned to other tasks. After two years Hamid Parsa called them in and showed them that the walls were impeccably tiled with glazes and workmanship of the highest quality and astonishing beauty.

After Hamid died, it was discovered that his frequent absences from the *Tekkia* were due to his having spent his time in a tile-yard, where he had made the necessary tiles himself. Later he had fixed them to the walls, without mentioning this to anyone except certain assistants whom he asked to say nothing about the matter.

His successor, Miran Jan, was asked:

'Why did the Pathfinder not tell us that he had done this work himself?'

Miran answered:

'His explanation to me was that if he told you, you would feel rebuked, and that you were not in a condition in which rebukes were useful. Or, he said, "They would in laziness, masquerading as proper admiration, regard me as some kind of wonder. Their trouble is laziness, my need was for the tiling. So I worked on the tiling and I gave them work to do to improve their condition of laziness."'

Learning of the Unripe

A man came to Khwaja Ahrar ('Master of the Free') and asked him a question.

When the Khwaja had given him the reply, he asked permission to go, and at once quitted the assembly.

Ahrar said:

'He was wise to ask the question.'

Allama Sadrudin said:

'Did he know why he asked it?'

'He did not know, but a part of him knew.'

Sheikh Mustafa Najur said:

'He was also wise enough to leave as soon as he had the required information.'

Ahrar replied:

'Yet that was another part of him. He was thinking that he should start off in time for congregational prayers in the Great Mosque.'

Haidar Gul inquired:

'Can a man then be wise inwardly, in some part of himself, when he is generally under the impression that he is unripe?'

'Were it not so, no man could attain wisdom in its fullness,' said the Master Ahrar.

Alacrity and Respect
Musa Farawani said:

'I served Sharif Abdalmalik for twenty years, and all I got from him was indifference. But I persevered, hoping that I would understand why he should pay so little attention to me. But I have never been able to solve this mystery.'

Daud, son of Zulfi, answered:

'Did you serve him with the same alacrity which you would have shown had he been the king?'

'I suppose not.'

'Did you serve him as faithfully as one serves the making of a complicated object, as does an artisan?'

'I suppose not.'

'Did you serve him with the alacrity which you would have shown if he had been a high official or a military commander, if you had been a petty official or a mere soldier?'

'I suppose not.'

'Then he was waiting for you to manifest those forms of service. The Sharif, himself serving something of the very highest, could not accept any service less than that which is manifested in lower concerns.

'You call something a "mystery" when you will not see it. You call something service which is not service at all. You have not yet begun to serve, therefore you cannot ask why your non-existent "service" has not been accepted.'

The Cripples

In a public square one day, some people were shouting:

'Down with the Throne!'

They were faced by a party of royal guards, who were trying to beat them and take them prisoner.

Sufi Zafrandoz, accompanied by a few students, was watching the scene.

'Which party should we aid?' asked a pupil.

'The cripples!' said Zafrandoz.

'Which are the cripples?'

'Both. The one party is incapable of ceasing to oppose authority. The other is unable to cease opposing them.

'People handicapped in such a manner are in the grip of a disability which hampers them. They are crippled in thought as surely as a lame man is crippled in body. Why, therefore, do we feel sorry for, and try to help, only the physically handicapped, who are such a minority?'

Names

Anwar of Nishapur was asked:

'Tell us one kind of Sufi whom we should avoid.'

He said:

'You cannot avoid any real Sufi. But if you want to avoid people, then avoid those who themselves use titles like "*murshid*" (guide) and who do not leave it to others to address them thus.'

Repetition

A foolish man came to Abdullah Manazil and asked him a question. Manazil answered, and at the end of the discourse, the man said:

'Please say that again.'

Manazil said:

'You asked me a question and I was ill-advised enough to expect that you would understand the answer. Now you have asked me to repeat my mistake.'

Bricks and Walls

They asked Minai:

'What are we to make of the work of the teachers of the past? We read their books and the accounts of their doings and sayings recorded for us. We perform their exercises, and we visit the places of their burial and teaching. Some people say, "Do not visit shrines"; others say, "Do not read books."'

Minai answered:

'The similitude of this situation is as the similitude of a strong wall built in the past. The old teachers are the original masons and the present teachers are the working masons. The disciples are like the populace, for whose protection the masons worked.

'The masons built walls, shall we say, to define certain limits. Those limits are there still, in some cases. In other cases the boundaries have changed. The present masons fix the boundaries again. In the same way, walls were formerly built for protection of the people. The climates and winds may have changed, or the people may have changed. They

461

look at the wall, and wonder how it may shelter them. But this old wall will not now do so.

'Consequently the present masons take the bricks, and make suitable walls for the people of the time. The books are bricks. Some masons ask you to read certain books. This is their instruction, for they can show you what wall to build. Some say, "Do not read books" because they mean, "This is not the wall we have to build"; or even, "We have not got to the stage of building a wall."'

The Hole and the Thread

A certain great Sufi was asked about the role and status of some of his predecessors.

He said:

'To erect a small building you may first have to excavate a large hole.

'To make a large carpet you may have to start with a single thread.

'When you can see the building or the carpet, your question is answered.

'But when your question is about the hole in the ground and the thread in the hand, you can only be answered in this parable.'

The Squirrel

Maulana Bahaudin was walking along a grassy bank with Alaudin of Nishapur.

Bahaudin said to him:

'I wish to know why it is that you have taken away from people the enjoyment of so many habits in Sufism. You may be right, and I will be the first to agree that you probably are, in saying that such practices are trivial. But you leave the people with nothing if you do not allow their companionship to become a source of joy for them.'

Alaudin said:

'There is a scene unfolding before us. Watch it and you will have your answer, if you can understand it, esteemed upholder of legitimate pleasures.'

In front of the pair several small boys were playing. They were throwing, from hand to hand, a squirrel which they had caught, and whose feet they had bound together. As they ran here and there, they roared with laughter, excitement and pleasure on every face.

After a few moments an older youth, seeing what they were doing, ran up to them from the roadside. He took the animal and removed the cord from its paws, and let it go. The players of the squirrel-game were furiously angry now, and they shouted all kinds of abuse at the older boy.

Alaudin says:

'Had it not been for this demonstration, I am sure that I would never have realized the relative situation and concealed dangers in what we assume to be legitimate pleasure. But ever since then, throughout my life, I have often found that what appears to be desirable is being done at the expense of something else; and that what pleases people, even "sincere" people, can be found to be making an appetite for an unsuspected vice.'

From: *The Dermis Probe*
Idries Shah

The Bolshevik School of Spies

By THE TIME I finished with the German spies in Persia and Afghanistan, a new scare arose in India. It was the peril of Red Revolution from the Bolshevik side.

This Moscow movement was gaining ground amongst the unemployed in the Indian cities; and the religious movement called the Khilafat, set up to reclaim the Sultan of Turkey, had added oil to the fire against the British in the minds of Indian Muslims.

The terrorist movement of the bomb-thrower in Bengal was not a patch on it, because the minds of eighty million Muslims residing in India were aflame; blaming the British for the downfall of their religious head in Turkey, they were willing to make a common cause with the Russians.

Those who preferred to leave the country, and to fight for the Turks against the English, were now leaving India in alarmingly large numbers via Afghanistan.

The Bolsheviks, of course, had an eye to business, because they saw in these fanatical young Indian Muslims excellent raw material for training as spies of Red Russia, who could be sent back to India to start a Communist Rising.

Since the route lay through Afghanistan – a familiar country to me – I, too, was walking through the dusty Khyber Pass with a caravan of over eight hundred men. Truly it was a Kafla of Lost Souls, for youths, scarcely knowing the reason of leaving their home and hearth in India, still in the budding stages of their career, still uncertain of the goal, dragged their weary legs along as we reached our first halt in Afghan territory at Jalalabad.

'Do you know brother,' a fellow traveller touched my arm, 'I have just heard that I am the proud father of a son.'

'And where have you left the light of your eyes?' I asked interestedly.

'Allah has so willed that my infant son shall remain in India,' came his sentimental reply, 'I go to fight against the English; but he must live.'

The Afghan Mahmandar was summoning us to the midday meal in the orchard of the *sarai*, which prevented our further conversation, and finding a place near my fellow traveller at the dinner table, I said, 'But you are still so young, Subhan.'

A shadow flitted across the young man's face – a shadow of doubt for his future escapades.

'Eat,' he said, 'and then we will talk, for you seem to have more understanding than these eight-hundred-odd travellers from India.'

Till late that night, Subhan and I talked. He told me of his aged father, his ailing mother, his young wife and infant son, whom he had left in India – for the holy cause of religion.

Assuming myself as one of them, I hazarded the thought of hardships which would be our lot in Bolshevik Russia on our way to Turkey.

'Who is going to Turkey?' he asked bluntly.

'Are we not all the soldiers of the sultan, going to fight in his ranks?' I explained.

The man looked rather blankly at me.

'Apparently you were not within hearing distance of the *kotwal*, when he told us of his news that we are not to be soldiers of the ordinary kind, but to be trained as spies of the Bolsheviks, to return secretly to our homeland and set India right.'

'Set India right?'

'Yes, set her in her rightful place as a self-governing and an independent country under the Russians,' came his reply slowly, deliberately.

My goal, of course, was the Bolshevik Spy School at Tashkent in Central Asia, where all these youths were going to land ultimately.

So after our route to the Bolshevik territory was determined to lie not right over the Oxus route, but via the northern Afghan town of Balkh, we finally crossed over the river at Takhta Bazaar. The terrible journey over the Hindu Slayer Range was one of my greatest tribulations in land travelling, for we drove on our mules and camels far too hard, slept under the stars in the chilly moonlight; and for food had only black bread, and tea made out of apple peelings.

Once in the Bolshevik territory we were received like princes; there was hot food, there were dance parties, fur coats were distributed to us, and cinema shows were organized where I stayed as a state guest at Induskaidom or the India House at Tashkent.

The important piece on the chess board of this intrigue was a Bengali Hindu, tall and thin and extremely irritable.

We rose to receive him. 'Welcome to you gentlemen,' he spoke as if in a great hurry to depart to Moscow whence he had come, 'but you have to work here, and work hard –'

Abruptly he turned to me, 'And you – what part of India do you come from?'

For a brief moment I was taken aback. 'From Kashmir,' I replied.

'Ah, hence the rosy complexion, and flashing eyes!'

I had become quite popular with the rest of the Bolshevik students in the school of espionage, and it was their delegation which suggested that I should accompany the Bengali Revolutionary as their spokesman to Moscow.

It was against my plans, and I refused, because the school term was now beginning, and I wanted to learn more than what they taught of revolutionary history at Tashkent.

It was exhilarating to read Karl Marx in faulty English, and to be told that Marx was less of a political leader, and more of a prophet; at the mention of whose name, the whole class had to say, 'Peace and glory to his name,' whilst I saw other classes forming and reforming in drilling squads in Teverskaya Boulevard.

In my studies, which began at nine in the morning, and did not terminate till five in the afternoon, but for a short break for a sparse lunch, I had to cram all that could be swotted about the French Revolution and the American War of Independence. But it was disquietening to read our own homely John Stuart Mill in the Russian language, and be told that Lord Morley's writings were really Bolshevik doctrines, if only we had wisdom to understand them.

Beyond the fact that I could take clear mental notes of all the methods of teaching imparted to the revolutionaries intended for India, I was able to do little more in persuading my ill-advised classmates that what they were learning was leading them only to a prison life in India, and the real mind of the stay-at-home Indian was not inclined to Bolshevism.

And yet, you never can tell. If every six months six hundred students were sent into India with an alien doctrine, the movement would soon make itself felt. More especially because we were thoroughly couched in the manner of manufacturing bombs, putting together rifle parts – which would be smuggled into British India – and pieced together by the agents there for use against the English official class.

After the first term, when I had gathered all my material regarding the school, I waited the starting of the first batch of spies India-wards. As the Bolsheviks had by now quelled a Turkestan revolt, the passes through to Golden Samarkand and Bokhara were free to travellers, and Bokhara was the first point at which such a number of these Indian spies would touch.

Aware of this, one fine night I disappeared from the school, and within a day and a half was securely installed as a carpet merchant in an obscure Bokharian market.

From here I dispatched a full report of the working methods of the school, and gave minute details of those who may at an early date be on their way to India. Adding, however, that possibly, the Afghans would not allow these agents of the Bolsheviks to go through their territory, so that winter though it was, the party might take some other route.

During the time that it took me to piece all this information together, I continued to trade in carpets in Bokhara, and none was any the wiser for it, till I announced to my nextdoor neighbour that I intended to go on a pilgrimage to Mecca, and sold the rest of my wares to him very cheaply.

However bad other Bolshevik arrangements might be, they keep their railway connection with north Persia in good trim, for the Transcaspian Railway line that connects the heart of Turkestan with the Caspian Sea is not only regularly but most efficiently run. Most efficiently, because at the door of each compartment sits a Bolshevik guard with a loaded revolver, and every train carries six secret agents, in order to examine the movements of all passengers.

And on its westward journey, Merv is a danger point, where I had to receive not only my instructions but make arrangements for some money to be sent to me, as I was embarking upon an uncharted journey.

At six-thirty our heavily laden train puffing and blowing arrived at the lonely Merv station. After the usual hurrying and shouting accompanying the arrival of a Central Asian train was over, I found the place in deep gloom. Not a *durakha* in sight, not a pedestrian on the footpaths, no lights could be seen anywhere, the place was dead. Merv was in the grips of malaria fever.

Not that I found this quiet atmosphere unwelcome, but my Turkoman agent was also shivering with a fever attack, and I found him under a load of quilts and moaning in pain, while his body was bathed in perspiration.

Whether it was my agent's illness, or my movements had given cause for suspicion, before I was able to do much business with the Turkoman there was a loud knocking at his door, and I found myself confronted by no less than six armed policemen.

At the police station my passport was examined, but although it was found to be in order, I was to be detained in a cell for the night, till they heard from Moscow.

'From Moscow,' I shouted, 'has Allah sapped your brains? What has Moscow to do with poor pilgrims bound for Mecca?'

The commandant winked at a sergeant.

'The Holy Man speaks good Turki!' The words were spoken rather scathingly.

I was searched, and having been relieved of twenty-three gold pieces which I had sewn in my shirt, I was allowed to go.

It was plain that was all they wanted.

The next morning when the Turkoman merchant had recovered from his fever, he gave me a full report of the party of the Bolshevik-trained Indians, who were reported to have been looted and left dying by Turkoman brigands, which seemed that my going any further was fruitless.

But one thing of important interest was that a Bolshevik Propaganda train was expected the next morning, and the Russian commissars had sent official orders to all to be present to receive and profit thereby.

SHAH

Perched on a mule, the Beg of the village rode towards the station. His hawk-bearers followed, then a party of Uzbek and Turkoman Elders walked in haste, but I was with the humbler trades folk and thus we saw the train arrive.

If was composed of three large wagons. The Third International was mightily played, and then the side of one of the central wagons was lowered to make an improvised raised platform. A comrade dressed in the garb of the peasants addressed us with emotionally dramatic gestures, describing the pitiable conditions of the farmers during the Czarist times, and gave a colourful description of the great service of the Soviets.

Sweets were distributed, each Elder received five gold pieces, and the village Beg a handsome sword and a robe of gold cloth. He would have preferred gold pieces, as with a bad grace he was strapping the sword at his middle.

We were subjected to another speech. This time from a mulla, who called upon his hearers in the name of Allah to consider that Bolshevism was no other than Mohammedanism, and later in the evening a news reel was projected on a side of one of the wagons.

More in jest than in earnest I laughingly remarked to my Turkoman friend: 'What if someone fires this train?'

His eyes dilated; an impish light played in them. 'Would you do it?' shaking with excitement. 'I will show you how.'

Well, the night was darker than other nights in Merv, as I crawled under the wheels of the wagons, and heard not a sound. The Propagandists, after their day's hard haranguing, had gone to pay a return call to the Beg. There was only one

472

soldier on duty. He, too, was in slumberland, and the deed was soon done.

Even as, standing in the shadows of mulberry groves outside Merv, I counted the three hundred beads of my rosary as carefully as the most pious mulla, the earth rose around the railway station enveloped in flames. A tremendous explosion shook the village, and an inferno of yelling and shouting could be heard everywhere.

Soldiers were now firing haphazardly into the night, but hitting no one, as the screeching and shouting mob surged towards the spot where the Propaganda train flared like fireworks.

The town was surrounded, but I was riding hard towards an unknown destination. This time I must try and catch a train going to the Caspian Sea, for on the Persian border town of Askabad another spy school existed, and was worthy of my attention.

A fair amount of cash, with which I had now been provided by the Turkoman at Merv, gave me a double chance of escape, because with a few gold coins added, I was able to persuade the station master at the next station to let me travel on an engine, which was to carry the news of the Propaganda train mishap to the junction at Tedjan, and bring help.

To the engine driver I was the special commissar on an urgent errand, and I will say he did let his old bus fly. There was no fear of a collision with any oncoming train, because the last one of the week had passed eastward, and the way was kept open for the Propaganda train.

At Tedjan I gave the full report, which tallied correctly with the previously interrupted telephonic report, and was asked to go at once to the chief commissar and give him also my report.

This chief, needless to say, never saw me, for I branched off, and wandered round the Persian border, which I knew like my own home town.

Had I known how greatly my little trick at Merv would dislocate the timing of the trains, I would have paused to think, for I was interested and in a hurry to get to Askabad to look at that other spy centre of the Bolsheviks.

Train after train passed to Tedjan without stopping; there was wild activity, and I did not envy the folk who were looking for the man who had mined the Propaganda train, but at last as a fast express pulled up just for the brief space of three minutes at Tedjan to pick up some official or other, I jumped on the roof of a wagon and clung to it like a limpet as it gathered speed in the chilly night. That cold took the skin from my face and knuckles.

Down the incline of Dushk, it roared its way to Lutfabad, and sped apace onward to Askabad, stopping nowhere on the way, till I saw the station of my destination fade in the haze of a hot sun. At Bami, it slowed down, and as I was famished, filthy and frozen with the intensity of the desert night cold, so I was baked and burned with the fierce rays of the day's sun, I slid in a lump down from my perch, and slunk stiffly past a reservoir.

As no trains were stopping at the place which I left behind, the only way out was to board another train, and get to the shores of the Caspian, where I could lounge about at that famous Bolshevik port of Krasnovodsk, and when the service was restored to some normality, to travel back to Askabad and see what I might be able to learn at the spy school there.

Within thirty hours, I found myself in that remarkable Caspian port of Krasnovodsk; and it opened my eyes to the danger which the Persian government was running by not protecting their northern frontier, for Krasnovodsk was chock-a-block with giant liners bringing arms and ammunition to the Bolshevik soldiers on the Persian border.

The vigil kept by the Bolsheviks, however, was great, and I had to lurk about the narrow and squalid sailor cafes and apartment houses to escape detection, but at last the police were too clever at their jobs, and I had to face a commissar.

'Ohe,' he cried upon seeing me with a tramp-like unshaven chin.

'Ohe, he does not answer to his description,' the commissar was looking at a photograph.

'Pull his beard,' he ordered.

And I yelled.

'It's not false, Comrade!' remarked the sergeant.

'But who are you?' the man eyed me narrowly.

'A pilgrim,' I replied simply.

'How do I know that you are a pilgrim?' he spoke suspiciously. 'Besides, do you not know that being in this port is forbidden without a pass?'

'Do pious pilgrims –?'

'Shut thy mouth with that religious stuff. Religion! Religion! I am sick of religion. Put him to work,' he thundered.

And my work was not of the easiest kind, being dockyard labour. After two hours one's back aches as if it were broken, for believe me it is no joke carrying cotton bales up and down a steamer – that is, if you are a novice at it.

Well, it had to be done. But day by day as I worked, I never seemed to grow to get used to it, much less like it, nor could I establish any contact with my agents in Merv, or Bokhara. No telegrams could be accepted, not even to Askabad. What business had a coolie with telegrams, anyway? In my present position the idea was fantastic – I would be questioned, and this was the last thing I desired.

The only plan was to board a train going towards Bokhara, and trust with luck to reach Askabad. But no one could travel without a passport, also no one was allowed within the barbed-wire entanglements surrounding the railway station at Krasnovodsk.

On the third day, a veritable giant of a boat named *Bokhara* steamed in. Only the more sturdy of the coolies were to unload it, for she had 'valuable cargo' – cases full of ammunition. We were, however, not required till proper berthing arrangements were made for her.

And when I heard that she had some bales of cotton as well in her hatches, a thought leaped into my mind.

More did the boat carry: oil from Baku, several tanks of it for the oil reservoirs of the port.

The third day came, and to speed up the unloading we were told off into shifts – day and night gangs. I so contrived that I should be in the latter.

Cotton and oil! Ha! How it would burn. The very thought warmed me.

A Kurdish labourer befriended me for a consideration, for he liked gold pieces, and to him I confided what was in my heart.

When he boarded the ship, like me he had been searched for matches and even for flint, but, being a well-drilled and notorious thief, he had hidden both near the hold.

On my night shift I soon found the matches. The oil tanks were very well known to us, and it was but a matter of a few seconds to ignite the cotton waste; it spread like wildfire, till it was nearing the tank, and closing my eyes, my heart in my mouth, I jumped over the gangway.

It came suddenly, as I was now hiding behind the dockyard. A terrific burst of flame and smoke belched forth from the man-hole, and a yell of dismay rose from the guards on shore.

Higher and higher leaped the flames, and almost from the first the fire burned with the fury of the fires of Hades.

Now was my time. I rushed to the chief commissar, reported the incident, and ran back with some of his office papers to the telegraph office; the officer's papers gave me the necessary credentials as I dispatched a carefully worded telegram to my friends in Bokhara.

Consternation was so great that practically all regulations were forgotten, I jumped into the station yard, hid in a luggage wagon of an east-bound train, awaiting to be carried to somewhere towards my destination as a stowaway, and hoping to jump off at some convenient station.

Although the whole town was in turmoil trying to extinguish the fire that had broken out on the ammunition-carrying *Bokhara*, I found that the train began to move, and was soon roaring on its way further and further from Krasnovodsk Bay. This was as I should have desired.

She pulled up at Guzul Arvat, before climbing to the heights of Bami, and I had opened the wagon just in time to be spotted, as I saw the guard run to close the door and gaze in wonderment as to how it had been opened of itself from the inside.

If I had not been in a hurry to gain the shelter of some bushes in the semi-darkness of the dawn, I would have liked to have shown the Comrade how to open a railway wagon, especially a Russian wagon from the inside. There is a way to do it, but they do not teach that to a railway guard. If he does not know, that is his own fault.

I was fully six weeks too late in reaching Askabad, for had I not been carried past it by the train after firing the Propaganda train, I would have seen how the Indian batch of spies, refusing to go to India, were shot dead as to one man they insisted on going to fight the English amongst the ranks of the Turkish army.

If it was to be that way, I thought that my little journey to Krasnovodsk had not been entirely in vain.

As that shooting affray at Askabad had created a major sensation amongst other students of espionage elsewhere in the heart of Central Asia, the Askabad training centre was closed down; some of them demanded to be sent back to India at once, so that they could start revolutionary work there without loss of time.

It was to watch this batch from Tashkent that I now journeyed to Bokhara.

From: *I Spy for the Empire*
The Sirdar Ikbal Ali Shah

The Clockmaker's Box

ONCE UPON A time there was a clockmaker whose clocks were regarded as the most beautiful mechanical objects ever created.

Adorned with fine tracery and exquisite detail, the clocks were extremely expensive to make. The only person in the kingdom who could afford to purchase them was the monarch. With an eye for excellence, and the funds to pay for it, he regularly ordered the clocks, which he presented to other kings.

Whenever one of the clocks was finished, the clockmaker would deliver it to the palace himself, displaying it on a simple silken cushion.

One day, the king, who had commissioned an especially splendid clock, sent word to the clockmaker, asking him to make a presentation box worthy of the timepiece. Following orders, the master craftsman fashioned a rather plain leather-bound box, in which the clock was presented to a visiting monarch.

The next time the king ordered one of the clocks, he asked that the box be a little more ornate – reflecting the sumptuous object it contained.

Time passed.

Each year, the king ordered more and more of the clocks. Utterly obsessed with them, he befriended other sovereigns merely so that he could present them with one of the marvellous mechanical objects.

Each time he placed an order, the king asked that the container be a little more ornate than the time before. Following instructions, the clockmaker added extra layers of golden filigree, finer grade leather, and lavish details that cost a small fortune.

With every order placed, the boxes became all the more magnificent, although the clocks themselves stayed very much the same.

By now, the boxes were so extraordinarily sublime that everyone followed the monarch's example, and became preoccupied with the containers rather than the mechanisms inside. The reversal of sense was so complete that the clockmaker himself was referred to as 'the box-maker'. Fearful at being singled out in making note of his opinion, the monarch's chief adviser held his tongue – even though it was obvious the sovereign was confusing contents with container.

When the king eventually passed on to the happy hunting grounds, a tremendous mausoleum was prepared, decorated with details from the legendary boxes the master craftsman had made. A special slab of marble was mined, and the king's long appellation and many titles were inscribed in lovely lettering upon it.

Beneath them, in pride of place, were etched the words:

KING, RULER,
LOVER OF BOXES

The reason I mention this story is because even a humble author is at times in danger of behaving, or rather misbehaving, like a king.

Just as the sovereign encased the clocks in boxes of astonishing delight, a writer risks falling prey to suffocating their work with introductions, prefaces, and afterwords.

I wrote the texts presented in this book as a way of complementing my own corpus, and in some cases the writing of others, so as to draw attention to certain themes and ideas, allowing the reader to observe the material in a different way.

When I had finished my first travel book, my father – the writer and thinker, Idries Shah – reviewed the manuscript. Having suggested I change the book's title, he urged me to delete the extensive introduction.

I asked him why.

'Because no one reads introductions,' he said.

'Why not?'

'Because they always think they'll be boring beyond belief.'

To anyone who happens to find *The Clockmaker's Box* in their hands, I offer apologies and thanks...

Apologies for boring you senseless, if indeed I do.

And thanks for supporting my need to release my work how I wish.

From: *The Clockmaker's Box*
Tahir Shah

Tales of a Parrot

AN ANCIENT SANSKRIT work, now lost, is believed to be the original of the *Parrot Tales*, which have been found in folk-recitals from Indonesia to Italy. The fourteenth-century Persian *Tuti Nama* (Parrot Book) by Nakhshabi is the collection of linked tales best known in the East, and it is still very widely read and recited. There is a derivative Sanskrit version, the *Seventy Parrot Tales*. Many of these stories, told by a parrot to divert his mistress while her husband is away, are found in the medieval *Seven Wise Masters*, which circulated for centuries in Europe with a popularity second only to the Bible.

The book is found in Greek, Hebrew, and other languages. The first European version is thought to have been prepared by the monk Johannes, of the French diocese of Nancy, in about AD 1184. The tales are thought to have been dispersed among the people of the West by wandering preachers. 'By such means,' says the eminent scholar Clouston, 'stories, which had their birth in the Far East more than two thousand years ago, spread into the remotest nooks of Europe; and jests, which had long shaken the shoulders and wagged the beards of grave and otiose Orientals, became naturalized from cold Sweden to sunny Italy.'

The frame-story of the *Parrot Tales*, split into three tales, was collected by the learned Giuseppe Pitrè, in Sicily, over a century ago, from peasant lips. Several versions have been found in Italy. The interest of this one, apart from its entertainment value, is the fact that, unlike most of the folktales of similar origins, it stems from the Sanskrit version, and not from an intermediate Islamic source, such as the Turkish, Arabic, or Persian collections. The medium through which a Sanskrit-based tale reached Europe is not known.

I

ONCE UPON A time there lived a king, who had an only daughter, who was the sun, moon, and stars to him. He gave her everything which she desired, and there was nothing in the world which she was denied.

On the day when this story begins, the king and the princess went driving out into the countryside, as it was springtime. So many beautiful flowers were in every valley that they drove quite a long way. They stopped the royal coach, walked about for a while, and after picking a few blossoms, drove back to the palace.

Now, no sooner did the princess return to the palace hall, than she saw with dismay that her favourite toy, a beautiful life-like doll, had been left behind somewhere – on a hedge, maybe. She was out of her mind with grief, for that doll had been hers since ever she could remember, and as she had no brothers or sisters, it was everything to her. The doll was dressed as she was, daily, and had almost as many jewels as the princess herself possessed.

So she decided that, without telling her father, she would slip out at the first possible moment and go to look for the doll.

It was not long before the king went to change his robes, and she found her chance to escape through a secret exit. Not being very used to going about alone, however, the princess was soon completely lost. Night was falling when she saw a fine palace in front of her.

Knocking on the door, she shouted, 'Who is the owner of this magnificent building?' She called out in a most regal way, and the captain of the guard who was at the entrance said, 'Lady, this is the palace of the Great and Glorious King of Spain!'

'I am a king's daughter,' she said, and she was at once admitted, and taken to a guest chamber. There she was undressed by several maids, and robed for the night with much ceremony. She soon fell asleep, and without any fear, since she was in a royal household, slept as if she were safe at home.

Next morning, she was taken before the King of Spain.

He was very impressed with her appearance, and with her manner and charm.

'Will you remain here with me and administer the palace as if it were your own?' he asked, for he had no daughter, and his wife had been dead some years.

'Certainly, I shall be happy to do so,' said the princess, and she soon felt that she had never lived anywhere else in the world.

But there was trouble in the palace among the courtiers. Twelve royal maidens who were related to the King of Spain by marriage felt that they had been passed over for a complete stranger.

Gossip and intrigue circulated and soon the courtiers had taken sides. Some were for the royal maidens, others were for the princess.

'How can we take orders and instructions from one so young and inexperienced in our ways as this girl!' they whispered. 'Who indeed is she, though she says she is a true princess? Let us plot her downfall!' So they went to her, and with smiles and giggles said, 'Oh, dear lady, why do you not come with us upon our next outing? There are many things we could show you, far away from the confines of the court!'

'Oh, no,' the princess shook her head, 'I am not sure that I can go anywhere without the permission of dear Royal Papa. He never likes me to leave his side.'

'But we know a sure method by which you can be spared,' said they. 'Let us tell you what to say to His Majesty.'

'What am I to say?' cried the princess.

'Just say "By the soul of your daughter you must let me go with the royal maidens!"' they murmured in her ear.

'Very well,' said the princess, 'I will try it.'

But no sooner had she said the fateful words to the devoted king, than the smile left his face, the light of anger came to his eyes, and he shouted, 'Ah! Wretched girl! How dare you speak to me like that! To the trapdoor with you!' And the unfortunate princess felt herself propelled towards a large trapdoor in the floor. She soon was falling through time and space, falling, falling in the most horrible darkness.

Suddenly, she stopped falling, and could feel the wood of another door. She turned the knob, blindly, and it gave way. Then she felt tinder and matches in her hand, and lit a lamp. Another door stood half-open, and slowly advancing, the princess saw in the light of the lamp a beautiful young girl, as fair as the moon on her fourteenth night. This unfortunate young creature had her hands bound and a silver padlock on her mouth, so that she could not speak. The princess looked at her questioningly, and the girl indicated that, under the pillow, was a silver key. The princess found it, and saw that it was set with a green stone in the top.

The princess unlocked the girl's lips, and she said, 'I am a king's daughter, stolen away by a wicked magician. He had left me here for I do not know how long, and feeds me when he comes. Every night at midnight he arrives, with two slaves carrying bowls of food and fruit.'

'But, tell me,' said the princess, 'is there any way in which you might be freed? This imprisonment must be torment for you!'

'I can only find that out by asking the magician,' said the other, 'so tonight conceal yourself under the bed, and listen to all that passes between us. I shall try to wheedle some sort of information regarding this out of him, so listen well, dear lady, and save me if you can.'

'That I shall do, with all my heart and all my strength, if it comes to that,' said the princess, and she got under the bed in readiness for the arrival of the magician.

When twelve o'clock came, the door flew open, and a strange-looking man, with a long dark robe, white beard, and fierce, piercingly blue eyes appeared, attended by two coal-black slaves of savage aspect. The magician took the key, unlocked the younger princess's lips and with every sign of affection, fed her with his own hands from the bowls.

While she was eating, he was paying her extravagant compliments, and she said, 'Now, just for argument's sake, if I were ever to escape from here, how could it be done? I pray you tell me, that I might be diverted by the telling of it!'

The magician looked taken aback for a few seconds, then he smiled and said: 'Well, since there is no chance that you ever could be able to do it, I will tell you.

'It would be necessary for someone to put gunpowder all around the palace, and, at midnight, when I appear, set light to it. Then it would blow a complete circle around the palace, and I would be blown up into the air. But eat these delicacies – you would not get food like this in the world except through my magical agency!'

The young girl laughed, and passed it off as though the idea meant nothing to her. After that, the magician caused one of the slaves to wash her mouth with rosewater, the magician dried it himself with a fine napkin, and he went away, not forgetting to lock her lips again with the padlock.

After a short while, the princess came out from under the bed and said, 'Sister, sister, have no fear, I will go and summon help from my adoptive father up there in the castle. Somehow you will be rescued, or we shall be blown up together!'

She crept out of the room, climbed through the trapdoor, and began to shout for the King of Spain.

The King of Spain, who had missed her after she had disappeared through the trapdoor at his command, came to her, and she told him the whole story from beginning to end.

He said, 'I will send for the captain of the guard, even though it be the middle of the night, to make a ring of gunpowder around the castle as soon as he possibly can get the men roused. I myself will light the powder at the very second twelve o'clock strikes. Leave it to me, and go back to your own room, my dear.'

'No, no, Father,' cried the princess, 'I have promised that poor girl that I shall rescue her, or we shall both get blown up together.'

'So be it,' said the King of Spain, and the brave princess vanished again down the tunnel. She comforted the girl with the silver padlock on her lips, as well as she could, and whispered words of encouragement to help her pass the hours of waiting.

The king's sappers began digging, and worked away with a will to prepare the mine. The day passed very slowly for the two girls. By the time it was nearly midnight, the gunpowder was ready in one large circle all around the castle.

When the clock struck twelve midnight, the magician came as usual through the door of the chamber. The princess was hidden under the bed, and the girl with the silver padlock on her lips looked as she always did, patiently waiting for him.

The torch set the gunpowder alight, the ring of powder ignited, and the magician was blown into the sky in a thousand pieces. The two girls were severely shocked for a few seconds, but soon began to laugh with joy and relief, though they had singed eyebrows, torn clothes and blackened faces.

When the King of Spain saw them, climbing out of the tunnel, he exclaimed, 'Ah, my beautiful daughter! Come to me and be with me here in harmony for the rest of our lives! You my dear,' he added to the brave princess who had effected the rescue, 'you shall have the crown after I am dead!'

'No, no, dear King of Spain,' cried she, 'I am a king's daughter myself, and I, too, have right to a crown!'

So a feast was prepared which took many days and nights of jollity.

This matter spread all over the earth, everyone taking the story to his or her own country, and everybody talked of the great courage and goodness of that beautiful princess who had saved another king's daughter from certain death and dishonour.

And all the chief actors in this tale (except, of course, the magician) enjoyed life and happiness in all the days of their sojourn in this world.

II

ONCE THERE WAS a king who had an only daughter who was as beautiful as any young girl ever born to humankind.

On her eighteenth birthday news came that the King of the Turks wanted to marry her.

'Oh, what do I want with a Turk for a husband?' she said, and refused to have anything to do with him.

Soon after this affair, she lapsed into a very unhappy state of health – she, who had never had anything wrong with her in her life before.

Her father the king sent for doctors from far and wide, but none could be found to help her, let alone to tell what was actually wrong with the princess.

She lay on her silken sheets, eyes rolling, body shivering, her limbs twisted under her.

Her poor father was in distress, and called the wise men of his capital city together. 'My friends, hear me at this time of my personal distress as you did when the country was in danger from enemies,' he said. 'Tell me what I am to do!'

'Your Majesty,' said they in unison, 'find the princess of whom we have just heard, who caused the rescue of the daughter of the King of Spain from the dreaded magician who hid her away and locked her lips. Find her, and she will find a way!' For the princess who wrought the miracle had

491

become the talk of every country in the world, and there was no quarter of the earth where her name was unknown.

The king ordered ships to set out that very hour to search for the lady. 'If the King of Spain will not let her leave him and come, then we shall go to war against Spain, though she be the mightiest country of Christendom!' spoke the monarch boldly, with eyes of fire.

The ships set off, and arrived off Spain very soon. All their guns blazed in salute across the bay, the envoy set foot on the earth of Spain, and bent down to kiss it in homage. 'A message, a message from a faraway king to the King of Spain,' was the cry.

The sealed letter borne by an envoy dressed in scarlet and gold was handed to the King of Spain.

He broke the seal, and let his eye wander over the message. But he clenched his fist and shouted, 'I will go to war, but I will never send my dearest adopted daughter on such a mission!' and he tore up the letter.

The princess came from behind the ivory screen and asked, 'What is it, Royal Papa? Who was that letter from, and what is this about?'

'Dear daughter, the king of another country has sent his ships to take you away to help in the affair of *his* daughter. You shall not go, I forbid it!'

'What are you afraid about? I will return to you, in time, after I have settled this thing,' she said.

So she went, after taking leave of him with great tenderness.

When she arrived, the king went to greet her.

'My daughter, if you cure this child of mine you shall have my crown!' he vowed.

'I am a king's daughter myself, and I already have a crown,' she said, as she had said to the other king. 'Let us see what the matter is, never mind about crowns or coronets.'

She was taken to the princess's bedchamber and saw her lying there, all wasted away.

Now, after a few moments' thought, the princess who had just arrived turned to the king and said, 'Your Majesty, have some soup made, and some chickens cooked. Also, cheese and fruit. Have these things brought to me here, and lock me in this room alone with your daughter for the space of three days.

'No matter what you hear, or even if I cry out for you to open up, do not do so. Within three days I will deliver your daughter to you alive or dead.

'Remember, whatever I say to you, do not open the door.'

Soon everything was done to her liking, and the great bolts were fastened on each side. But when she went to sit beside the princess as the light from the windows failed, she discovered that they had forgotten the tinder to light the candles at night. So, she poked about in cupboards, with the unlit candle in her hand, looking for a tinder-box. One of the doors led to a small room, and, looking out of the window, she saw a light in the distance. She could not stand the dark, so she descended from the window with a ladder of silk to try to find the light.

When she got near the light she saw it was a huge black cauldron placed on a fire. There was a tall Turk stirring something in the pot with a stick.

She greeted him with, 'What are you doing, O Noble Turk?'

And he replied, 'My king wanted the daughter of this king, but she did not want him, so he is having this done as a bewitchment.'

'Oh, poor Turk,' she said, laying her hand on his sleeve, 'you must be tired, stirring like that for so long and so bravely.'

'Yes,' said the Turk, 'I am rather tired now, and I wish that someone else would help me.'

'Why, I will help you,' said she. 'You just lie down there, and I will continue stirring for you.'

'That is extremely kind,' said the Turk, yawning, and he lay down. She took the stick and began to stir.

'Am I doing it correctly?' asked the princess.

'Yes, indeed, beautiful lady,' the Turk replied. 'If only I could sleep for a little while…'

'Well, you take a sleep now and I will stir,' said she, and the Turk fell into a doze.

When he was asleep she bent down, and, with her amazing strength, threw him into the boiling cauldron. When she saw that he was dead, she lit her candle at the fire and returned up the silken ladder to the bedchamber.

She sat beside the sick princess's bed, and saw that she seemed to be better. For three days and three nights she nursed her and fed her with the delicacies which the king had provided. When the princess got up on the morning of the third day, perfectly well again, the girls embraced each other, and called through the door for the king to open it. He came in at once, and kissed them both with great joy.

'Ah, my daughter,' he said to the princess who had wrought the miracle, 'I owe you my kingdom and my daughter's life! What in the world can I give you to repay you? Tell me, I am at your command.'

'Nothing my gifts have brought me are of any value; I only work by the power vested in me by Providence,' she replied.

'Stay with us here,' pleaded the king, 'and you shall be as dear to me as my own daughter.'

'No, you threatened my father with war if I did not come, remember,' she said, 'and my father will declare war upon your country if I do not return at once, so let me go, with your leave.'

Sadly, the king agreed, and thanking her again, gave a great feast in her honour. Loaded with costly presents for herself and her father, she soon departed, and returned to the King of Spain's palace.

III

ONCE UPON A time there lived a king and queen, who had a handsome son whose only diversion in life was to go hunting. Morning and noon he hunted, attended by many huntsmen. Now, one day, he was far afield when he saw a most beautiful doll lying on the ground. It was dressed like a real live princess would be attired, and even had real jewels in its ears and round its neck. He looked everywhere to see where the owner of this fabulous doll might be, but there was no one to be seen in any direction. So he took the doll up onto his horse, as if it had been a lady, and declared to the others, 'We shall return home at once now,' and they rode back to his father's kingdom.

In his private room the prince examined the doll, and placed it upon his mantelpiece, looking at it long. 'What a beautiful doll,' he said again and again to himself. 'If the doll is so beautiful, what must its mistress be like? Surely it is made in her image.' After he had taken the doll to his room the prince would not leave it, gazing upon it fondly hour by hour, murmuring, 'Just think of the mistress, if the doll is so beautiful!'

When he had not seen the prince for several days, and the court physician told him he had been keeping to his private apartment, the king went to see him. He found the prince looking at the doll on the mantelpiece, muttering feverishly, 'If this is the doll, how beautiful must be the mistress!'

'My boy!' cried the king. 'Are you completely out of your wits! What are you doing with that image? Have you become an idol-worshipper in the space of a few days since you came back from your last hunt? Tell me the truth of the matter at once.'

The prince turned lacklustre eyes upon his father and said in a low voice, 'If this is the doll, just think how beautiful the mistress of such a doll must be! Just think of the mistress, if this is only the doll!'

Horrified at his son's wasted appearance and strange manner, the king went back to the throne-room and summoned all his courtiers.

He said: 'See what has happened to my son, he has become mad! What is to be done? The physician says he has no physical ill, no fever, no broken bones, but his mind has completely gone. Such a man cannot possibly take my place as ruler when I am gone. What is to be done?'

One aged sage stepped forward and bowed before the throne.

'Speak,' said the king.

'Your Majesty, people are talking about a miraculous princess who goes from kingdom to kingdom, curing people. She is said to have found the King of Spain's lost daughter, and to have cured another princess only recently. Send for her, and if she will not come, declare war upon her father!'

'Well said,' agreed the king. 'Send an envoy for her at once. I will brook no delay. My son must be cured for the sake of the country and the people, if not for mine.'

So a suitable courtier was sent with a long retinue and a sealed letter from the king.

When these foreigners arrived, the hall of audience was full of people thronging through it. The princess looked from behind the carved screen and said to the king, who was reading the letter, 'What ails you, Father?'

'Nothing, nothing my dear,' said the king, frowning and biting his nails, tossing the letter into the corner rolled up into a ball.

'There must be something wrong. Who are all these strangers at court, and what news does that foreign envoy bring in that letter which you have thrown away?' she asked gently.

'It is war,' said the king testily, 'unless I allow you to go on yet another of these ridiculous journeys to the far corners of the world!'

'Is someone ill again?' she asked.

'Yes, this time a young prince, who is behaving very strangely and seems to be quite out of his wits. I do not think that I should expose you to these dangers...' said the king.

'I must go, I shall soon come back, I promise, dear Father,' said she, and after he had embraced her, she set off.

With many attendants and soldiers, the princess's journey took quite a time, but at last she arrived at the prince's private room. He was looking at a beautiful doll and sighing deeply, murmuring to himself the while, 'Oh, what a beautiful doll. If this is the doll, just think how wonderful the mistress of this doll must be!' But as he was now so feeble, he said it all under his breath.

So the princess said to the king: 'Close me up in this room with the prince for three days. Lock the doors and do not come in until I call you to open them. Leave some food here for me to give him daily, and in three days I will bring him out alive and well, or dead.'

They did as she asked, and she sat with him, feeding him chicken broth sip by sip, until she made him stronger.

At last, when he was able, he called in quite a loud voice: 'Oh, what a beautiful doll! If that is the doll, how much more beautiful must be the mistress!'

'Ah, wretch,' cried the princess, 'so it is you who has got my doll!'

He raised himself on one elbow and said, 'Are you the owner of the doll?'

'Yes,' she said, 'I am. Now drink this chicken broth and get well.'

When he was able to get out of the bed, they called through the door to his father that he was cured.

So the king and the courtiers came in, and carried the prince out to the people, happy and well, looking even more handsome than he had been before.

The princess took down her doll from the mantelpiece, and hugged it for sheer joy.

Soon the prince told her he was in love with her, and begged her to marry him. 'For though the doll is beautiful,' he said, 'you are so much more beautiful, as I knew you would be. Will you marry me and become in time the queen, when I am king?'

And so she answered that she would.

The king, delighted to have such a wonderful daughter-in-law, gave her many jewels, and the people were wild with joy at having the famous princess for their prince's bride.

Several letters were written and sent with trusted messengers right away, among them one to the King of Spain to tell him that she would not be returned to him as a daughter, but later, she would go back with her prince to pay their respects; and another letter to the king whose daughter she had cured.

At the time of the wedding, which was one of great splendour, all the monarchs came together and helped to make the princess's good fortune complete. And she lived in great peace and happiness till the end of her days.

From: *World Tales*
Idries Shah

The Haunted Carpet

I HAD NO real reason to dislike the Prince of Jutpore in whose territory I entered as a guest, but that I did dislike him, nay detest him, had been obvious to me from the moment he had engaged me as his secretary. I loathed the atmosphere of his gloomy palace on the outskirts of the ancient little city, I hated the dreadful room in which I was compelled to work. But I was not the master of my own fortunes, and therefore could not but endure the surroundings I execrated.

Not only was the prince haughty and monosyllabic, mysterious and, to my mind, ill-balanced, but he was certainly the most ill-favoured human being I had ever set eyes on. His pale, unhealthy face had all the cold horror of a death mask in plaster, and the lustreless eyes, which could scarcely be said to light it, resembled those of a dead man. The great room in which he laboured so ceaselessly at his work of reading and transcribing was stifling, dark and neglected, for he would permit no one to lay an orderly hand upon its dire confusion. Almost directly behind his chair stood an immense piece of furniture of a type and workmanship altogether unfamiliar to me. It was made of some exceptionally hard wood, and every square inch of its surface was richly carved with grotesque symbols, regarding the purport of which I could not even hazard a guess.

Serpents writhed and twined upon its sides, and in the centre of each of its two doors, leering faces, crowned with feathers, were surrounded by an intricate wealth of ornamental detail, which had for me not the faintest significance. A lamp of bizarre appearance and extraordinary workmanship hung from the roof, and even the chair in which the prince sat had a weird and antique shape.

But, most striking of all the curious things that this repellent yet fascinating room contained was the wonderful carpet which occupied a portion of the spacious stone-flagged floor, and which lay in all its arresting display of colour and pattern between my employer's desk and the door. As no furniture was placed upon it, not even a chair or settee, it was easy to get a full view of it in all its beauty or hideousness – for to this day I cannot make up my mind regarding the essential quality through which it appealed to me, at times attracting, at others repulsing me by virtue of the strange properties which seemed to reside in its unusual colours and eccentric design. Of what material it was made I could not at first satisfy myself, but I found later that it had been woven from the fibre of the jute plant, and the details of its workmanship left no doubt in my mind that it had been fashioned by native weavers.

The ground of this peculiar carpet was a shade of golden-yellow or honey colour, with which a mysterious and perplexing design had been interwoven. Fringing the border was a series of discs in blue and red which seemed to me to represent eyes – not human eyes, but round, birdlike orbs, half closed, yet unwinking, holding the solemn stare of the owl and the brooding menace of the vulture. Within this border, ranks of great red spiders with human faces sprawled to meet a row of interlacing serpents and spotted toads. The centre was occupied by a grim yellow skull, from the sockets of which a pair of eyes similar to those fringing the edges of the carpet looked out balefully. The effect of the whole was that of a craftsmanship barbarous, yet artistic, and I did not know which to admire more, the almost unique skill shown in the wonderfully involved design, or the warm shades of the brilliant and realistic dyes with which it had been coloured. But, this notwithstanding, the aversion I felt at times to this singular piece of workmanship was so intense, that I could scarcely bring myself to remain in the same room with it. At other times I could scarcely tear myself away from the contemplation of its striking pattern and gorgeous hues.

By degrees I came to the conclusion that the carpet was a thing accursed. Its extraordinary symbolism haunted me. I dreaded it, while it fascinated me. The prince evidently observed the attention I paid to it, and once said unsmilingly:

'If you will take my advice, Mr. Secretary,' for this was always the way in which he addressed me, 'you will not look upon that carpet too curiously. It – well, it has a history.'

And then something happened which aroused my slumbering fears to active terror. One night, about eleven o'clock, I suddenly recalled that I had left some unfinished work upon my desk. I hastened to the great room to lock it away. Entering abruptly, I beheld a sight which I cannot yet think of without horror and aversion.

The prince stood in the centre of the room. Where the lamp glowed brightly, an oasis of light in a desert of gloomy shadow, he stood. His face wore a fixed and terrible expression. To my amazement I saw that his cheeks were daubed with red and black paint; he was dressed in a flowing robe of crimson – and his arms were red to the elbows with blood. The doors of the great armoury behind him (I do not know how to describe it otherwise) stood wide open, and I had a glimpse of barbaric implements, gilded, carven, grotesquely appalling in their shining and symbolic hideousness.

Coming suddenly upon such a sight, was it surprising that I exclaimed loudly – cried out in horror? As I did so, his weird languorous eyes turned quickly in my direction, and lit up with cruel yellow fires, like those of a savage beast.

'How dare you come here?' he thundered. 'Go – at once – instantly.'

I went – quickly. What in heaven's name had I witnessed? I could not even guess. I spent a night of anxious and troubled surmise. When I entered his room next morning, he beckoned me to his desk.

'Mr. Secretary,' he said in his ordinary level tones, 'I would prefer that you did not enter this room after ten o'clock at night. I frequently engage in experiments here, the delicate nature of which scarcely admits of sudden intrusion. Do I make myself plain?'

I falsely assured him that I perfectly understood his dislike of interruption.

I did my best to put what I had seen out of my mind, but with only partial success. Indeed, I grew almost morbidly interested in the personality of my strange employer. The prince might be insane, his midnight performance might be dictated by a diseased mind, but how was I to account for the extraordinary situation, the weird costume in which I had surprised him on that night – how to explain the painted face, the blood-red robe? Surely the whole thing was too outrageous to exist outside of a house of detention!

Strive as I might, I found it impossible to banish the memory of what I had glimpsed that midnight. The whole fantastic circumstances had burned themselves into my brain. They were with me at my rising up and my lying down. And the more I brooded upon them, the more I became conscious that meditation upon the strange nature of my surroundings was bringing me into touch with some force, some power, subtle and malignant. As I sat at my work, I recalled my first entrance into this room, the instinct of repulsion I had experienced. I cursed myself for a fool, rallied myself in that spirit of irony which is perhaps the surest indication of fear. But to no purpose. And then, one day, certainty took the place of surmise.

As I sat alone at the window of the prince's room one late afternoon busied with my work, I became conscious of a certain slackness, an interruption of the sober spirit of occupation. At the imperious call of some outer impulse, I raised my eyes from the papers with which I was engaged and looked behind me. The great room was full of the shadows of the hour before evening. At first, from where I sat I could scarcely see the wall opposite me. But as my eyes grew accustomed to the gloomy interior, I could perceive no signs of human presence. I knew that the prince was in the city. And yet I could have been certain that that which had made me glance so hurriedly over my shoulder was born of the natural instinct we experience when under observation. Urged by an unaccountable nervousness, I rose and walked halfway to the door. But strain my eyes as I might in peering down the dark length of the place, I could see nothing; listen as intently as I might, nothing was to be heard.

I returned to my seat. In another moment I was engrossed as ever in my work. For perhaps a quarter of an hour I scribbled on, looking neither to the right nor to the left. Then I became dimly conscious of a rustling like the movement of a light and nimble body. I swung round in my chair, every sense strung to its uttermost by instinctive panic. The rustling noise continued. Straining my eyes through the fast-gathering darkness, I saw the outline of something huge and yellow writhing in slow and sinuous agitation. The carpet…was moving!

Leaping from my seat, I seized a heavy stick which always lay beside the prince's chair, and ran forward. The carpet lay absolutely motionless. A rat, I supposed, had got beneath it. I struck at it again and again, in the passion of resentment which comes of sudden shock.

I did my utmost to forget about the carpet, telling myself that I had been the victim of a mere hallucination. All the same I found it impossible to rid myself of the feeling that something uncanny lurked within its brilliant folds. This sentiment was by no means allayed by an incident which occurred not many days later.

Selecting at random a book for evening reading, I chanced upon a manuscript volume in the prince's library. It was evidently a personal diary written by an English official about a century ago in the John Company days, and in turning its yellow leaves, I abruptly encountered the following passages:

'Indeed my Maria has a profound objection to the carpet, and insists, the dear creature, that it has a life of its own. Strange, is it not, that we discovered the syce quite dead, wrapt in its hideous folds? How grossly superstitious the people here are, to be sure. But that Maria should harbour such absurd conjectures... When I put down my pen just now it was because of cries in the courtyard below. It seems that Fanny, our Yorkshire nurse, rushed screaming into the withdrawing room shrieking out that the carpet had risen at her, and struck out at her with one of its corners, for all the world like a great serpent. I must rid myself of the pestilential thing. I shall sell it – or burn it, preferably the latter. The cook assured me it is the property of Kali, the dreadful goddess of human sacrifice.'

A page or two farther on I found the following passage:

'Lord have mercy upon us! The accursed carpet. My unhappy child! What a catastrophe! I can write no more.'

What the nature of the 'catastrophe' had been, or who the 'unhappy child' referred to, I never discovered, for here the manuscript ended. I was in the act of replacing it in the bookcase when a sinuous motion beneath my feet made me leap backward. That part of the carpet between the window and the desk was agitated violently as though by a gust of wind, although it was a calm and windless evening. Then, to my horror, it rose in the air a full three feet and more.

How I managed to escape from that dreadful room I cannot say. I only know that I found myself on the other side of the window in the bright moonlight, trembling and utterly demoralized. Making my way out of the garden, I walked for miles into the country like a man in a dream, before I found the courage to return to the house.

And as I did so, I remembered. It was the night of the full moon, the night of the immemorial sacrifice to the goddess Kali, the most fiendish and barbarous of all the deities of the Hindu faith. I was aware, of course, that her horrid worship had been proscribed and absolutely forbidden by the English Raj, but as a good Mohammadan, I trembled with pious fear even to think of the abomination manifestly dedicated to her which lay on the floor of that detestable room. But the better part of my pluck had returned, and as I entered the garden and saw a light burning in the prince's apartment, I felt sufficiently emboldened to march right up to the window and see how he was busying himself at that late hour.

As I peered through the glass I recoiled in horror. Once more, with distorted countenance and blood-red hands, the prince stood in the middle of the room, making what seemed to me magical passes, the light of fanatical frenzy in his eyes. He had pushed back the carven desk so that nothing now encumbered the carpet, which lay, as it seemed to me, like a dragon half asleep, its frightful half-closed eyes yet balefully awake.

'Kali!' shrieked the prince. 'Hear me, Kali! This very night shall I render to thee the heart's blood of the accursed Mohammadan who sleeps above, and who is in my power. Six lives hast thou had in as many years, and with this, the seventh, my task shall be complete, and I shall henceforth be thy high priest. Kali! Kali! Hear me, goddess of the abyss!'

So it was for this that the prince had engaged me as his 'secretary'. A terrible revulsion of feeling surged over me. From fear I rose to the heights of an angry disgust. That this demon should have selected me as his quarry appeared to me not only as a deep personal wrong, but as an infamy both to my own faith and to the noble Hindu religion which I respected and even admired for its beauty and spirituality. This degraded creature of a savage cult horrible to all true men, ruinous to India, must be made to suffer for his infamies. Yes, tonight, despite his rank, I would see to it that he was placed beyond the possibility of further outrage.

Suddenly, as I stood there trembling, I noticed that on which the prince stood move slightly. Then there was a swift and voluminous uprising of something…something which surged and billowed round him in vast and enveloping folds, like great yellow waves flecked with a many-coloured foam. He stood for an instant in awful amazement. Then a look of such terror crossed his face as I have never seen in that of a living man.

Even as he screamed, the carpet, with its riot of dreadful symbols, wound itself about him, its sides shrouding his head, its corners writhing around his limbs like the tentacles of an octopus. The serpent and spider shapes with which it was covered seemed to move in an awful mimicry of life, while from every part of the whirling mass the dreadful half-closed eyes looked out, alight, as it seemed, with demon fire. Powerless to aid, and, as I believe, in the grip of some malignant and arresting force, I stood at the window while the yells of the suffocating wretch grew fainter and fainter. Through the folds of the woven mass which surrounded him, I could see the writhing of his limbs. His shrieks died away to a low moaning. At last, when the power of volition returned to me and I rushed forward, a dreadful stillness had taken the place of the anguished struggling of the moment before. The carpet lay flattened and creaseless upon the floor. And upon its bizarre background huddled the prince, the secret priest of the goddess Kali, with purple and distorted face – dead.

From: *The White Terror of the Khyber*
The Sirdar Ikbal Ali Shah

Continues in

A Son of a Son

Volume II

BIBLIOGRAPHY

1918	*Eastern Moonbeams*	The Sirdar Ikbal Ali Shah
1918	*A Briton in India*	The Sirdar Ikbal Ali Shah
1922	*Exploits of Asaf Khan*	The Sirdar Ikbal Ali Shah
1923	*The Wanderings of Asaf*	The Sirdar Ikbal Ali Shah
1925	*Best Indian Chutney*	The Sirdar Ikbal Ali Shah
1927	*Afghanistan of the Afghans*	The Sirdar Ikbal Ali Shah
1928	*Bahadur Khan Warrior*	The Sirdar Ikbal Ali Shah
1928	*Westward to Mecca*	The Sirdar Ikbal Ali Shah
1930	*Eastward to Persia*	The Sirdar Ikbal Ali Shah
1931	*Peeps at Many Lands: Arabia*	The Sirdar Ikbal Ali Shah
1931	*The Golden East*	The Sirdar Ikbal Ali Shah
1932	*Mohamed: The Prophet*	The Sirdar Ikbal Ali Shah
1932	*Peeps at Many Lands: Turkey*	The Sirdar Ikbal Ali Shah
1933	*Alone in Arabian Nights*	The Sirdar Ikbal Ali Shah
1933	*Extracts From the Koran*	The Sirdar Ikbal Ali Shah
1933	*Fighting Through*	The Sirdar Ikbal Ali Shah
1933	*Islamic Sufism*	The Sirdar Ikbal Ali Shah
1933	*The Book of Oriental Literature*	The Sirdar Ikbal Ali Shah
1933	*The Prince Aga Khan*	The Sirdar Ikbal Ali Shah
1933	*The Tragedy of Amanullah*	The Sirdar Ikbal Ali Shah
1934	*Afridi Gold*	The Sirdar Ikbal Ali Shah
1934	*Kemal: Maker of Modern Turkey*	The Sirdar Ikbal Ali Shah
1934	*Lights of Asia*	The Sirdar Ikbal Ali Shah
1934	*The White Terror of the Khyber*	The Sirdar Ikbal Ali Shah
1936	*Fuad: King of Egypt*	The Sirdar Ikbal Ali Shah
1936	*Lion of the Frontier*	The Sirdar Ikbal Ali Shah
1936	*My Life From Brigand to King*	The Sirdar Ikbal Ali Shah

1936	*The Lion of the Frontier*	The Sirdar Ikbal Ali Shah
1937	*Fifty Enthralling Stories From the Mysterious East*	
		The Sirdar Ikbal Ali Shah
1938	*Nepal: Home of the Gods*	The Sirdar Ikbal Ali Shah
1938	*The Golden Treasury of Indian Literature*	
		The Sirdar Ikbal Ali Shah
1938	*Through the Garden of Allah*	The Sirdar Ikbal Ali Shah
1938	*Brothers in Arms*	The Sirdar Ikbal Ali Shah
1939	*I Spy for the Empire*	The Sirdar Ikbal Ali Shah
1939	*The Spirit of the East*	The Sirdar Ikbal Ali Shah
1944	*Pakistan: A Plan for India*	The Sirdar Ikbal Ali Shah
1952	*Occultism: Its Theory and Practice*	
		The Sirdar Ikbal Ali Shah
1956	*Oriental Magic*	Idries Shah
1957	*Destination Mecca*	Idries Shah
1957	*The Secret Lore of Magic*	Idries Shah
1960	*Vietnam*	The Sirdar Ikbal Ali Shah
1961	*A History of Secret Societies*	Idries Shah
1962	*Witches and Sorcerers*	Idries Shah
1964	*The Sufis*	Idries Shah
1966	*Special Problems in the Study of Sufi Ideas*	
		Idries Shah
1966	*The Exploits of the Incomparable Mulla Nasrudin*	
		Idries Shah
1967	*Tales of the Dervishes*	Idries Shah
1968	*Caravan of Dreams*	Idries Shah
1968	*Reflections*	Idries Shah
1968	*The Pleasantries of the Incredible Mulla Nasrudin*	
		Idries Shah
1968	*The Way of the Sufi*	Idries Shah
1969	*The Book of the Book*	Idries Shah
1969	*Wisdom of the Idiots*	Idries Shah
1970	*The Dermis Probe*	Idries Shah
1971	*Thinkers of the East*	Idries Shah
1972	*The Magic Monastery*	Idries Shah

1973	*The Subtleties of the Inimitable Mulla Nasrudin*	
		Idries Shah
1974	*The Elephant in the Dark*	Idries Shah
1975	*Black and White Magic*	The Sirdar Ikbal Ali Shah
		(posthumous)
1977	*Neglected Aspects of Sufi Study*	Idries Shah
1977	*Special Illumination*	Idries Shah
1977	*A Veiled Gazelle*	Idries Shah
1978	*Learning How to Learn*	Idries Shah
1978	*A Perfumed Scorpion*	Idries Shah
1978	*The Hundred Tales of Wisdom*	Idries Shah
1979	*World Tales*	Idries Shah
1980	*Escape From Central Asia*	The Sirdar Ikbal Ali Shah
		(posthumous)
1981	*Evenings with Idries Shah*	Idries Shah
1981	*Letters and Lectures of Idries Shah*	Idries Shah
1982	*Observations*	Idries Shah
1982	*Seeker After Truth*	Idries Shah
1986	*Kara Kush*	Idries Shah
1987	*Darkest England*	Idries Shah
1988	*The Natives Are Restless*	Idries Shah
1990	*Sufi Thought and Action*	Idries Shah
1991	*The Middle East Bedside Book*	Tahir Shah
1992	*Spectrum Guide to Jordan*	Tahir Shah
1993	*Cultural Research*	Tahir Shah
1994	*The Commanding Self*	Idries Shah
1994	*Journey Through Namibia*	Tahir Shah
1995	*Beyond the Devil's Teeth*	Tahir Shah
1998	*Knowing How to Know*	Idries Shah (posthumous)
1998	*Neem the Half-Boy*	Idries Shah (posthumous)
1998	*The Farmer's Wife*	Idries Shah (posthumous)
1998	*Sorcerer's Apprentice*	Tahir Shah
2000	*The Boy Without a Name*	Idries Shah (posthumous)
2000	*The Englishman's Handbook*	Idries Shah
2001	*The Lion Who Saw Himself in the Water*	
		Idries Shah (posthumous)

SHAH

2001	*The Magic Horse*	Idries Shah (posthumous)
2001	*Trail of Feathers*	Tahir Shah
2002	*In Search of King Solomon's Mines*	Tahir Shah
2003	*The World of Nasrudin*	Idries Shah (posthumous)
2004	*House of the Tiger King*	Tahir Shah
2005	*The Clever Boy and the Terrible Dangerous Animal*	
		Idries Shah (posthumous)
2005	*The Man With Bad Manners*	Idries Shah (posthumous)
2005	*The Old Woman and the Eagle*	Idries Shah (posthumous)
2005	*The Silly Chicken*	Idries Shah (posthumous)
2006	*Fatima the Spinner and the Tent*	Idries Shah (posthumous)
2006	*The Man and the Fox*	Idries Shah (posthumous)
2006	*The Caliph's House*	Tahir Shah
2008	*In Arabian Nights*	Tahir Shah
2011	*Travels With Myself*	Tahir Shah
2012	*Timbuctoo*	Tahir Shah
2013	*Casablanca Blues*	Tahir Shah
2013	*Eye Spy*	Tahir Shah
2013	*Scorpion Soup*	Tahir Shah
2013	*Three Essays*	Tahir Shah
2014	*Paris Syndrome*	Tahir Shah
2018	*Speak First and Lose*	Idries Shah (posthumous)
2018	*The Ants and the Pen*	Idries Shah
2018	*The Onion*	Idries Shah (posthumous)
2018	*Hannibal Fogg and the Supreme Secret of Man*	
		Tahir Shah
2019	*After a Swim*	Idries Shah
2019	*The Horrible Dib Dib*	Idries Shah (posthumous)
2019	*The Idries Shah Anthology*	Idries Shah (posthumous)
2019	*The Tale of the Sands*	Idries Shah
2019	*Jinn Hunter: Book One – The Prism*	
		Tahir Shah
2019	*Travels With Nasrudin*	Tahir Shah
2020	*Casablanca Blues: The Screenplay*	Tahir Shah
2020	*Godman*	Tahir Shah

2020	*Jinn Hunter: Book Two – The Jinnslayer*	
		Tahir Shah
2020	*The Anthologies: Africa*	Tahir Shah
2020	*The Anthologies: Ceremony*	Tahir Shah
2020	*The Anthologies: Childhood*	Tahir Shah
2020	*The Anthologies: City*	Tahir Shah
2020	*The Anthologies: Danger*	Tahir Shah
2020	*The Anthologies: East*	Tahir Shah
2020	*The Anthologies: Expedition*	Tahir Shah
2020	*The Anthologies: Frontier*	Tahir Shah
2020	*The Anthologies: Hinterland*	Tahir Shah
2020	*The Anthologies: India*	Tahir Shah
2020	*The Anthologies: Jungle*	Tahir Shah
2020	*The Anthologies: Morocco*	Tahir Shah
2020	*The Anthologies: People*	Tahir Shah
2020	*The Anthologies: Quest*	Tahir Shah
2020	*The Anthologies: South*	Tahir Shah
2020	*The Anthologies: Taboo*	Tahir Shah
2020	*The Arabian Nights Adventures*	Tahir Shah
2020	*The Clockmaker's Box*	Tahir Shah
2020	*The Reason to Write*	Tahir Shah
2020	*Timbuctoo: The Screenplay*	Tahir Shah
2021	*Congress With a Crocodile*	Tahir Shah
2021	*Jinn Hunter: Book Three – The Perplexity*	
		Tahir Shah
2021	*The Misadventures of the Mystifying Nasrudin*	
		Tahir Shah
2021	*The Peregrinations of the Perplexing Nasrudin*	
		Tahir Shah
2021	*The Voyages and Vicissitudes of Nasrudin*	
		Tahir Shah
2021	*Tales Told to a Melon*	Tahir Shah
2021	*The Man Who Found Himself*	Tahir Shah
2021	*The Tahir Shah Fiction Reader*	Tahir Shah
2021	*The Tahir Shah Travel Reader*	Tahir Shah

A REQUEST

If you enjoyed this book, please review it on your favourite online retailer or review website.

Reviews are an author's best friend.

To stay in touch with Tahir Shah, and to hear about his upcoming releases before anyone else, please sign up for his mailing list:

✉ http://tahirshah.com/newsletter

And to follow him on social media, please go to any of the following links:

🐦 http://www.twitter.com/humanstew

📷 @tahirshah999

f http://www.facebook.com/TahirShahAuthor

▶ http://www.youtube.com/user/tahirshah999

📌 http://www.pinterest.com/tahirshah

g https://www.goodreads.com/tahirshahauthor

http://www.tahirshah.com

www.ingramcontent.com/pod-product-compliance
Lightning Source LLC
Chambersburg PA
CBHW031023030726
47497CB00004B/974